► SPECIALIZED TECHNIQUES IN

PSYCHOTHERAPY

► SPECIALIZED TECHNIQUES IN

PSYCHOTHERAPY

Edited by

GUSTAV BYCHOWSKI, M.D.

and

J. LOUISE DESPERT, M.D.

BASIC BOOKS, INC., Publishers • New York

First Printing, June 1952
Second Printing, January 1953

$$\frac{\text{B}}{\text{B}}$$

► TABLE OF CONTENTS

Those of us who have witnessed the spectacular development of psychoanalysis have felt the need of applying analytic psychotherapy to ever wider groups of suffering individuals. The content of this book is a demonstration that this need is being increasingly realized, a proof of the rapid development of psychotherapy in our time. It is indeed indicative of the growing interest in and the expansion of psychotherapeutic methods that the Salmon Lectures, an annual psychiatric lecture series taking place in the New York Academy of Medicine, were devoted in 1951 to "The Place and Scope of Psychotherapy."

Today concrete form has been given to the stirring vision of Freud who, as far back as 1918, in a paper delivered before the Fifth International Psychoanalytic Congress in Budapest, said: "I will cast a glance at a situation which belongs to the future—one that will seem fantastic to many of you, but which I think, nevertheless, deserves that we should be prepared for it. You know that the therapeutic effects we can achieve are very inconsiderable in number . . .

"Now let us assume that by some kind of organization we were able to increase our numbers to an extent sufficient for treating large masses of people . . . Then clinics and consultation-departments will be built, to which analytically oriented physicians will be appointed, so that the men who would otherwise give way to drink, the women who have nearly succumbed under the burden of privations, the children for whom there is no choice but running wild or neurosis, may be made by analysis able to resist and able to do something in the world." *

It is a mark of the great progress achieved in a relatively short time that, a little over thirty years later, the "clinics and consultation-departments" which he then considered as a utopia

---

* Freud, S., "Turnings in the Ways of Psychoanalytic Therapy." *Collected Papers.* II, 400–401. London, Hogarth Press, 1950 (1924).

have become part of our psychiatric reality. The necessity for extending the benefits of psychoanalysis, then the privilege of only a few, he foresaw with a realistic vividness and tangibility which today seems almost incredible to us.

At that time Freud also postulated "that the application of our therapy to numbers will compel us to alloy the pure gold of analysis plentifully with the copper of direct suggestion; and even hypnotic influence might find a place in it again, as it has in the treatment of war-neuroses. But whatever form this psychotherapy for the people may take, whatever the elements out of which it is compounded, its most effective and most important ingredients will assuredly remain those borrowed from strict psychoanalysis which serves no ulterior purpose." * This book then is dedicated to the objective of describing various forms of this psychotherapeutic "alloy," and in this way spreading the knowledge of various modifications of psychotherapy and of the methods for its application which have been evolved in recent time and are still in the process of evolving.

The widening of the scope of psychotherapy has altered the position of the psychiatrist. He had been isolated during the initial phase of intramural psychiatry and had become isolated again, although in a different way, in the classical period of psychoanalysis. Now he stands at the very center of psychiatric activity, no longer an isolated figure in the therapeutic process. He has been enriched by the communication of knowledge acquired through his increasing contact with various disciplines such as psychology, social work, anthropology, and social sciences, and has lost nothing in the sharing of his experience.

Psychotherapy, being in a constant state of flux, precludes any rigid and final formulation. What we call techniques are really approaches evolved in the course of research and experimentation. Our contributors present the substance of their firsthand experience, as a contribution to knowledge of specific dynamic and therapeutic problems they have encountered and as a stimulus for workers in their respective fields. The reader will appreciate the wide range of the clinical material, and the

---

* *Ibid.*, 402.

great variety of individual approaches, despite their common conceptual structure. This structure rests on the basic tenets of Freudian psychoanalysis. What has been crystallized in this joint effort are the results of the evolution of psychoanalysis as applied to various therapeutic problems and to ever-widening groups of individuals. Although proud of their origins, these psychotherapeutic methods differ from the original classic psychoanalysis.

Certainly all the various modifications recorded in this volume cannot be described as forms of psychoanalysis, since psychoanalysis implies certain prerequisites described by Freud and his followers. On the other hand, we have the right to regard as psychoanalytic every psychotherapy which deals with such basic elements of psychoanalysis as the concepts of the unconscious, transference, and resistance. We feel that the present day development of theoretical knowledge and clinical experience permits us to forego that defensive rigidity which was understandable in the more heroic era of our science. We can today allow ourselves more flexibility and elasticity in our methods of approach to the healing of the mentally and psychically ill.

In the course of its development one principle of psychotherapy remains as a cornerstone upon which rests every method—that is, of course, the therapist-patient relationship. The subtle shadings of this significant relationship are clearly reflected in the following contributions. Based on research and experience and well-substantiated theory, these contributions are dominated by a single practical objective—to provide psychological help to the patient.

This book is one outcome of a project of the past seven years which aims at providing an exchange of information and ideas for workers in the field of psychiatry and allied social sciences. The project is known as the Psychiatric Forum Group. Over a hundred psychiatrists and workers in related fields have been gathering monthly in New York in an attempt to integrate their varying approaches to mental illness, and to hear the presentation by their associates of new experiences, ideas, approaches and techniques. Many of the contributors to this volume, including the editors, have taken an active part in these gatherings.

The editors wish to extend a special word of thanks to their colleague and friend, Dr. Victor W. Eisenstein, whose initiative and vision were instrumental in originating the Psychiatric Forum Group and in planning this volume.

Finally we wish to thank the editors of *The American Journal of Orthopsychiatry, Psychiatry,* and the *Psychiatric Quarterly* for permission to reprint three papers which first appeared in their journals.

G. B.

J. L. D.

New York

▶ NARCODIAGNOSIS AND NARCOTHERAPY

By Paul H. Hoch, M.D., and Phillip Polatin, M.D.***

INTRODUCTION

Historical Note

In 1929 Bleckwenn used sodium amytal by mouth for the first time, in the production of hypnosis in patients whom he could not hypnotize by ordinary methods. Lindemann in 1932 discovered that comparatively small doses of sodium amytal injected slowly intravenously produced a marked effect both in normal individuals and in patients suffering from psychiatric illness, which was sufficient to alter their mental states.

General Discussion of Applicability

In normal individuals the intravenous injection of sodium amytal produces a sense of well-being and a feeling of serenity. There is a friendly attitude toward the environment and a marked desire to come into contact with it, which together with a great ease in verbal communication will result in increased talkativeness. A lack of inhibition manifests itself, and the individual is able to talk very freely about his intimate thoughts and experiences if he wishes to do so.

The action of sodium amytal and sodium pentothal is similar in certain respects to the effects of alcohol, ether, and cocaine. Amytal leads to a lack of inhibition of words. Alcohol, on the other hand, produces release of inhibition in actions as well as words. In some individuals, however, where certain

* Principal Research Scientist (Psychiatry), New York State Psychiatric Institute; Assistant Professor of Psychiatry, College of Physicians and Surgeons, Columbia University.
** Associate Clinical Psychiatrist, New York State Psychiatric Institute; Assistant Clinical Professor of Psychiatry, College of Physicians and Surgeons, Columbia University.

1

types of mental pathology are present, a psychomotor discharge may occur with sodium amytal or sodium pentothal as occurs in some types of war neuroses. The response to alcohol and cocaine is markedly influenced, among other factors, by the underlying personality structure of the patient. A more uniform response is produced by amytal in spite of the many different underlying personalities involved and, therefore, it can be better standardized.

Sodium amytal intravenously was first used in mental patients to eliminate negativism, mutism, and refusal of food such as occurs in the catatonic form of schizophrenia. Later it was used to overcome the resistance of the patient and to induce him to communicate his ideas and experiences. Thorner, working with a series of 100 patients under sodium amytal intravenously, indicated that about half of this group expressed ideas not previously indicated and that these ideas were pertinent to the structure of the psychosis.

The term "narcoanalysis" was first employed by Horsley (19), (20), (21). He used the barbiturates intravenously in conjunction with hypnosis and later developed a technique which was essentially along psychoanalytic lines; this was applied while the patient was under the influence of sodium pentothal intravenously. This procedure was somewhat similar to the technique described by Bleckwenn.

In World War II, sodium amytal and sodium pentothal intravenously were used in the war neuroses in many variations, either as straight sedation, or in conjunction with suggestion, or combined with psychoanalytically oriented psychotherapy. After World War II, sodium amytal intravenously was used with increasing frequency for diagnostic purposes and mainly as a form of short-term psychotherapy in certain forms of civilian neuroses.

General Technique

Sodium amytal or sodium pentothal injection is given intravenously with the patient always in the recumbent position. A 5 or 10 per cent solution of the drug is used, and the drug is injected slowly in an antecubital vein, not more rapidly than one grain per minute. The injection proceeds until the patient appears relaxed and in a state of good contact, which is usually determined when the patient's speech becomes slurred. As the injection proceeds the patient is asked some indifferent or impersonal questions, which tend to reassure him and thus lead to a better rapport. At the same time the examiner can determine whether the speech is slurred, thereby establishing the depth of the semi-narcotic state. The questioning of the patient or the actual therapeutic work should begin when the patient appears to be flushed, shows slurring of speech, and when nystagmus is observed by the examiner testing the patient's eye-muscles with his finger. The amount of drug which is needed to produce the desired state varies in different individuals. The needle is left in the vein while treating the patient, and if the effects of the drug wear off, an additional amount can again be introduced slowly. If too much drug is given, the patient becomes somnolent, unintelligible, unresponsive, and falls into a deep sleep in which no therapeutic procedure can ensue.* Sodium pentothal usually intoxicates more rapidly than sodium amytal. In other words the gap between the therapeutic and narcotic effects of the drug is much narrower with sodium pentothal than with sodium amytal.

The safety of this drug in general use has been demonstrated over many years in many patients. Certain precautions, however, should be kept in mind. The drug should not be used in patients who are acutely ill with some major physical disorder or in patients with liver or kidney disease. In hypertensive cases it should be applied cautiously. If during the course of the sodium amytal injection, the patient begins to manifest a marked panic reaction or shows psychotic behavior, both of which conditions however are not common, an additional amount of the drug should be quickly injected so that the patient falls asleep rapidly. The patient should not be permitted

---

* Brickner worked out a form of therapy during which the patient is actually asleep under the influence of amytal. Intensive psychotherapeutic work is then done while under the narcosis.

to leave the interview in the continued panic state or while manifesting psychotic symptoms.

If the drug is given in an ambulatory setting such as an outpatient department or in the private office of the physician, it is important to avoid the possibility that the patent will sleep too long after the interview or will leave in a too-drowsy state. As a consequence 10 mg. of benzedrine sulfate can be given orally shortly before the amytal interview begins. Benzedrine should not be given for this purpose intravenously after the interview is terminated and the patient appears too drowsy. Otherwise there will be a markedly stimulating effect and the patient will become very restless; there will be a lack of sleep and occasionally an intensification of his emotional symptoms. The patient in this ambulatory setting should be forbidden to take alcohol following the amytal interview, should be accompanied by a responsible person when leaving the office, and should be strictly forbidden to drive a car following an amytal session.

USE IN DIAGNOSIS

Discussion

Sodium amytal interviews can be used effectively to differentiate psychotic states from psychoneurotic ones. The technique is especially useful in differentiating a psychoneurosis from schizophrenia. It is less reliable in differentiating manic-depressive states from psychoneuroses. Many schizophrenic patients under sodium amytal show a biphasic reaction. That is, in the early phase of the drug reaction the patients manifest a disinhibition and a tendency to contact the environment; their defenses are usually reduced, and they talk more freely about the content of their disorder. Later on, in the second phase of the reaction, a normalization takes place in which these patients usually feel quite well, and readily discuss their difficulties, since often they become somewhat detached from the emotional impact. Reticent, uncommunicative, and hostile patients verbalize their conflicts much better with than without the drug. They often readily admit delusions and hallucinations which they did not discuss before. This is especially true of dissimulating or evasive paranoid patients. Here hypochondriacal ideas, bizarre interpretations, and all rationalizations of their behavior and conduct are easily and rather quickly elicited. It would be very time-consuming and often impossible to obtain such a mass of material from a schizophrenic patient without applying the drug. The relationship of the patient to reality is fairly quickly ascertained under sodium amytal intravenously. This is often difficult in patients not under the influence of the drug because of the presence of anxiety or depressive features. The sexual organization of the patient also becomes apparent. Incestuous wishes, fears, homosexual preoccupation, oral, anal, sadistic and masochistic tendencies are often elicited; their structure can be differentiated readily from similar neurotic expressions.

This method is especially valuable in the investigation of incipient, latent, or pseudoneurotic schizophrenics. These constitute a large group of patients with whom clinical examination often does not permit a differentiation between schizophrenia and psychoneurosis, or permits such differentiation only after prolonged observation and treatment. In this group, the often typical schizophrenic reactions can be elicited under the influence of the drug.

It must be emphasized that the diagnostic work with sodium amytal is not an automatic one except in rare instances. By this we mean that the simple injection of the drug will not necessarily recover psychotic material by the spontaneous admission of the patient. It requires skillful verbal maneuvering on the part of the examiner. Consequently a diagnostic test of this type requires the physician to be very well versed in clinical psychiatry and in psychodynamic knowledge and understanding of the structure of the neuroses and psychoses. Limitation of space prevents us from enlarging on the differential diagnostic elements. Success in eliciting psychotic material depends primarily on the skill of the examiner, and only secondarily on the use of the drug. This explains why in some hands this method yields valuable information while in others very little is obtained from this procedure.

It is well known that drug intoxication can modify the psychic reaction of a patient. The doubt was therefore expressed that some of the material obtained could not be interpreted properly because of the toxic disturbances of the drug. We will return to this point later in discussing the medico-legal implications of this method. After our extensive experience we can state briefly that even though it is undoubtedly true that the drug modifies the patient's productions, in most instances it does not produce such a reaction that the patient displays a toxic psychosis. If a psychotic picture evolves, it represents usually the release of a schizophrenic or manic-depressive reaction and not that of a superimposed organic psychosis. We must, therefore, emphasize the technical point mentioned above, namely, that during the interview the patient should be in good contact with the examiner, with clear sensorium. The material obtained otherwise should be used with caution, especially when the patient is in such a state that the narcotic effect of the drug is marked, the patient half asleep, incoherent in speech, or where answers are elicited only by constant prompting.

In diagnostic work we prefer the use of sodium amytal to sodium pentothal or to other barbiturates because sodium pentothal and the other barbiturates intoxicate rather rapidly and the patient is not clear during the interview. If pentothal is used, it is preferable to wait until the patient comes out of the pentothal half-sleep and is again in good contact, with his sensorium clear. In spite of the fact that sodium amytal produces a disinhibition of verbal productivity, a patient none the less does not have to admit psychotic material if he does not want to do so. Therefore, if such material is not obtained it does not necessarily mean that the patient does not have a psychosis. Confabulation can occur under sodium amytal but a conscious or unconscious simulation of a psychosis is rarely observed in patients who are not under legal investigation. If significant material suggestive of a psychosis is obtained, it is necessary to cross-check and to confront the patient with the material in a drug-free interview, or else repeated sodium amytal interviews have to be undertaken in order to test the validity and consistency of the patient's statements. The patient is usually not aware of the significance of the material released and, therefore, purposeful admission of psychotic material under the influence of sodium amytal is not seen in non-legal cases.

The drug interview is also used to differentiate between organic and psychogenic conditions. There are, for example, certain neurological disorders such as extra-pyramidal disease, nerve injuries, etc., where it is difficult to determine, on the basis of a neurological examination alone, whether the condition is organic or psychogenic or a combination of both. Organic conditions like tremors and rigidity are diminished under the drug and sometimes eliminated, but only temporarily. When the drug effect wears off, the neurological disturbance usually returns in full force. In addition, no material is obtained which would indicate a motive for psychogenesis. In psychogenic disturbances the reverse is true, and usually the alleged neurological disorder disappears for hours or longer after the interview. It is taken for granted that in such diagnostic work it is essential that the examiner be conversant with the clinical manifestations of organic disorders as well as with the psychogenic disturbances. Often in such cases it is demonstrated that even when an organic disease is present, it is superimposed by psychogenic mechanisms which re-enforce or prolong the organic disturbance. It was also suggested that the amount of amytal consumed is indicative of the presence or absence of an organic disorder. This is not borne out in general by scientific observation.

The drug is also used to supplement the clinical differentiation between malingering and psychogenic disorders. Here, however, errors can be made in one way or another, and a marked familiarity with the method is necessary to arrive at true conclusions.

The sodium amytal interview is quite valuable in ascertaining rapidly the focal points in a psychotic or neurotic structure. It is first necessary to examine the patient in a drug-free interview in order to obtain some impression of his conflicts. Under the drug these sensitive areas are clarified, and because the patient is cushioned against anxiety and depression and is in a better transference situation, he will elaborate more readily and will release important material more rapidly than is otherwise the case. It is not unusual for patients to speak freely about emotional traumata which they appear to minimize or conceal in drug-free interviews. Quite often under the influence of the drug, apparently simple anxiety reactions are revealed as deeply structuralized phobic or obsessive symptoms. This intravenous interview properly conducted is especially useful in eliciting sexual material, as well as the patient's evaluation of himself and how he handles social situations, especially aggression.

Medico-legal Implications (Truth Serum)

We are in agreement with practically all other workers in this field that sodium amytal interviews should be used only with great caution in medico-legal work. If an individual agrees to submit to such a test without coercion as he might submit himself to a "lie detector" test and if he is aware of the implications of such an exposure, there would be no objection to its use as an auxiliary to a properly conducted psychiatric examination. We must, however, emphasize that material obtained from such a test alone should not be used as evidence for or against the accused. While it is popularly believed that a sodium amytal or sodium pentothal interview is a form of "truth serum" and that the person subjected to it invariably reveals the truth about his actions and motives, this is not the case at all. Many persons, even under the influence of the drug, are able to withhold information. As a matter of fact, many are able to lie and fabricate, and this is especially true about psychopathic defendants. Further, under the influence of the drug, many individuals are so suggestible that they will agree to questions improperly phrased or formulated. They are also often unable to differentiate between thoughts and actions. For instance, an idea of killing someone could be formulated as actual action, for ordinarily the patient would be able to indicate clearly that he merely had homicidal thoughts, as many neurotics have, although he had never been able actually to carry them out. In drug interviews in non-legal cases, such confessions are of secondary importance since the misunderstandings and mis-statements can be rather easily clarified and verified. This, in a legal situation, often becomes impossible. Consequently, considering all the foregoing material, we definitely feel and wish to emphasize that drug interviews are not admissible in medico-legal practice, with the exception as indicated above.

Prognosis

Sodium amytal or sodium pentothal interviews are also used for prognostic purposes. While their value here is not fully ascertained, there are some indications that they may have value for prognostication.

It is obvious that the prognosis would be different if the patient suffers from a psychosis rather than from a neurosis. The structure revealed in the psychoses and the neuroses would constitute valuable prognostic hints. The evaluation of the material as to future development is no different than if the material were obtained in drug-free interviews. In patients suffering from functional psychoses an effort to evaluate the prognosis with shock therapy can be made in terms of the sodium amytal interview. Here the structure of the psychosis or neurosis is not as important as is the degree to which the patient is able to normalize under the influence of the drug. Depressed or manic patients, for example, may lose their depressive or manic symptomatology for an hour or more. This would indicate a favorable outcome with electroshock therapy. If the manic or depressive symptomatology does not disappear or is not markedly influenced by the drug, then the outcome with electroshock is not favorable.

Even more significant are the findings concerning schizophrenia. If a schizophrenic patient shows regressive symptoms, and if under sodium amytal he re-integrates fairly well, this would indicate a good response to insulin or electroshock treatments. Schizophrenics who manifest deterioration indicating a fixed regression and who usually do not normalize under sodium amytal, remaining emotionally blunted, unresponsive, and intellectually disorganized and scattered, will either not show any improvement with shock therapy or, if some relief is experienced with such treatment, will respond only temporarily.

Sodium amytal was also used in interviewing patients who were candidates for lobotomy, topectomy, and similar brain operations. It was found that if a patient does not normalize under sodium amytal, the prognosis with the above-mentioned brain operations is not good, or at least must be considered as quite guarded. Normalization under sodium amytal, however, does not necessarily mean a good prognosis with the operation. In some patients the outcome corresponded closely with the normalization obtained under sodium amytal. In others, in spite of normalization under the drug, the operative outcome was not favorable. Here, therefore, sodium amytal has only a negative prognostic value—if the patient does not normalize, the outcome is usually not good.

THERAPY

In War Neuroses

In World War II, first in England and then in the United States, sodium amytal or sodium pentothal was used extensively in the treatment of the war neuroses. This treatment used by different workers was variously labeled. One spoke about "narcosuggestion," another about "narcocatharsis," another about "narcoanalysis" and still others about "narcosynthesis." Each of these treatments conveys the use of a somewhat different technique even though in many instances the same form of treatment was applied, but under different names.

Two main types of treatments emerged from this narcotherapeutic approach: the covering-up form of treatment or narcosuggestion; and the uncovering type of therapy, namely, narcocatharsis, narcoanalysis, and narcosynthesis. The first or the simple narcosuggestive method emerged as a consequence of the immediate need to sedate rapidly the emotionally upset and especially the severely anxious members of the armed forces. In addition to the sedation, suggestion was applied to reinforce the sedative effect. Here, while the sodium amytal is being injected, it is pointed out to the patient that he is relaxed and quiet, that the action of his heart is normal, that he does not perspire and that the doctor is capable of stopping his symptoms. If necessary, the patient also receives a short and concise explanation regarding the genesis of his symptoms and is reassured as to his anxiety conflicts. At the end of the interview it is suggested that the patient should sleep, and reassurance is given as to his future well-being. Such treatment can be carried out in a few minutes. Some workers, instead of using ordinary suggestion, employed the hypnotic technique while the patient was under the influence of the drug.

In the uncovering form of treatment, narcocatharsis was the first method used and was based on the idea that abreaction (catharsis) facilitates the cure of a war neurosis. The techniques used here were reminiscent of early psychoanalytic techniques in which the release of repressed emotions was in the foreground of therapeutic concern. In narcocatharsis after the injection of sodium amytal, the patient is asked to tell about his war experiences. He generally will begin with some conscious memory but as he continues to talk he begins to bring up repressed material. Some therapists permit the patient to associate freely, while others attempt to elicit the traumatic experience directly by questioning. The most common approach is the method of limited free association in which the patient is permitted to speak about anything he wishes but also receives directive questions in order to clarify vague points; often he is pressed back to the traumatic experiences which are assumed to be the causes of his conflicts. Usually during such a procedure, the patient develops a marked emotional state and relives anxiety, hostility, rage, guilt, and other emotional experiences connected with the traumatic situation. The patient again and again in the same or repeated interviews is taken over the same material until the emotional tension connected with it is discharged, and he gains mastery over the original situation with which he was unable to cope previously. Such sessions may last from one-half to one hour. Usually a number of sessions are needed to treat the patient. This method is especially useful with an acute war neurosis, in which the conflictual situation is still not fixed, and the defense mechanisms of the patient are still flexible. The material which is uncovered during such interviews should be explained to the patient. This can be done in either a sedated or non-sedated state. It is preferable to present a summary of the material in the non-sedated state since amnesia is often present in association with the state of sedation. If necessary this narcocathartic treatment can be combined with narcosuggestion.

The narcoanalytic approach in the war neuroses does not differ much from the above-described narcocathartic method. The difference may be that narcoanalysis is more similar to the technique used in the civilian neuroses where free association is more extensively used, interpretations are given, and the whole treatment-approach is less concerned with abreaction than with the total therapeutic mechanism involved in a transference situation.

Grinker presented an elaborate scheme for the conduct of an uncovering form of treatment which he called "narcosynthesis." He suggested this term because he felt that abreaction alone was not sufficient for the treatment of war neuroses. He also believed that the suggestive form of approach had only temporary value. He stated that in narcosynthesis the patient establishes an identification with the therapist. Based on this experience the patient is reassured and is able to view the world as a not altogether hostile place; later he is educated to become independent of the therapist. Narcosynthesis uses all the mechanisms of the above-employed techniques but in addition stresses the need for ego-support of the patient. In Grinker's technique the drug is far less important than the psychotherapy which is given after the patient comes out of the drug sleep. Consequently, the patient is first narcotized and is made to sleep and then, when he comes out of this state and is alert and responsive, the therapeutic work is initiated.

In our own experience with war neurotics we found that any of these methods can be used to considerable advantage. In the more superficial and more acute cases such as acute anxiety, hysterical and fatigue states, and especially when there is no time or facility for intensive treatment, the narcosuggestive method is best utilized. In cases where the war neurosis shows a rather deeper structuralization such as obsessive-compulsive, phobic, or paranoid states, the narcoanalytic method is more useful. The narcoanalytic method is the one of choice in all war neuroses if the patient is removed to a hospital where facilities are available for his treatment, and especially if the neurosis is already a few weeks old. The success with the narcoanalytic method in ingrained, chronic war neuroses is not fully determined. Some investigators believe that it is more successful than non-drug-connected psychotherapy, while others disclaim this. Statistically speaking, and omitting some conspicuous successes in individual cases, the therapeutic outcome with these drug methods in chronic war neurosis is unimpressive. This is also true with all other forms of treatment of the non-drug variety.

In Civilian Neuroses

After World War II the narcoanalytic methods were used in the United States and abroad in the civilian neuroses. It was understood that the dynamic structure of the civilian neuroses in many respects was different pathogenetically from the war neuroses. In spite of this it is a fact that in anxiety neurosis, conversion hysteria, and in some psychosomatic conditions many of the mechanisms are similar. The anxiety experience, the somatic vegetative symptoms of anxiety, and some of the dissociation and symbolic conversion mechanisms are similar, even though some of the fundamental and causative and motivational factors are not the same. The use of sodium amytal or sodium pentothal interviews in the civilian neuroses is essentially for short psychotherapeutic use. It is not advocated for the prolonged psychoanalytic therapy except for certain indications which we shall enumerate later. The question of the use of sodium amytal interviews in the civilian neuroses is intimately connected with the problem of short psychotherapy versus prolonged psychotherapy. This issue is by no means settled and most likely in a generalized sense will never be settled. There is ample evidence to show that some patients respond well to short psychotherapy while others have a successful outcome with prolonged psychotherapy, and still others do not respond to either of these approaches. Therefore, generalizations that a psychotherapy must always be prolonged or must always be short is, in our opinion, unrealistic. Unfortunately, we know very little about the type of patient or the clinical picture which will respond best to one or the other therapeutic approach. The clinical symptoms and even the psychodynamic factors give only a general hint, and by no means a reliable one, as to how the patient will fare with short or with prolonged psychotherapy.

PROLONGED PSYCHOTHERAPY. The use of sodium amytal interviews interpolated into the psychoanalytic or into the prolonged psychotherapeutic approach is sometimes indicated, especially if the patients' productions are meagre or if the material is very deeply repressed or if the emotional response produces such intense inarticulateness that little is being accomplished by the standard technique. In these cases when sodium amytal interviews were used, the patients became more cooperative, more verbally productive, the transference relationship became more intense, and the repressive forces were loosened with a resultant upsurge of associative material. Many patients, however, even with this additional technique, did not progress in the course of psychoanalytic therapy. At present it cannot be stated with certainty how frequently a bogged-down analytic patient will respond to an interpolated sodium amytal interview. In some patients the use of amytal will be contraindicated, especially if applied by the same analyst or the therapist who treats the patient. The indications and contraindications of this form of therapy must be decided in each individual case.

Acute panic states occurring in the framework of psychoanalytic therapy or prolonged psychotherapy often necessitate the use of special methods. Such conditions are disagreeable occurrences for the patient and therapist alike since they are often associated with unpleasant vegetative manifestations, sui-

cidal ideas, or certain phobias. These often become so dominant as to prevent the patient from leaving his home. In such
instances the use of sodium amytal intravenously in connection
with the regular therapy is quite often beneficial. It eliminates
the anxiety state and permits, after a short period of time, the
original form of therapy to be resumed. Similar indications are
present in some obsessive-compulsive patients in whom the
obsession or the compulsion becomes so dominant that the patient is unable to give much attention to anything but his symptoms. Here again the interpolation of narcotherapy permits the
temporary reduction of the emotional charge behind the symptoms, and soon the original treatment can be resumed without
resorting to hospitalization.

In the treatment of some psychosomatic patients we also
at times see, especially during analysis, an intensification of the
somatic symptomatology. This is very disturbing to the patient
and often seriously interferes with the transference relationship.
On the other hand, the somewhat rapid reduction of somatic
symptoms which occasionally occurs in these cases may lead
to emotional outbursts, anxiety, or hysterical reactions. In all
of these instances the temporary use of sodium amytal as an
adjunct of psychotherapy is indicated and its employment advocated more often than is common today. Otherwise we do not
believe, with the exception of some rare instances, that the
narcotherapeutic method as it is used currently is indicated in
the framework of a prolonged psychoanalytic treatment.

SHORT-TERM NARCOTHERAPY. It was previously mentioned
that there is no definite agreement as to which type of patient
should be treated with short-term psychotherapy and which type
with prolonged psychotherapy. There is even less agreement as
to whether short-term therapy should be used alone or in conjunction with hypnosis, sodium amytal, and similar drugs. We
do not feel that the drug technique is able to do more than
ordinary psychotherapy, although it will be able to shorten the
treatment considerably if the patient is a suitable one for any
form of short-term therapy. It also enables us to give treatment
to patients who are so reticent or uncooperative that it would

take a long time to establish a transference relationship with them.

The most suitable cases for short-term narcotherapy are found to be those patients suffering from anxiety states, especially an acute one, and from hysterical reactions. Much less responsive were cases of obsessive-compulsive neuroses, those with phobic reactions, and those suffering from marked sexual maladjustments such as homosexuality, exhibitionism, voyeurism, and similar disturbances. We have also obtained gratifying results in psychosomatic patients, even when the disorder has been present for a considerable period of time. Some cases of schizophrenia, especially the well-integrated pseudoneurotic schizophrenic group, are also amenable to this approach even though the therapeutic results are not as good as in the neuroses. In cases of manic-depressive psychosis, overt schizophrenia, and psychopathic personality states, this form of regular short-term narcotherapy did not yield satisfactory results, except in a few cases, and this approach is definitely inferior to other methods of treatment used today with psychotic patients. We did not use this method in alcoholics or drug addicts, but Lemere reported a series of alcoholic patients who benefited a great deal from narcotherapy.

The advantages of the short-term narcotherapy are obvious. There is a large number of neurotic patients in offices and clinics awaiting treatment; these treatments as employed today are cumbersome, expensive, and time-consuming. Any method which will condense treatment-time is, therefore, welcome, even though the results at times will show more symptomatic improvement than profound insight cures. In spite of this, a considerable number of patients respond to such narcotherapy and remain well. If the short-term narcotherapy is unsuccessful, no harm is done and a prolonged treatment can then be instituted.

Psychotherapy with sodium amytal given intravenously of course does not mean psychotherapy by the inexperienced, with the drug compensating for lack of skill and psychotherapeutic acumen. It does require that the person employing this technique be well versed in the psychodynamics of therapy in general and should signify that the short-term narcotherapy is being employed because the therapist feels that ordinary psychotherapy will not help the patient sufficiently. Narcoanalysis will not replace psychoanalysis or psychotherapy. Nevertheless it is an important adjunct in the treatment of some patients. It must be emphasized that narcotherapy is not the last word in such treatment and that probably in the future even more potent therapeutic measures will be devised in which psychotherapy will be linked with drugs having a specific somatic influence on the emotions, especially that of anxiety.

The technique of narcoanalysis must be acquired by constant practice in the same way as skill in psychotherapy can be acquired only by experience. Owing to limited space, we cannot discuss in detail how such a treatment can be adapted to the different kinds of neurotic patients. This treatment too, as in psychotherapy, must be individualized. Stereotyped application will yield only stereotyped or unimpressive results.

In this therapeutic technique we must first consider the fact that the drug alters the psychic state of the patient by making him more suggestible, and that this condition produces certain therapeutic disadvantages as well as advantages. The advantage is that patients are more impressionable to interpretation. On the other hand, if improperly handled, suggestive questions or suggestive interpretations could lead to an acting-out of interpretations. Consequently how such interpretations are made must be weighed much more carefully than in a standard psychotherapeutic technique without the use of drugs. There is no particular rule as to whether the narcotherapy should be conducted on a free-association basis or on the basis of a verbalized question method as used by Deutsch. We usually permit the patient to associate freely in one or two drug sessions. If significant material emerges, this is clarified by questioning. Interpretations given to the patient are similar to those given in psychoanalysis or prolonged psychotherapy. Because we are dealing with short-term psychotherapy, interpretations are handled more actively than in prolonged psychotherapy. This does not mean that the therapist must overwhelm the patient with interpretations, thus permitting the treatment to degenerate into a form of interpretative persuasion. It is important to formulate the interpretations clearly and simply because of the drugged condition of the patient. Elaborate interpretations and re-discussion of the material should be undertaken in a drug-free interview. This applies to patients who after a drug session show some amnesia about the material and interpretations.

Some patients progress very rapidly, and at times it is necessary to avoid a precipitous emergence of traumatic material which the patient is not able to handle in a drug-free state. In such instances while the patient is in a drug-free session, it is best to refrain from interpretations and to discuss the material obtained rather cautiously. Then while the patient is under the influence of the drug, the same traumatic points can again be brought up in order to determine whether there is a marked difference in handling the material in the drugged and in the drug-free sessions. We alluded above to the method of handling such patients in which a rapid emergence of traumatic material leads to panic or psychotic states.

Short-term psychotherapy is more ego-supportive than the usual prolonged psychoanalysis. Narcoanalysis is no exception to this rule. With this method, anxieties and other disturbing emotional situations emerge more rapidly and much more actively, and consequently the ego, in order to handle all this, will need much more support than if the ego has to handle the material in minute doses. The technique for this ego-support is the same as in other psychotherapeutic techniques which are active in interpretations. Reassurance, suggestion, encouragement, and advice in handling situations, are more liberally utilized than occurs in psychoanalysis proper.

The transference and counter-transference situations in short-term psychotherapy, especially under the influence of a drug, were not studied as extensively as in the standard psychoanalytic treatment. More work will have to be devoted to this aspect in future research. Usually the transference is established rapidly. On the other hand, many of the nuances of interpretation relationships which occur in a prolonged treatment are not as manifest. In short-term narcotherapy the interpretation of transference situations is utilized much less than in a Freudian psychoanalytic approach. Even so, rather pointed remarks and attitudes will emerge from the patient, indicating his feelings toward the therapist, especially on sexual issues, aggressive impulses, or in relation to early parental feelings. The handling of this material requires more presence of mind than is necessary in prolonged psychotherapy because of the uninhibited state of the patient. The counter-transference is also developed more rapidly because the patient is more pliable and complacent, particularly if he manifests rapid improvement. This, of course, ingratiates the therapist to a considerable degree. Generally, however, we feel that the problems which come up in the transference and counter-transference situations are no more complicated than they are in patients treated without drugs.

CONTRADICTIONS AND COMPLICATIONS. Some patients express a great deal of fear in relation to submitting to sodium amytal intravenously. These are patients who are afraid that they will release some material which could be very damaging to themselves or who are afraid of the physical procedure, especially of injection. Other patients become panicky at the thought that they will become sleepy, unconscious, or intoxicated. In many patients it is often possible to allay these fears prior to the interview. In spite of this, however, a few patients will resist and will refuse to submit to this narcotherapeutic technique. We feel, therefore, that this approach should not be used with patients who are very opposed or antagonistic to it.

Some investigators expressed the fear that the treatment could lead to habituation to barbiturates. Theoretically this is possible, especially in certain patients who are already addicted to alcohol or to other drugs and in those who take barbiturates habitually by mouth. This group could readily crave the drug for its relaxing and euphorizing effects and not for the psychotherapy which is given with it. Practically, however, we did not encounter any such habituation in patients who were submitted to no more than about fifty sessions of treatment. In the literature the apprehension regarding addiction was recorded, but properly documented cases were not produced, indicating that such habituation does not occur with any frequency.

The most important complication is the possibility of the release of a psychosis under the influence of sodium amytal intravenously, especially in patients who were formerly apparently well-integrated. The release of latent schizophrenia, and particularly of paranoid or catatonic excited states, can occur under sodium amytal or sodium pentothal intravenously. This situation, however, is not too frequent. If, in the course of narcotherapy, a patient releases psychotic material, it is best not to interrupt the session but slowly to inject enough amytal or pentothal to induce sleep in the patient and to permit him to sleep for an hour or two. Usually when the patient wakes up there is amnesia for the released psychotic material. In rare instances, if the frank psychosis continues, hospitalization of such a patient may be necessary. In a hospital setting if such psychotic episodes occur during the course of narcotherapy, these situations can be readily handled by the usual hospital methods.

SUMMARY AND CONCLUSIONS

The foregoing material presents an outline but not a comprehensive review of the work being done with the specialized techniques of narcodiagnosis and narcotherapy. We would like to stress that these techniques should be regarded as adjuncts to ordinary diagnostic and psychotherapeutic methods current in psychiatry, not as substitutes for such methods. As adjuncts, employed with skills in suitable cases, narcodiagnosis and narcotherapy present a very helpful aid in the diagnosis, prognosis, and treatment of many mental disorders. Further experimentation is needed to improve the technique and to elucidate its theoretical background, still not well understood. We hope with this outline to focus attention upon this valuable auxiliary in diagnosis and therapy, and to promote further studies.

BIBLIOGRAPHY

1. ADATTO, C. P., "Observations on criminal patients during narcoanalysis." *Arch. Neurol.*, LXII, 82–92, 1949.

2. BARBARA, D. A., "An evaluation of the therapeutic role of narcoanalysis in mental disorders." *J. Nerv. & Ment. Dis.*, CIV, 414–424, 1946.

3. BLECKWENN, W. J., "Schizophrenia." *Assn. Res. in Nerv. and Ment. Dis.*, X, 1931.

4. BOBON, J., "Impuissance datant de trois années, analysée et guérie en une seule séance de subnarcose." *Acta. Neurol. et Psychiatr. Belg.*, XLIX, 361–364, 1949.

5. BRICKNER, R. M., PORTER, R. T. AND OTHERS, "Direct reorientation of behavior patterns in deep narcosis." *Arch. Neurol. & Psychiat.*, LXIV, 165–195, 1950.

6. CORNIL, L. AND OLLIVIER, H., "Considérations sur la narcoanalyse psychosomatique en psychiatrie infanto-juvenile." *Ann. Medico-Psychol.* (Paris), 3, 318–321, 1948.

7. COUMEL, P., VELLUZ, J. AND HOSOTTE, "Narco-analyse d'une contracture avec tremblement." *La Presse Médicâle,* 54/62, 844, 1946.

8. CRAIGIE, H. B., "Treatment of acute war neurosis." *Brit. Med. J.*, Dec., 1942.

9. DELAY, J. AND MALLET, J., "Application du sodium amytal en neuro-psychiatrie et en médecine psychosomatique." *L'encephale* (Paris), 37/38, 99–108, 1948.

10. DE OLIVEIRO, W. I., "Erfahrungen mit Narkoanalyse bei funktionellen Psychosen." *Neurobiologia* (Pernambuco), XII, 99–126, 1949.

11. DEUTSCH, F., *Applied Psychoanalysis.* New York, Grune and Stratton, 1949.

12. D'HOLLANDER, L., "Quelques résultats de la narcoanalyse des psychonévroses." *Acta. Neurol. et Psychiatr. Belg.*, XLIX, 369–373, 1949.

13. DOMINICI, F., "La narco-analisi nella prassi medico-legale." *Minerva Medica,* (Turin), 1/17, 505–509, 1949.

14. EVRARD, E., "Exploration du psychisme et traitment sous sub-

narcose barbiturique." *Acta. Neurol. et Psychiatr. Belg.,* XLIX, 351–361, 1949.

15. FISCHER, G., "La narco-analyse ne peut être admise dans l'expertise judiciare." *Le Concours Médical,* (Paris), 71/14, 741, 1949.

16. FLORDH, P., "Södersjukhusets Psykiatriska AVD., Stockholm Narkoanalysen Och Dess Kliniska Avändbarhet." *Svenska Lakartidningen,* (Stockholm), 46/9, 477–484, 1949.

17. HOCH, P. H., "The present status of narcodiagnosis and therapy." *J. Nerv. & Ment. Dis.,* CIII, 248–259, 1946.

18. ———, "Narcodiagnosis and narcotherapy in the neuroses and psychoses." *N. Y. St. J. Med.,* XLVII, 2694–2698, 1947.

19. HORSLEY, J. S., "Narcoanalysis." *Lancet,* I, 55, 1936.

20. ———, "Narcoanaylsis." *J. Ment., Sc.,* July, 1936.

21. ———, "Narcoanalysis." *Brit. Med. J.,* August, 1942.

22. KALINOWSKY, L. B. AND HOCH, P. H., *Shock Treatments.* New York, Grune and Stratton, 1946.

23. KAMENEVA, E. N. AND YAGODKA, P. K., "Sodium amytal: its therapeutic and diagnostic uses." *Am. Rev. Societ. Med.,* III, 328–331, 1946.

24. LARIVIERE, P. "La Narcoanalyse et les névroses de guerre." *J. de L'Hôtel-Dieu de Montreal,* VI, 367–375, 1945.

25. LINDEMANN, E., "The psychological effects of sodium amytal." *Proc. Soc. f. Exp. Biol. and Med.,* XXVIII, 864, 1930–31.

26. ———, "Psychological changes in normal and abnormal individuals under the influence of sodium amytal." *Am. J. Psychiat.,* XI, 6, 1932.

27. MALLINSON, W. P., "Narcoanalysis in neuropsychiatry." *J. Royal Navy Med. Serv.,* XXVI, 281, 1940.

28. POLATIN, P. AND PHILTINE, E. C., *How Psychiatry Helps.* New York, Harper, 1949.

29. SARGANT, W., "Some observations on abreaction with drugs." *Dig. Neurol. & Psychiat.,* (Hartford), XVI, No. 4, 193–206, 1948.

30. SCHNEIDER, P. B., "Die Narcoanalyse, eine diagnostische und

therapeutische Methode bei psychischen Störungen."
Deut. Med. Rundschau, (Mainz), 3/3, 61–64, 1949.

31. SHORVON, H. J. AND SARGANT, W., "Excitatory abreaction with special reference to its mechanism and the use of ether." *J. Ment. Sc.,* XCIII, 709–732, 1947.

32. STRATTON, H. G., HOBBS, G. E. AND CARSCALLEN, H. B., "Subcoma insulin and pentothal sodium as aids to psychotherapy." *Am. J. Psychiat.,* CIV, 56–59, 1947.

33. STROTZKA, H., "Ueber die Verwendbarkeit der intravenösen Halbnarkose in der Psychiatrie." *Wien. med. Wochenschr.,* XCVIII, No. 17–18, 192–193, 1948.

34. ———, "Narkodiagnose, Grenzen und Möglichkeiten." *Wien. klin. Wochenschr.,* 160, 1949.

35. SUSSELMAN, S., FELDMAN, F. AND BARRERA, S. E., "Intravenous injection of sodium amytal as a test for latent anxiety." *Arch. Neurol. & Psychiat.,* LVI, 567–580, 1946.

36. TEIRICH, H. R., "Bemerkungen zur Narko-Analyse." *Wein. klin. Wochenschr.,* 659–661, 1949.

37. ———, "Dynamische Psychotherapie." *Wien. med. Wochenschr.,* 460–462, 1949.

38. TILKIN, L., "The present status of narcosynthesis using sodium pentothal and sodium amytal." *Dis. Nerv. System,* X, 215–218, 1949.

39. THIODET AND MICHAUX, "A propos de la subnarcose chimique et de son intérét médico-légal." *L'Algérie Médicale,* 53/4, 139–145, 1949.

40. VON BLARER, A., "Uber die Anwendung von Sodium Pentothal in der amerikanischen Armee." *Schweiz. Zeitschr. Psychol.,* VII, 133–139, 1948.

41. WILDE, J. F., "Narcoanalysis in the treatment of war neuroses." *Brit. Med. J.,* 4–7, July, 1942.

► HYPNOANALYSIS AS A PSYCHOTHERAPEUTIC TECHNIQUE

*By Robert M. Lindner, Ph.D.**

INTRODUCTION

Over the past decade psychotherapists have seen the revival of hypnosis as a treatment adjuvant; some of us have participated in its further development as a curative instrument. Hypnosis has been recalled from the opprobrium to which it had been consigned (for reasons which we need not consider here), and fitted into the framework of theory and practice which psychoanalysis provided. Thus it has acquired a new respectability founded upon its inherent—but until recently unrealized—potentiality for rendering service in the struggle against human distress. The credit for this resurgence of interest in and use of hypnosis in therapy belongs, of course, to psychoanalysis. Without the referential frame provided by psychoanalysis and without the clinical orientation and insight implicit in the parent approach, hypnosis could not have returned so triumphantly from the scrap-heap of therapeutic hopes abandoned. This should never be lost sight of in the enthusiasm of re-discovery which we are observing today, an enthusiasm testified to by a rash of clinical papers, reports, and books; by the founding of new societies and the appearance of new journals to study, promote, and advance the arts of hypnotherapy.

DEFINITION

The very word "hypnotherapy" involves us in a crucial dis-

---

* Chief Consultant Criminal Psychologist to the Maryland Board of Correction.

tinction that has to be made before we can proceed with this discussion. Technical accuracy calls upon us to separate hypno-analysis from hypnotherapy. The latter may be regarded as a generic term applicable to all forms of treatment wherein hyp-nosis is depended upon for the results to be obtained. As such, it covers a wide range, from the old-fashioned direct suggestive methods, through the more subtle indirect techniques, to hyp-noanalysis itself. Hypnoanalysis is but one form of hypnother-apy, then, albeit the most specialized and the most complex. In this article our preoccupation will be with hypnoanalysis.

What is hypnoanalysis? Briefly, it is a therapeutic com-pound in which there is a proportionate blending of psycho-analysis and hypnosis, a blending theoretically justified by the nature of both and practically warranted by certain obvious benefits to be achieved from its judicious employment in care-fully selected cases. From psychoanalysis it takes its orienta-tional setting and its wholesale direction, as well as its inter-pretative core; from hypnosis it derives a penetrative technical instrument that obviates many of the time-consuming ele-ments which often render ordinary psychoanalysis objectionable and, in some cases, impossible. In a variety of instances, be-cause of these virtues, hypnoanalysis has become the treatment of choice. In the management of that usually treatment-deflect-ing collection of traits that compose the psychopathic person-ality, in the phobias, and with certain of the compulsive forms of neuroses, hypnoanalysis finds its most fertile fields and most rewarding employment.

APPLICABILITY

The operational limits of hypnoanalysis are not difficult to define, and the bases on which selection of cases can be made are rather clear. Its range is somewhat narrower than that of psychoanalysis in one sense; in another it is wider. Broadly speaking, anyone who can be hypnotized can be hypnoana-lyzed. From the technical and clinical points of view, however, this generalization has to be modified, for there are many addi-tional considerations which an experienced clinician will want to examine, considerations depending upon the specific nature of the case at hand. Research over the last decade has made it clear that there are two quite definite and important contra-indications for hypnoanalysis. Significantly, these relate also to the question of hypnotizability, and so they actually consti-tute almost self-limiting factors which will ordinarily give the conscientious clinician pause.

CONTRAINDICATIONS

The first contraindication for hypnoanalysis applies to the condition of the patient's conscious ego. By and large, it is true that where the conscious ego is fragmentated or far gone in debility—as in actively psychotic cases—hypnosis is impos-sible; but in addition it is also dangerous even if a rare case should demonstrate a capacity for entering the hypnotic state. Hypnoanalysis, therefore, requires first of all that the conscious ego of the patient be relatively intact. This requirement natu-rally limits its applicability to the non-psychotic and, for the most part, also to those who are not incipiently psychotic, with egos already showing the first if faint signs of conscious-ego destruction. Moreover, to violate this limitation is a hazardous and clinically ill-advised undertaking. It is not only wasteful of effort and unproductive of results, but the risk is thereby run—with, incidently, a statistical likelihood approaching absolute-ness in this writer's experience—of precipitating a psychosis or, in the presence of psychosis, of shattering beyond repair what remnants there are on which other therapy could have capital-ized. In view of recent work with the psychoanalysis of psy-chotics, and in the face of the fact that the borderline psychotic shows a fair prognosis with psychoanalysis, here is one respect in which hypnoanalysis has a considerably narrowed operational range compared with its parent therapeutic form.

A second contraindication for hypnoanalysis narrows the range still further. It limits its use to cases in which strongly latent homosexuality either is nonexistent or, at the least, does not play a major role in the presenting distress. This means that overt homosexuals can be hypnoanalyzed. So also can latent homosexuals with adequate defense systems that contain their homosexuality, and also such individuals as possess, at the outset of treatment, some insight with regard to their latent homosexuality. However it excludes the rather numerically extensive individuals with weak and inadequate defenses, the fearful character-type whose homosexuality is strongly featured in the ontogeny of his neurosis, and the neurotic whose unconscious conflict is founded upon latent homosexuality. With all of these —except for a certain type of latent homosexuality characterized in men by marked effeminacy, complete passivity, and near-total dependency—hypnosis is almost impossible of attainment and, where achieved, is useless for therapeutic purposes.

Attempts to hypnoanalyze the types described routinely meet with failure. They cannot be hypnotized because they so strongly fear being assaulted that they are preoccupied with fantasies about being attacked; or the experience of hypnosis is itself unconsciously interpreted as an assault. In the infrequent cases where hypnosis is possible, moreover, an ordinary occurrence is for the trance to pass over into real sleep. By this latter means a defense is wrought that withdraws the ego from participation in—or awareness of—the assault it expects to be practiced upon it. So the second contraindication is seen likewise to represent a constriction of the operational effectivity of this method when compared with its forebear; and psychoanalysis remains the single therapy offering hope in just such cases as hypnoanalysis has to exclude.

SPECIAL APPLICATIONS

A widening of the effective range of hypnoanalysis, when compared with psychoanalysis, is evident on the score of its success—by now amply documented in the literature—with certain diagnostic categories and types. They are the ones before which psychotherapy at large confesses helplessness and psychoanalysis in particular admits either defeat (in the one instance) or prolonged and intensive struggle with the expectation of only equivocal success. In the category of psychopathic personality, for example—a category heretofore regarded with therapeutic nihilism—hypnoanalysis can claim achievements regarded in some quarters as remarkable. As we all know, the chief problem with which the therapist is confronted in such cases is that of "holding" the patient in therapy until a beachhead can be gained and occupied by insight into his personality. This is the very problem of their therapy, as Wittels, Dooley, and others too numerous to mention have stressed. But with hypnoanalysis this "problem" no longer exists since the nature of the method permits the utilization of post-hypnotic suggestion which becomes—until first transference and then insight take over—the binder of patient to treatment. The same applies to a wide range of the addictions, including alcohol. Many of these are found among the psychopathic personalities or other similar character distortions. With them, hypnoanalysis performs both as an investigative and synthesizing technique. At the same time it provides strength for those positive elements in the personality that the discomfiture of the patient informs us must be there, assisting him in the battle against the neurosis by what amounts to "shoring up" of the ego. In the instances of addictions arising within the constellations of perversion and impulse neuroses, precisely the same applies.

Among the phobias and certain of the compulsions, hypnoanalysis offers gains ordinarily achieved more slowly and more painfully with psychoanalysis. This statement however has to be qualified by the reminder that the contraindications as stated above will limit the number of cases to which the technique can be applied. Nevertheless, if attention is paid by the clinician to the structural aspects of his compulsive or phobic patient's personality, and if then treatment is instituted with appropriate safeguards, there is a likelihood of early success. Again, the integrated and positive ego-elements receive nourishment as a by-product of the method, and gains made against disruptive forces within the patient have a chance to become quickly incorporated into the total personality. Thereafter these gains assist the therapist by alignment with his goals and aims.

The further dynamics of this process refer, of course, to the transference and its special nature within hypnoanalysis, as well as to the handling and fate of resistances. A discussion of these most important factors, however, has to be reserved until we outline the methodology of the technique.

METHODOLOGY

Treatment by hypnoanalysis begins with a period of training-in-hypnosis for the patient. At one time such a patient–training period was entered upon abruptly and without ceremony, but the wisdom of prefacing this training period by an antecedent discussion with patients of their preconceived biases, fears, or popularly-derived notions regarding hypnosis has been acknowledged by most practitioners. Wolberg, in particular, has stressed the importance of this introductory phase. He has pointed out not only the salutory effect it is likely to have on patients who retain cultural prejudices against hypnosis with attendant apprehension, but also the effectiveness of the few hours' time devoted to it in overcoming unconscious resistances that often create artifacts on which the whole course of treatment is likely to founder.

The present writer recently witnessed a striking illustration of this in a case where a patient had been under prolonged psychoanalysis which, despite certain marked successes, was held inconclusive because of a peculiar amnesia covering a series of events that both the analyst and the patient considered essential to recover. The assistance of the writer was requested in this matter and, although the entire procedure was regarded as somewhat irregular, the attempt at recovery of the missing period through hypnosis was made. Despite intensive efforts, however, the patient seemed unable to enter the hypnotic state. Questioned closely about this, it soon developed that the resistance the patient demonstrated to hypnosis was, indeed, an artifact. It appears that when the project was discussed with his analyst, the latter made an incautious observation to the effect that "you can try it, but it won't work." Thereafter this casual comment stood as a barrier to hypnosis even though the patient was —as it developed once the matter was clarified—an excellent hypnotic subject. Unconsciously the patient had interpreted this chance remark as a command not to be hypnotized. Nor was this all; we later discovered that these words had led to the formation of an additional unconscious block against hypnosis: if the patient permitted himself to be hypnotized then thereby his own analyst would be proved wrong, and—so the resistance ran—if his analyst was proved wrong in this, then he was likely to have been wrong throughout the long analysis. This the patient could neither permit nor tolerate; so he simply "refused" to be hypnotized.

Such may be the stuff of which resistances to hypnosis are made.

The actual period of patient training-in-hypnosis will vary in length depending upon the patient's aptitude for the work and the amount of time required to find the "level" of trance—again a highly individualized matter—best suited to the continuance of treatment. Clinicians vary with respect to the optimal level, some maintaining that a light trance featured by relaxation is required; others believe that trance at the somnambulistic level increases chances for positive results. In practice, however, no strict rule can be followed, since patients show a striking facility for selecting for themselves, as it were, the level of trance-depth at which they can function most efficiently and, in any case, close observation discloses that that level varies from time to time during treatment and with the analytical material being handled.

However, by the end of the training period, three criteria demand to be met: the patient should be able to enter a hypnotic state of trance without difficulty, on the signal of the hypnoanalyst; he should be able expeditiously to carry out post-hypnotic suggestions, particularly suggestions relating to post-hypnotic amnesia; and he should, without difficulty, be able to accomplish memorial reversion. Regarding the latter requirement, it has to be noted further that this entails the ability not only to remember in the sense of recall, but also to re-experience in the sense of re-live.

TYPES OF MEMORIAL REVERSION

At this point we encounter a distinction not often given the weight or the meaningfulness it should have in the minds of analysts who employ hypnoanalysis. There exist, in essence and for the purposes of this kind of therapy, two kinds of memorial reversion of equal importance for the method: regression and revivification. "Regression" is the term used to describe remembering where the patient merely recalls and regards the products of recollection with his present outlook. "Revivification" is the literal psychic return to a previous biographical setting or situation in which the patient re-participates in events. Since these alternative forms of memorial reversion are particularly germane to hypnoanalysis, and since they each have a specific role to play in the treatment, much care has to be exercised in insuring that patients become talented in the employment of both, before the initial period of training is brought to a close.

TRANSFERENCE, RESISTANCE, AND ABREACTION

Treatment by the method of hypnoanalysis may be said to begin for the patient with the close of the training period and the opening of the analytic phase which follows immediately. This, however, is not completely true, since therapy is always initiated with the first exchange between clinician and patient and, in hypnoanalysis, by the time the second phase is reached not only have certain resistances and defenses already been clarified, but a manifest positive transference has been developed. This latter observation requires explanation which must be delayed. Suffice it to say at this juncture, however, that the charge made in some quarters that hypnoanalysis works only with a manifest positive transference falsely imposed upon the patient, that it ignores all other transference aspects in defiance of absolute therapeutic standards and to the detriment of the patient, is false and based on little knowledge of the process. Nevertheless, the midphase of therapy by hypnoanalysis does imitate the process of psychoanalysis and utilizes free association. Exactly as in psychoanalysis the patient is called upon to produce material—associations, dreams, recollections, etc. —which are interpretatively handled by the analyst. It is only when marked resistances are encountered that the patient is hypnotized, by the use of the appropriate signal, and the resistance in question thus undercut.

Now it is precisely at this point, more than elsewhere, that hypnoanalysis has been subject to criticism resulting from a serious lack of understanding. We are aware that psychoanalysis is, essentially, the analysis of resistance and transference. Some have held that the efficacy of hypnoanalysis is reduced by this undercutting of resistance and that, because of it, the treatment must be superficial. The objection disappears, however, when the facts are known. In the first place, not all resistances are dispelled by hypnosis. The usual reluctances, hesitancies, and more shallow blocks are manipulated in routine fashion through discussion, interpretation, and evocation through insight into the mechanisms of defense. The more serious resistances, those that relate to the fundamental personality structure and the character determinants, as well as resistances due to amnesia for traumatic events or defense mechanisms habitually employed and eventuating in neurosis, character malformation, and distortion through symptom-formation—these are called upon to respond to hypnosis. The patient is simply hypnotized and requested to continue his free associations in this state. At this point the analyst may press for the material excluded in the waking state and resisted against, or he may call upon either regression or revivification, if the matter is of an historical nature. When the material has been liberated, however, and thoroughly exhumed in the hypnotic trance, the state of hypnosis is dispelled, the patient returned to the waking state, and the usual analytic procedure again enjoined.

Here, once more, a clinical caution has to be interjected. Although there are some analysts who follow a vagrant fashion of therapy and currently de-emphasize—if they do not entirely disregard—the principle of abreaction, experience with hyp-

noanalysis regularly confirms its necessity for total therapy and
lasting therapeutic benefit. Therefore, abreaction in hypnoanalysis is sought. Yet it is not alone necessary that abreaction
occur in the hypnotic state; the clinician has also to insure
that the total organism participates in it. To do this and to
guarantee that the compound personality shares in the therapeutic process, post-hypnotic amnesia for each trance state is
imposed.

NECESSITY FOR POST-HYPNOTIC AMNESIA FOR TRANCE

The imposition of post-hypnotic amnesia for trance when
it is utilized in recovery of lost, repressed, rejected, or otherwise deflected memory—or in the disintegration of resistance
—is, in the opinion of this writer, an absolute condition of hypnoanalysis. It has been observed that the function of this procedure is three-fold. Through the operation of a phenomenon
referred to in the literature as the "interim phenomenon," once
material has been expressed in the trance state, the ego of the
patient is slowly but subtly and surely prepared to receive
what has up until then been unconscious. In other words, in
the interim between the disclosure of significant but repressed
memories or other resistance-forming material, and waking
free association, the ego is readied for the reception of what it
had formerly rejected for any one or a combination of possible
reasons. It can be estimated by the reader what this means for
the therapeutic process and how valuable for treatment such a
phenomenon is. Technically, it replaces the lengthy "analysis
of resistances" phase of usual psychoanalysis which also functions to prepare the ego for the reception of that which it has
formerly deflected or defended itself against.

In the second place, with the introduction of post-hypnotic
amnesia for the events of trance, it always transpires that a
spontaneous production of that for which the amnesia was imposed comes about. Accordingly, nothing pertinent to therapy
is lost, and the total organism not only is permitted to participate in the therapy but—and this is the third benefit—the va-

lidity of the material of the analysis is constrained to remain consistently high as the clinician obtains a two-way check on production.

To return to the subject of transference, in the course of the middle phase of hypnoanalytic therapy, transference is managed and analyzed as it is when psychoanalysis is employed. When necessary, it is subject to examination, and no regular rule for it can be laid down. Nevertheless, there are matters pertaining to transference that call for further exposition. Nominally, the transference in hypnoanalysis is similar to that observed in the course of employment of the parent technique. It is liable to the same vicissitudes of movement and function and, on the surface at least, cannot be distinguished from the form usually encountered. Yet there is a qualitative difference between transference in psychoanalysis and hypnoanalysis, a difference that may be of theoretical interest and importance when it comes to answering the question as to the nature of hypnosis itself.

THE TRANSFERENCE AND THE NATURE OF HYPNOSIS

Scientists concerned with the mind have never ceased to pose this question of the nature of hypnosis nor has anyone yet provided the kind of answer that will satisfy all requirements. Most formulations of the hypnotic state and of the special nature of the accord between hypnotist and subject have been unsatisfactory in one way or another, and the biases of the investigators and theoreticians on the subject have been displayed in a regrettable tendency to romanticize the observed phenomena. Thus, hypnosis has been regarded as a variant form of "falling in love," of "role-playing" in regard to the projection of a parental image, as having "an erotic root," as "surrender to dependency and submission," and the like.

When, however, the concept of transference is applied to the relationship between hypnoanalyst and patient in the course of treatment, the relationship that allows hypnosis and actually permits the treatment to be carried out, a certain amount of clarification of the problem results, and a better answer to the question naturally presents itself. Such answer is to the effect that, due to the narrowing of the attentional field and the creation of a new social gestalt, the figure of the analyst is introjected and incorporated into the unconscious ego of the patient. From this literal engulfing of the analyst into the patient's unconscious ego, there is created a highly special and unique form of rapport which accounts for the rapidity with which exploration of the unconscious takes place in hypnoanalysis. In other words, in the process of entering hypnosis, and while under hypnosis, the analyst by introjection becomes incorporated with the patient. He loses the chameleon quality that is projected upon him out of the patient's resistances and defenses, when the patient is working in the waking state; at the same time he retains the quality as an object to be reacted to, in accordance with the demands of the historical nature of the personality and its formative influences.

Thus the analyst, when the patient is under hypnosis, has thrust upon him a dual and complex role: that of participator or sharer in the unconscious ego and, at the same time, that of object. It is to be supposed that this is, more or less, an intensification of the situation behind transference in psychoanalysis, with the qualitative difference that herein the introjective process operates to localize the therapist's image—during trance—in the unconscious ego rather than elsewhere (for example, in the superego where the image of the therapist so often comes to rest during certain phases of ordinary psychoanalysis).

Transference in hypnoanalysis has, in addition, further responsibilities. In recalcitrant cases—for example, in cases of psychopathic personality—transference is deliberately exploited for the continuity of treatment. Finally, and due to its special nature as described, it is a powerful instrument in the third phase of the therapeutic process.

The end-phase of hypnoanalysis is wholly synthesizing. It differs not at all from the closing stages of psychoanalytic therapy except as it continues to employ hypnosis wherever the analyst considers it necessary. He will find it necessary in at least one, or at the most two, places. The first of these is in respect to habit systems. Here it lends itself to the re-enforcement of newly-acquired response-and-reaction patterns, assisting the patient's insightful determination toward change. It operates to invade, to break down—and eventually to destroy—motor organizations employed in the maintenance of former defenses or systems for achieving satisfaction when these systems and defenses are no longer necessary. With post-hypnotic suggestion bolstering the new personality organization acquired by understanding, the struggle to acquire operative integration becomes less painful and less time-consuming. Especially is this true in cases where the motor system of the organism is deeply involved in the structure of the neurosis.

The second of the places where hypnosis may be necessary toward the close of hypnoanalysis is in the dissolution of transference. Here the analyst receives help in his attempt to redistribute the energies of the analytic relationship, energies that were formerly of pathogenic significance. At this juncture, of course, special qualities within the analyst are called upon to guarantee that the re-distribution follows carefully the lines dictated by the entire course of the therapy to that point. Here, particularly, the analyst's qualifications for employing hypnoanalysis come to the fore. On the whole, however, apart from those cases where an organized and habituated motor system needs to be destroyed, hypnosis in the end-phase of hypnoanalysis is not to be recommended, nor will clinicians call upon it very often. It has, indeed, been the experience of this writer that the final stages of this mode of therapy regularly show a diminishing need for hypnosis, and that ordinarily the techniques of termination employed in psychoanalysis suffice.

REQUIREMENTS FOR PRACTICING HYPNOANALYSIS

The question now arises, who shall practice hypnoanalysis? This is not an idle question; its answer involves considerations often of little moment where other modes of therapy are concerned. In hypnoanalysis we are confronted with certain unique situations having properties nowhere else encountered among the psychotherapies. The accord between patient and analyst is closer and more intense than in other forms of treatment. The tools of therapy are sharper, more incisive. The temptations confronting the therapist are more numerous, more insistent. Who, then, is qualified to employ this technique?

A first condition is self-knowledge on the part of the clinician. This means that only the analyzed practitioner can be permitted to wield the tool called hypnoanalysis. For not only is there called for the special knowledge demanded by this dependent variety of psychoanalysis—a knowledge which cannot be taught or communicated otherwise than through personal experience—but a control over the self is an acute and ubiquitous requirement exceeding every other. The nature of the situation demands it no less than the nature of the mode of therapy.

A second condition is training. Unfortunately, training in the employment of hypnoanalysis is nowhere to be obtained. Although the method is regarded with respect in professional quarters, in most places it is either still confused with hypnosis and consequently vilified, or it is given only passing and grudging recognition. In the curricula of the psychoanalytic institutes, in the universities and schools where psychotherapy is taught, during the internships and residencies of medical men preparing to do psychotherapy, hypnoanalysis is ignored and hypnosis is hardly discussed, much less required to be learned. As the situation stands, an occasional psychotherapist may present himself to the few specialists who practice hypnoanalysis and ask for training. Too often the motives involved in such a presentation are suspect; too often the candidate has first to be sent for psychoanalysis. Usually his own curiosity and self-instruction prepare the practitioner to employ hypnoanalysis, and in these schools mastery is hard-won, if indeed it is not also expensive to the well-being of patients.

SUMMARY

Hypnoanalysis is a valid technique of therapy which can point to an impressive history although that history is a brief one. By its accomplishments to date it can claim a place among other forms of treatment that have carved for themselves a niche in the Aesculapian temple. Surely it is time that provision be made for training and qualifying practitioners in the art of its use. This must be done to satisfy not only the earnest seeker after knowledge and the devoted minister to the well-being of his fellows, but also a public that makes ever-increasing demands upon the psychotherapeutic profession.

BIBLIOGRAPHY

1. BRENNAN, M. AND GILL, M. M., *Hypnotherapy*. New York, Internat. Univ. Press, 1947.
2. ERICKSON, M. R. AND KUBIE, L. S., "The successful treatment of acute hysterical depression by a return under hypnosis to a critical phase of childhood." *Psychoanal. Quart.*, X, 583, 1941.
3. GILL, M. M. AND BRENMAN, M., "Treatment of a case of anxiety hysteria by an hypnotic technique employing psychoanalytic principles." *Bull. Menninger Clinic*, VII, 6–14, 163, 1943.
4. LINDNER, R. M., *Rebel Without a Cause*. New York, Grune and Stratton, 1944.
5. ———, "Hypnoanalysis in a case of hysterical somnambulism." *Psychoanal. Rev.*, XXVII, 325, 1945.
6. ———, "Hypnoanalysis: Some theoretical and practical considerations." *Personality Disorders*. B. Glueck, ed. New York, Grune and Stratton, 1946.
7. WITTELS, F., "The position of the psychopath in the psychoanalytic system." *Internat. J. Psychoanal.*, XIX, 471, 1938.
8. WOLBERG, L. R., *Hypnoanalysis*. New York, Grune and Stratton, 1945.
9. ———, *Medical Hypnosis*. 2 vols. New York, Grune and Stratton, 1948.

► THE USE OF THE TELEPATHY HYPOTHESIS IN PSYCHOTHERAPY

*By Jule Eisenbud, M.D.**

INTRODUCTION

The term "telepathy" was defined in 1882 by F. W. H. Myers as "the communication of impressions of any kind from one mind to another independently of the recognized sensory channels." Today this is felt to be a rather loose definition which begs certain difficult questions, yet it is nevertheless sufficiently applicable to a broad class of observable phenomena to be provisionally useful for our purposes. In the present context we may disregard the distinction between telepathy and clairvoyance (the direct "perception" of inanimate objects independently of recognized sensory channels and without the intermediation of another perceiving mind). We may also ignore the difficulties inherent in such a term as "mind," as well as in the conception of the fundamental nature of the postulated interactions. Nor do we need to touch upon other aspects of what have come to be known as *psi* processes (of which telepathy is but one) which too, according to present indications, will ultimately take their place among the conditioning factors in human behavior. For the present we will limit ourselves to the discussion of phenomena in which what is known to most people as "telepathy" figures, by presumption, as the major or only *psi* process involved. In this presentation when we speak of *psi*-conditioned behavior we will for the most part

---

* Formerly Associate in Psychiatry at Columbia University School of Medicine, lecturer at the New York Psychoanalytic Institute and instructor at the New York School of Social Work.

be implying a telepathic process. The important distinction to be made here is between what we call telepathy and other processes which may be broadly grouped under "intuition"— mostly unconscious manipulation of data gathered sensorially, however occultly.

HISTORY

The fact that people could become aware, through some method, of events that were happening at such distances and under such circumstances as to eliminate the practical possibility of ordinary means of knowledge has seemingly been known from earliest times. However, although individual men of science occasionally showed some interest in these phenomena, science as a whole remained aloof from such alleged happenings, while informed opinion in general held them to be the result of superstitious illusion or outright trickery. Indeed, the mess of fraudulent and mercenary practices which came to surround the subject, from the weaseling divinations of the ancient soothsayers to the spiritualistic pimping of the seance room, seemed to justify such scorn. Only the Church gave its serious if grudging attention to the question of separating fact from fancy in the realm of the occult. Over the centuries its courts of enquiry were the only bodies even making a pretense of looking into the evidence; but wherever something turned up that looked like fact, both the fact and the witness were customarily consigned to the devil, thus posing certain awkward philosophical and scientific problems while disposing, perhaps, of the more threatening theological and administrative ones. The burning of thirty thousand witches during the period of the Church's most active interest in these matters was probably not the least factor in the development of the antipathetic attitudes toward the occult which came to prevail.

But scepticism and contempt notwithstanding, the phenomena had a way of recurring, spontaneously, ubiquitously, and with a stubborn perversity that defied the pronouncements of the Church and of the somewhat settled chairs of Science. In 1882 a group of Cambridge scholars decided that the will-o-the-wisp phenomenology of the occult was just as worthy of the attentions of science and of the application of scientific method as the more favored aspects of natural law then under investigation. Out of their resolve was born the Society for Psychical Research.

The major contribution of this group of investigators was to gather, sift, and evaluate the evidence for "psychic" occurrences according to the strictest canons of scientific enquiry. Over a period of years some of the best scientific, critical, and philosophical brains of England and the continent were devoted to this task. The results, a mountainous collection of first-hand evidence of spontaneously occurring phenomena, documented, cross-documented and critically worked-over with almost obsessional zeal, were certainly such, on any fair comparative standards, as to establish the presumptive fact of telepathy on a foundation as firm as anything else in the realm of natural phenomena.

However, what apparently was demonstrated by all this labor was less the assumption of telepathy than the great difficulty of making evidence alone, however striking, extensive, and sound, compel even interest, let alone belief, when such interest or belief were opposed by the profound and structured resistances of an entirely contrary way of life and thought. None other than T. H. Huxley, the eloquent advocate of Darwin's then-disturbing hypotheses, dismissed the work of the Society with the remark that true or false, telepathy could hold no more interest for science than the chattering of a bunch of old ladies. The final dictum of the great Helmholtz was that "Neither the testimony of all the Fellows of the Royal Society nor the evidence of my own senses could ever lead me to believe in [what is] clearly impossible."

Although the Huxleys and the Helmholtzes are still with us, attitudes today toward telepathy and other *psi* phenomena are considerably more enlightened than they were a half-century ago. Scientists of diverse fields are not quite so careless in shrugging off the entire subject as of no interest, or in declaring the alleged phenomena to be "clearly impossible," meanwhile many are taking an active part in research. This is in no small measure due to the efforts of workers at Duke University (Durham, North Carolina) and other places to develop methods of investigation which could be repeated anywhere under laboratory conditions, and the results of which could be evaluated according to the most refined and unequivocal mathematico-statistical techniques available. The cumulative evidence for what has been termed "extrasensory perception" that has been collected over the last twenty years by these patient and practically foolproof methods—methods utterly without flair and not likely to appeal to anyone's deeper needs for magic—has effectively dimmed the "reasonable doubt" to which the conservative scientist clings as a last token of individual liberty to be surrendered only before the *force majeure* of the calculus of probabilities. There is no longer any particular difficulty today in demonstrating that he who would deny the actuality of *psi* phenomena is either uninformed or unreasonable, and in the latter case, that the use of magical thinking is all on his side.

However, despite the increasing intellectual acceptance of the evidence, *psi,* including telepathy (perhaps its least inherently baffling form), tends to remain an odd, useless curio in the attic of science. Our capacity to integrate the still strange presumptive forces at work into any fairly meaningful and consistent scheme of things lags far behind our ability to demonstrate the simple existence of the phenomena. We still tend to regard *psi* events solely as phenomena, as disembodied and almost depersonalized outside happenings, instead of as manifestations of behavior that subserve, presumably, the same basic adaptational laws as all behavior. We continue to hold the data rigidly at arm's length and to keep their implications at a safe distance where they cannot touch our favored conceptions of ourselves, our actions, and our relationships.

This dissociative tendency, this isolation of knowing from affect and from significance, is particularly fostered by present-day trends in *psi* research. For all their historical usefulness and promotional value, these trends tend still to preserve a picture of *psi* as an insipid, devitalized phenomenon operating somewhere on the ineffectual and happily meaningless fringe of personality. To some extent this is an artifact of focus and methodology. We can no more expect today's professional para-psychologist, preoccupied as he is with the minutiae of experimental and evaluative techniques, to be able meaningfully to relate *psi* to the fundamental concerns of purposive human striving than we could expect the biochemist to tell us much about sexual behavior and love from his highly abstracted data on the steroid hormones.

THE PSYCHIATRIST AND TELEPATHY

On the other hand, the psychiatrist and psychoanalyst, whose business it is to study man in a larger context, has been understandably cautious about inclining even tentatively toward hypotheses which suggest a possible reality behind the complex of ideas that has always peculiarly characterized the thinking of the mentally disturbed. These "delusions," moreover, have just been triumphantly demonstrated to have their origin in the prelogical, magical thinking of the infant in a stage of development where reality-testing is still an embryonal function of the emergent ego and where behavior is dominated almost exclusively by narcissism and notions of omnipotence.

Actually the seemingly slow progress, from the scotomatized outlook which sees only discrete *psi* phenomena, to the broader concept of *psi*-conditioned behavior, is not entirely an artifact of methodology. Nor is it the result of what may appear to be empirically derived prejudice. The forces of resistance against the over-all implications of facts which perhaps nobody today can view in their ultimate significance, lie far deeper. They are no doubt themselves responsible for the attitudes of denial implicit in both the safe "scientificism" of the laboratory and in the sane, if not always logical, empiricism of the consulting room. These both are effective defenses against awareness of specific aspects of man's (or perhaps I should say, "one's," since the struggle is intensely personal in each investigator) unconscious behavior, aspects which are in certain ways more disturbing than the findings that psychoanalysis has thus far brought to light.

However, the gradual liberation of the thinking part of

man from untenable assumptions, both positive and negative, and irrespective of source, is what characterizes progress in science. This is what must take place before *psi* phenomenon can be brought into a more integral relationship to other natural events. As it happens, today's psychiatrist and psychoanalyst is particularly well situated to take part in this advance. This is not only by virtue of the fact that he is somewhat more capable than his confreres of identifying and dealing with his irrational resistances, but also because he is by training and temperament committed to the holistic approach which the data now demand. Furthermore, this type of investigation at last places him in a position to look just a little deeper than his findings to date. It enables him to gather much-needed data on the problem of where the delusions popularly held by infants really come from, and whither, in the course of the development of the sometimes overbearing sense of reality under which the chastened child labors through life, they go. This in itself should be an inviting prospect.

The foundations of a dynamic behavioristic concept of telepathic phenomena were actually laid down in the 1920's in the observations of Stekel and Freud, and have since been added to in a slow, piecemeal way by the work of a handful of psychoanalytic and psychoanalytically oriented investigators. Stekel's main contribution was to show that "thought-transference," as telepathic phenomena were characteristically designated at that time, did not occur as the idle offshoot of a virtually accidental sensitization of the minds of the agent and percipient, but that it proceeded along the lines of strongly charged emotional relationships. The content of the material that was conveyed and picked up, he showed, was apt to reflect the conflictful affects of love, hate, jealousy, etc., in terms of which the participants in a telepathic episode related to each other.

It remained for Freud, however, to make the penetrating observations about the nature of the telepathic process that, for some reason, Stekel had just fallen short of stating in an explicit way. Hitherto it had been possible to identify a telepathic occurrence as such only if the representation in dreams or otherwise of the percipient corresponded in an unusually striking and unambiguous way with what had been "transmitted" by the presumptive agent. What was looked for was a prima facie case against chance. The spontaneously occurring cases collected by the Society for Psychical Research and other groups had all been of this variety. Freud had only the most meager data to work with, but he concluded nevertheless that the telepathic communication must, for the most part, occur on an unconscious plane and hence must be subject to the same laws of unconscious mental functioning, most significantly the processes of distortion and symbolic representation, as any other material dealt with by the unconscious. He showed that unraveling the distorted derivatives of unconsciously elaborated material by means of psychoanalysis could bring to light latent correspondences which made it possible to unmask telepathic events that would otherwise not be identified as such.

CASE MATERIAL

An example will illustrate the basic principle of this approach:

A patient dreams: "I am climbing across a picket fence. My red purse slips from me and I tell someone to see that it doesn't fall through the fence, but to give it to me when I alight."

The patient associated "red purse" to uterus and thought that the dream might be premenstrual. But on second thought she felt that the dream probably had to do with the imminent termination of her treatment (climbing across a fence) and her fear of continued dependency (leaving behind a rather costly erotic attachment).

All of this was more or less relevant as far as it went. A fairly acceptable interpretation of the dream's meaning could have been formulated on this basis alone. However, one had to admit that the stamp of irreducible specificity was somehow lacking from such a patternization. For one thing, a really significant day's residue does not seem to have been dealt with, since the anticipated termination of the patient's treatment had been set months earlier, and the imminence of menstruation could not be reasonably construed as the sole provocation of such a dream elaboration. Presumably these factors plus something else concealed in some still missing, latent thoughts would be necessary for an adequate understanding of all the manifest elements. What, for instance, might account for one of the salient features of the dream, namely the *picket* fence?

On the morning following the dream the patient received a letter from a friend in another city. The friend, a surgeon, wrote that on the day he had received her last letter he had treated an unmarried woman who ostensibly had come to have some varicosities removed, but who on examination turned out to be six months pregnant. The doctor felt that this was a remarkable coincidence, because in her letter to him the patient had spoken of her discouragement at not having conceived after trying for many months. Here at hand was a woman who had become pregnant without wishing to. He hinted that an arrangement might be made whereby the patient, if she were considering adoption at all, could adopt this woman's child.

The patient's conscious reaction to this proposal was entirely negative. Her wish for a child was the culmination of a long-delayed acceptance of the feminine role that had ostensibly come about as the result of her treatment, and she wanted to become pregnant as a mark of graduation *cum laude,* so to speak. The fact that she was long since past her biological prime had only intensified her stubborn determination in the matter (the remains of a strong masculine identification), and she had by no means given up hope of achieving her desire with her own equipment. But in any case she would have nothing of private, bootleg transactions. If it ultimately turned out that she could not become pregnant, she would of course proceed through the ethical, if somewhat bureaucratic, channels of an officially licensed adoption agency.

In her dreams, however, the patient's attitudes are revealed to be considerably less rigid. If we assume her unconscious telepathic awareness of the proposal which is about to break upon her consciousness in the form of the surgeon's letter, we can look upon the dreamwork as a buffer process which enables her to deal in advance with certain problems before they confront her conscious ego. In the dream she reacts favorably toward the idea of getting a quick baby without either physiological fuss on her part or the bother of agency red tape and delay. In climbing across a picket fence she is indeed crossing a picket line, indicating that she is quite willing to avail herself of the cheap, scab "labor" that has been offered. She is also not above circumventing the difficulties of a regular agency (which represents organized "labor") by utilizing a fence (disposer of illicitly gotten goods). The representation of her uterus as a purse, finally, appears overdetermined by the allusion to the equivalence of the two in relation to securing a baby: she doesn't have to make excessive demands on her middle-aged uterus when she can buy a baby, produce one out of her purse, so to speak.

With the addition of this dimension in the structuring of the dream (a dimension achieved simply by the assumption that its latent thoughts are conditioned by a significant residue that could have been perceived only telepathically), we are able to arrive at an interpretation. Such an interpretation not only takes adequate account of the manifest dream elements otherwise only partially explained or totally unexplained, but also penetrates far deeper and with greater consistency into the patient's still unresolved conflicts. In the absence of the data which the assumption of unconscious telepathic percipience provides, we get a picture of the dream's meaning that is comfortingly ego-syntonic. The meaning is acceptable as a matter of fact not only to the patient's ego but to the therapist's as well, since it represents the patient as confidently taking the hurdle of ending her treatment with but one thing as the only still-unfinished business—the matter of seeing to it that she does not leave behind, and still attached to the therapist, her newly acquired feminine strivings. With the telepathic dimension, however, we are led to confirm our suspicion that the reasons for the patient's continuing inability to become pregnant may lie deeper than the natural limitations of her age and her physiological status: that she may actually be eager to escape from the treatment with a still menstruating, nongravid uterus; that her professed desire to become pregnant is a flight into health according to the most acceptable cultural standards—at best, perhaps, a transference-induced wish to please the analyst; and that her real aim is to get out with the compromise of a quickly and illicitly acquired baby while her continuing unproductiveness remains yet unanalyzed. All this is now contained in the red purse that she does not wish to leave behind.

THE APPLICATION OF THE TELEPATHIC HYPOTHESIS

Freud's basic observations have since been repeatedly confirmed by an increasing number of analysts during the course of their work. Moreover, continued investigation along these lines has revealed that the application of the telepathy hypothesis is a much more potent tool than might originally have been surmised (although in hindsight, of course, it seems perfectly natural that such a useful hypothesis could not long remain isolated from the major problems of behavior). A goal of science is to demonstrate orderly relationships between events. Those assumptions which appear successful in doing just this, in maximizing our ability meaningfully to organize apparently unrelated data, gradually achieve an increasing validation as their application becomes broader and more inclusive. It frequently happens, moreover, that two sets of independently derived assumptions become mutually supportive in terms of the results of their combined use. This is the case with the assumptions of psychoanalysis and the hypothesis of telepathy.

The application of the telepathy hypothesis to data gathered in the course of clinical investigation is able to reveal significant relationships behind events that would otherwise appear totally unrelated. At the same time such patternization indicates that the telepathic process (whatever it is, since we do not as yet have any adequate physical analogies for it) is not limited solely to idle and ineffectual "perceptions" which merely increase the load of the dreamwork, but that it also con-

ditions our affects and actions—in fact, every area of our functioning—in definitely observable ways. Conversely, a great deal
in our observable affects, actions, and behavior in general, both
morbid and normal, can frequently not be meaningfully pattern-
ized without the aid of an hypothesis such as that of telepathic
interaction and intercommunication between individuals.

CASE MATERIAL

A middle-aged woman in an incipiently manic state is
brought by relatives for observation. Several weeks earlier
she had suddenly gone into a *status asthmaticus* which had
lasted without a break for seventeen days, although previously she had not had the slightest asthmatic symptom for
years. This distressing state came to an abrupt end when
she received notice that her airforce pilot son was listed as
missing in action. One week later, the symptoms of manic
excitement having already begun, she received official noti-
fication that her son had been killed, shot down over France.
The date of his death was given as the exact date on which
her asthma had had its sudden onset. Curiously enough,
neither the patient nor her relatives had noticed the coincidence.

A young married woman is entertaining a few guests in
her home when she suddenly falls into a stuporous condition from which she emerges several hours later with tetra-
plegic paralysis and anesthesia. At precisely the time of her
seizure—10:30 p.m.—a former lover with whom she had
broken and whom she had not seen in almost a year, had
had a fatal heart attack. It finally emerged during questioning prompted by the patient's casual mention of the "curious" coincidence that she had later learned about, that she
had had secret expectations of being left a sizeable fortune
by this wealthy, elderly man. The will disclosed the completely unrealistic nature of this fantasy.

A young man who has abjectly followed a rejecting mistress all over Europe in the hope of getting her to marry
him, finally loses her trail and returns to the United States
in a deepening depression. About two months later the de-

pression lifts one day as if by magic, and the young man suddenly finds himself restored to life. This happy state is to last only two short weeks, however. At this time he gets word that his errant former mistress had shortly before gotten married. The date of her marriage, in fact, coincided precisely with the date on which his depression had miraculously lifted. With the receipt of this news his depression returned, worse than before and, according to him, not so very miraculously.

VALUE OF THE TELEPATHIC ASSUMPTION

These instances are not cited as proof of the reality of telepathy. From the purely evidential point of view they would not be given a second thought by the trained parapsychologist or indeed by anyone else who had his feet solidly on the ground. But they merit a very searching second thought by the psychiatrist and psychoanalyst. This is because they enable him to see more in his data and to utilize these data more intelligently, if they are viewed with the reported facts integrated by means of the telepathy hypothesis than if they are viewed as meaningless coincidences. We may grant that it is impossible to determine the precise probability of the operation of a telepathic factor in cases of this sort. Nevertheless, if we make the assumption that an unconscious telepathic percipience (which on entirely independent grounds we know to be possible), may in each such instance be the provoking stimulus of a seemingly inexplicable reaction, then we are in a position to suspect—and more important, to communicate to our patients—something significant about their functioning that might otherwise pass unnoticed.

In the first instance, the *status asthmaticus* is a valuable clue to the deeper meaning of this woman's relationship to her son. When her ego has no conscious knowledge of the loss, she reacts not with unrealistic denial which develops when the ego is formally confronted by the news, but in terms of a primitive organ language which acknowledges the loss in a way that tells us plainly where it hurts the most—and, by inference borne out by subsequent investigation, why.

In the second case, our ability to relate the patient's extremely regressive though transient symptomatology to its presumptively provoking cause tells us, as little else can, what is wrong with her marriage in the first place and what it is fundamentally that she expects in her relationships with all people. It also tells us exactly where the aggression behind her present depression stems from, an aggression which must be directed squarely against its rightful target before therapy can be really effective. Except for the searching beam of the telepathy hypothesis this target might have remained indefinitely hidden.

In the third case, the use of the telepathy hypothesis to relate the sudden lifting of our young man's depression to the marriage of his elusive mistress tells us what he himself would never have told us, what in fact he was effectively and affectively hiding from himself: that he was secretly relieved and glad to be rid at last—through forces happily beyond his control, as it were—of a woman who had brought him only humiliation and bedeviling uncertainty. Of course when his ego got wind of the event, he reacted with appropriate demonstrations of injured narcissism. The actual object-loss, however, as experienced on an entirely unconscious plane, was not only secondary but apparently salutary. Compare this reaction with that of the woman who lost her son.

We see that the assumption of telepathy, if we but give it the same kind of fair trial as we would give any other kind of assumption that had a reasonable amount of evidence in its support, is able to sharpen somewhat our clinical focus and to increase our effectual knowledge of the many still hidden determinants of human behavior. In our enthusiasm and excitement over the last half-century's advances in dynamic psychology and psychiatry, we tend to lose sight of certain facts: that for the most part we are still abysmally ignorant about how the human being functions, individually (if he can be said to do this at all) and in groups; that we still spend long hours in the consulting room listening to material out of which we are able to make sense only now and then; and that, if we face the facts quite candidly, our therapeutic efficacy falls far short of our sometimes suspiciously effusive technical and theoretical raptures. In view of these circumstances, it would seem the part of methodological conservatism to entertain provisionally, rather than to abandon, any hypothesis that gave promise of decreasing, however minimally, the many gaps in our knowledge.

The usual difficulty in getting used to a new hypothesis stems from our tendency to use it too little and too timidly. If we use an hypothesis at all we should use it boldly, imaginatively. Only in this way, which is perfectly sound from a logical point of view, providing we never let go of the controls, can we apply an hypothesis constructively and not merely as a passive vessel into which we can pour all our hopes for easy thinking. At the start we often have to force things. There are many areas, for instance, in which the telepathy hypothesis may not appear suitable until after a certain amount of preliminary organization of the data has been accomplished. It might be suggested as a working rule that before any data, however dead they may seem, are sent to the mortuary of chance or left to rot in the atmosphere of an indolent, unacknowledged indeterminism, a trial poke with the telepathy hypothesis can always be profitably attempted. An unsuspected vitality, one might almost say *joie de vivre,* is sometimes immediately manifest. Especially is this so in what has been dubbed the psychic-pathology of everyday life, a newly discovered realm with horizons far beyond, as a matter of fact, the limits of even simple telepathy to explore. However the assumption of telepathy alone can often take us a goodly distance, as the following example can show.

CASE MATERIAL

A woman patient seized the temporary absence of her husband on a business trip to consummate a flirtation that had been spasmodically percolating for some time. The next day in her analytic hour she passed the whole matter off very lightly and denied any feelings of guilt about her escapade. I tried to show her that guilt feelings were not always consciously perceived, and cited the onset of certain physical symptoms as an illustration. I also suggested that her very bravado in taking her lover into her own home, which she knew to be dangerously indiscreet, far from indicating the absence of guilt pointed in fact toward an unconscious wish to be caught and punished. All this the patient denied, rationalizing her symptoms and behavior on other grounds.

That afternoon she was again to be with her new lover for several hours, after which she was to meet her mother-in-law for dinner and theatre.

Arriving very late to meet her mother-in-law, the patient gave as an excuse the story that she had unexpectedly run into a Mr. and Mrs. X, with whom she had stopped in somewhere for a friendly cocktail. This couple had moved out of the patient's community and social set several years before and hence, according to the patient, had occurred to her on the spur of the moment as absolutely safe and perfectly suited to lend the necessary touch of casual documentation to her lie. The mother-in-law had known of the X's but had never met them.

At the theatre, who should take a seat directly in front of the patient but Mrs. X! The patient was overcome with confusion but was powerless to prevent the imminent catastrophe. Mrs. X immediately spotted the patient whom she greeted effusively as a long-lost friend. She hastened to explain that her husband too was away on business. Introductions were unavoidable. The patient tried to slur over Mrs. X's name, but the surprised and then frozen stare of the mother-in-law showed at once that this attempt at concealment had only succeeded in underlining the significance of the telltale name. Afterwards, the patient, as if ferreted out by the magic beam of divine omniscience, had all she could do to keep from blurting out the whole story. As it was, the lie she invented to cover the lie in which she had been caught was so silly and so obviously contrived that the mother-in-law was inevitably led to suspect something pretty close to the truth.

In this example of what would usually be referred to as

"the long arm of coincidence," we are forced by one significant circumstance to consider a more satisfactory hypothesis
than the meaningless operation of blind chance. This was
the patient's repressed sense of guilt about her affair and
her unconscious need for exposure. (This, it should be remembered, had been pointed out to the patient before the
event.) The fact that the chance meeting with Mrs. X in
the theatre would seem to satisfy this need, forces us to examine the means whereby the patient chose the X's, seemingly at random, as the focal point of her lie.

The patient had gotten her theatre tickets about two
weeks in advance. Mrs. X had bought her seat from a ticket
agent the night before (a fact the patient later ascertained,
at my request). For the sake of convenience and simplifica-
tion we will assume that the primary fact of Mrs. X's position directly in front of the patient at the theatre represents
a chance event. The question now is whether my patient's
seemingly random choice of the X's for her lie was also a
chance event—that is, unconsciously determined, of course,
but in no relation to the fact that she was later to find Mrs.
X right under her nose—or whether it was in some way
conditioned by that very, already determined fact. (An analogy would be somatic compliance in the "psychogenesis" of
an organic symptom.)

This question cannot be given a definite answer in the
absence of a clearly circumscribed set of probabilities relating to the events under scrutiny. We are in a position,
nevertheless, to consider several significant data: First, investigation of the patient's introspections surrounding the
whole constellation of events failed to reveal any already
existing associative link to account for the X's popping into
her head at the moment of her lie. Second, if we assume the
possible operation of unconscious telepathic perception, the
patient could easily have been in possession of the knowledge that Mrs. X was within the next hour or two going to
be in a position to confront her. Finally, the patient's repressed sense of guilt could conceivably have led her to
utilize this knowledge in the manner described, just as she
might have used any other readily available means to fulfill
her unconscious need.

It is the business of science to attack and harry chance wherever it seems to present itself. Here, in a specific case where there are certain known facts to work with, the use of psychoanalytic insight in conjunction with the hypothesis of telepathic or *psi* functioning enables us measurably to shorten the long arm of coincidence. It might also be noted that the interpretation of her behavior which I was able to formulate for the patient on this basis had a much more marked effect than my earlier attempt to make her aware of the deviousness of her sense of guilt.

UTILIZATION OF *PSI*-DERIVED MATERIAL IN PSYCHOTHERAPY

It is perhaps too early to formulate a number of specifically valid principles for the utilization in psychotherapy of telepathic or *psi*-derived material. There are many types of psychotherapy, not all of them based on bringing unconscious material to consciousness. However, insofar as the objective in any particular situation may be to investigate and ultimately to make the patient aware of the reasons for his behavior, there would appear to be no demonstrable reason why all presumptive determinants of this behavior should not be included in this program. If it can be ascertained that telepathic determinants play some role, that a given segment of behavior is at least to some extent *psi*-conditioned, the responsible factors should be brought to consciousness along with any other determinants of which the patient is unconscious.

So far there have emerged no categorical contraindications to the use of interpretations to the patient based on such concepts. My own observations, derived from over ten years' experience with many cases of depth-therapy, in every one of which the behavior turned out to be in some degree *psi*-conditioned, would indicate that the generally sanctioned rules of interpretation are as applicable (insofar as they are valid at all) in the case of *psi*-derived material, as in the case of material derived in any other way. The essential goals and techniques of therapy are in nowise altered. Questions of what to interpret, if to interpret, how to interpret, and when to interpret, are decided in terms of the over-all clinical picture and not in terms of whether or not the material at hand is presumptively *psi*-derived.

It has invariably appeared that patients who are given a straightforward explanation of how an interpretation incorporating *psi* concepts is arrived at, react exactly as they react to any other type of interpretation. They do not jump up and make for the door with a frightened backward glance. If the interpretation seems to be correct and acceptable it will result in precisely the same type of transformation of affect, resistance, and behavior as any other correct and well-timed communication to the patient. No great perturbations result from the fact that the possibility of telepathic functioning is taken as much for granted as the possibility of any other kind of unconscious behavior. On the contrary, the most surprising revelation of continued clinical work with these concepts is that patients seem ready to recognize such factors in their behavior with an intuitive grasp that suggests a profound intrapsychic awareness of the *psi* level of functioning. Such reactions are fairly easily differentiable from the tendency of some patients to swallow any old camel when in a positive phase of transference, or from the narcissistic need to believe oneself the possessor of hidden sources of magic. This latter reaction, when it arises in connection with the identification of *psi* factors in behavior, can be handled in the same way as when it arises in any other connection. I believe that this experience fairly parallels that of other therapists, particularly psychoanalysts, who have begun to make active use of the telepathy hypothesis in their clinical work.

Difficulties on the Side of the Therapist

The greatest difficulty in the way of the free use of telepathically derived material in psychotherapy does not, as a matter of fact, arise from the side of the patients, but from the characterologically unique resistances of the therapist himself. This has been shown to be related to the fact that *psi*-conditioned events occurring during the course of depth-therapy, particularly as they manifest themselves in dreams and associations, are apt in a very penetrating way to reflect the therapist's specifically defended-against repressed material. It is, as the Hungarian psychoanalyst Hollós once expressed it, as if there were a return from repression of the analyst's own repressed content in the dreams, slips, actings-out, etc., of the patient. It thus happens that before the therapist can freely perceive and meaningfully integrate the discretely emerging *psi* data, he must first somehow have worked-through or be ready to work-through foci of conflict in himself that may be very closely related to those problems which the patient is dealing with in a *psi*-conditioned way. Although, on the one hand, the therapist is thus provided with a useful potential means of observing and controlling the counter-transference, he is, on the other hand, considerably blocked in his ability to appreciate and work with the *psi*-conditioned material latently around. The ins and outs of this somewhat distressing complication, which can best be observed in the relationship between doctor and patient during the course of psychoanalytic therapy, is under continued investigation. Unfortunately it cannot be described fully in this paper.

CONCLUSIONS

At this time one can hardly evaluate the ultimate place of *psi* factors in human behavior. We do not know whether they play an as yet unperceived great part or a part that is destined to fade into relative insignificance when stacked up against determinants now known and others yet to be discovered. (We cannot say, for instance, what role these factors may play in the overt psychoses, although Ehrenwald, for one, has published some interesting observations and theories in this regard.) The future will undoubtedly provide perspective. We can be certain that the role of telepathy and other *psi* factors will become increasingly clear as more and more clinical observers gain confidence in the ability of such concepts to diminish the role ordinarily ascribed to chance in the still but poorly understood field of human interrelationships.

BIBLIOGRAPHY

1. BENDIT, L. J., *Paranormal Cognition*. London, Faber and Faber, 1944.
2. BURLINGHAM, D. T., "Child analysis and the mother." *Psychoanal. Quart.*, IV, 69–92, 1935.
3. DEUTSCH, H., "Okkulte Vorgänge während der Psychoanalyse." *Imago*, XII, 418–433, 1926.
4. EHRENWALD, J., "Neurobiological aspects of telepathy." *J. Amer. Soc. Psych. Res.*, XLII, No. 4, 132–141, 1948.
5. ———, "Precognition in dreams." *Psychoanal. Rev.*, XXXVIII, 17–38, 1951.
6. ———, "Presumptively telepathic incidents during analysis." *Psychiat. Quart.*, XXIV, 726–743, 1950.
7. ———, "Psychopathological aspects of telepathy." *Proc. Soc. Psych. Res.*, (London) XLVI, 224–244, 1940.
8. ———, "Psychotherapy and the telepathy hypothesis." *Am. J. Psychother.*, IV, 51–79, 1950.
9. ———, "Quest for 'psychics' and 'psychical' phenomena in psychiatric studies of personality." *Psychiat. Quart.*, XXIII, 236–247, 1949.
10. ———, "Telepathy in dreams." *Brit. J. Med. Psychol.*, XIX, 313–323, 1942.
11. ———, *Telepathy and Medical Psychology*. New York, W. W. Norton, 1948.
12. ———, "Telepathy in the psychoanalytic situation." *Brit. J. Med. Psychol.*, XX, 51–62, 1944.
13. EISENBUD, J., "Analysis of a presumptively telepathic dream." *Psychiat. Quart.*, XXII, 1–33, 1948.
14. ———, "Psychiatric contributions to parapsychology: a review." *J. Parapsychol.*, XIII, 247–262, 1949.
15. ———, "Psychoanalysis and parapsychology." *J. Parapsychol.*, XII, 1948.
16. ———, "The dreams of two patients in analysis interpreted as a telepathic *rêve à deux*." *Psychoanal. Quart.*, XVI, 39–60, 1947.

17. ——, "Telepathy and problems of psychoanalysis." *Psychoanal. Quart.*, XV, 32–87, 1946.

18. ELLIS, A., "Telepathy and psychoanalysis: a critique of recent 'findings'." *Psychiat. Quart.*, XXI, 607–659, 1947.

19. FODOR, N., "The Poltergeist-psychoanalyzed." *Psychiat. Quart.*, XXII, 195–203, 1948.

20. ——, "Telepathic dreams." *Am. Imago*, III, 61–87, 1942.

21. ——, "Telepathy in analysis." *Psychiat. Quart.*, XXI, 171–189, 1947.

22. FREUD, S., "Dreams and the occult." *New Introductory Lectures on Psychoanalysis*. New York, W. W. Norton, 1933.

23. ——, "Ergänzungen and Zusatzkapitel zur Traumdeutung." *Ges. Schr.*, III, 172–184. (Trans.): "Some additional notes upon dream interpretation as a whole, 1925." *Int. J. Psycho-Anal.*, XXIV, 71–75, 1943.

24. ——, "Traum und Telepathie," *Imago*, VIII, 1–22, 1922. (Trans.): "Dreams and telepathy." *Int. J. Psycho-Anal.*, III, 283–305, 1922.

25. GLEY, E., "À propos d'une observation de sommeil provoqué à distance." *Rev. Phil.* (Paris), XXI, 425–428, 1886.

26. GURNEY, E., MEYERS, F. W. H. AND PODMORE, F., *Phantasms of the Living*. Abridged ed., London, Kegan Paul, 1918.

27. HÉRICOURT, J., "Un cas de somnambulisme à distance." *Rev. Phil.* (Paris), XXI, 200–203, 1886.

28. HOLLÓS, I., "Psychopathologie alltäglicher telepathischer Erscheinungen." *Imago*, XIX, 529–546, 1933.

29. HUMPHREY, B. M., "The relation of ESP to mode of drawing." *J. Parapsychol.*, XIII, 31–46, 1949.

30. HYSLOP, G. H., "The biological approach to psychic phenomena." *J. Am. Soc. Psych. Res.*, XXXVI, 50–56, 1942.

31. JANET, P., "Note sur quelques phénomènes de somnambulisme." *Rev. Phil.* (Paris), XXI, 190–198, 1886.

32. ——, "Deuxieme note sur le sommeil provoqué à distance et la suggestion mentale pendant l'etat somnambuliqué." *Rev. Phil.* (Paris), XXI, 212–223, 1886.

33. MEERLOO, A. M., "Telepathy as a form of archaic communication." *Psychiat. Quart.*, XXIII, 691–704, 1949.

34. PEDERSON-KRAG, G. "Telepathy and repression." *Psychoanal. Quart.*, XVI, 61–68, 1947.

35. PEERBOLTE, M., "Een telepatische droom." *Tijdschr. voor Parapsychologie,* III, 121, 1937.

36. ———, "Psychoanalysis and parapsychology." *Psychiat.-neurol. Bladen,* 1938.

37. RHINE, J. B., STUART, C. E., PRATT, J. G., SMITH, B. M. AND GREENWOOD, J. A., *Extra-Sensory Perception after Sixty Years.* New York, Henry Holt, 1940.

38. RICHET, C., "Experience sur le sommeil à distance." *Rev. Phil.* (Paris), XXV, 435–449, 1888.

39. ———, "Further experiments in hypnotic lucidity or clairvoyance." *Proc. Soc. Psych. Res.* (London), VI, 66–83, 1889–1890.

40. ———, "Relation de diverses expériences sur la transmission mentale, la lucidité, et autres phénomènes non explicables par les données scientifiques actuelles." *Proc. Soc. Psych. Res.* (London), V, 168, 1888–1889.

41. RÓHEIM, G., "Telepathy in a dream." *Psychoanal. Quart.* I, 277–291, 1932.

42. SCHMEIDLER, G., "Personality correlates of ESP as shown by Rorschach studies." *J. Parapsychol.,* XIII, 23–31, 1949.

43. SERVADIO, E., "La baguette des sourciers." *Rev. franc. psychoanal.,* III, 1935.

44. ———, "L'ultima Helene Smith." *La Ricerca Psichica,* Nov., 1933.

45. ———, "Otto sedute col medium Erto," *La Ricerca Psichica,* Nos. 8–12, Parte riservata, 1932.

46. ———, "Psychoanalyse und Telepathie." *Imago,* XXI, 489–497, 1935.

47. ———, "Psychoanalysis and Yoga." *Bull. Bombay Med. Union,* Nos. 3–4, 1947.

48. ———, "Sul meccanismo psichico delle alluzioni telepathiche." *La Ricerca Psichica,* X, 577, 1933. (Trans.): "The

psychic mechanism of telepathic hallucinations." *J. Am. Soc. Psych. Res.*, 149–159, June, 1934.

49. STEKEL, W., *Der telepathische Traum*. Berlin, Johannes Baum Verlag, 1921.

50. WARCOLLIER, R., *Experiments in Telepathy*. New York, Harpers, 1938.

► FREE PAINTING AS AN AUXILIARY TECHNIQUE IN PSYCHOANALYSIS

By Max M. Stern, M.D.[*]

INTRODUCTION

Free paintings are paintings in the production of which any goal-directed intention is excluded, whether there be the intention to reproduce a certain effect as in works of art, or a technical purpose, such as science, advertising, or the like.

Analagous to the use of the terms "free idea" and "free association" to designate the psychoanalytic technique, we may describe any spontaneous, not reality-directed action (affective organization of behavior) as a "free expression." If free expression takes the form of free arrangement of a material, we arrive at a projection of its specific dynamics onto this material. In the free painting we use free expressions in the form of paintings produced by the patient. "In drawing without aim, we obtain an expression of a specific order" (22).

This paper describes experiences with the application of the psychoanalytic method to the free paintings of adult neurotics. Since its very beginnings, psychoanalysis has accepted the method of free expression in the form of pictures, as a representation of unconscious processes (Pfister, Silberer, Bertschinger, Marcinowski, Rorschach, N. D. C. Lewis, Kris, Bychowski, Despert, Mosse, Naumburg, among others). In 1925, Nolan Lewis recommended this method as a generally applicable auxiliary technique in psychoanalysis and described its most important features. The fact that the method nevertheless has not been gen-

---

[*] Associate Psychoanalyst, Collaborating Staff of the Psychoanalytic Clinic for Training and Research, Columbia University.

erally adopted in the treatment of adult neurotics may be due to the lack of clarity with respect to both its technique and its results. In contrast to the extensive literature dealing with paintings of psychotics and of children, only a few clinical publications exist on the subject of free paintings of adult neurotics. In none of these studies was a strict application of the psychoanalytic method to free painting carried through; some of them even indicate that this was refrained from intentionally. In the highly interesting case of Bychowski (4) for example, the patient gave her interpretation, as had been previously arranged, as late as two months after completion of her analysis; seemingly Bychowski was interested mainly in the effect of nonverbalized painting on the course of the treatment.

THE TECHNIQUE OF FREE PAINTING

When the analysis is under way, the patient is informed that the treatment may be intensified by his painting pictures at home.* (I generally advise the use of tempera or water colors.) It is left to the patient whether or not he will follow the suggestion. The patient is instructed to take a brush and to put onto paper whatever comes into his mind, to let himself be guided solely by his hand and by the intentions which may emerge while he paints. In short, he is to exclude all conscious direction as much as possible, and thus to produce a picture which corresponds to a free idea (*freier Einfall*). Or, the production may take some definite idea, experience, mood, fantasy, or dream as a starting point; in this case, it would correspond to a free association. In any case the patient is asked to abstain from any evaluation or criticism while he paints—whether or not the drawing meets his expectations and whether or not he finds it pleasing. After a few attempts, the patient usually acquires a certain amount of practice in using this technique just as he does in free association.

---

* For many reasons the practice of having the patient paint during the analytic session (17), which has been used successfully in the treatment of children and psychotics, in my experience proved to be unsuitable for consistent application in the analytic treatment of adult neurotics.

When the patient has brought a picture, I request him specifically to associate to each detail of the picture and to omit nothing, however trivial or unimportant it may seem, exactly as in the analysis of a dream. It must be stressed that general explanations about the meaning of the picture, and the like, are merely opening associations sometimes constituting no more than the patient's resistance. What has in the literature been described as free associations to paintings has rarely gone beyond this phase.

THE PATIENT'S REACTION

While he paints, the patient frequently experiences a peculiar state of more or less intense excitement, working as though under a pleasurable compulsion. The after-reactions vary. Patients may register a certain fatigue which in many cases is pleasantly satisfying and which in others may take the form of complete exhaustion. Depressive moods or states of anxiety either may appear, or on the contrary may be relieved during painting. Frequently patients paint several pictures in succession.

RESULTS

I have been using this method for fourteen years. After initial hesitations my assurance in handling it has grown with my increasing insight into the laws which determine it. I now use it regularly, as a reliable and generally applicable method, side by side with the more generalized techniques (dream analysis, etc.) Like dreams, the paintings thus produced are determined by unconscious processes; they, too, reveal their latent meaning only through free associations; sometimes, in a surprising fashion, only in later sessions. The pictures, seeming devoid of any meaning at first, mostly turn out to be fascinating representations of the underlying, unconscious thoughts.

The findings may be formulated as follows: The patients' associations to the pictures lead, in almost all cases, first, to the *memory of the recent experience* which occasioned the painting; second, *to an abundance of childhood memories,* mainly with *traumatic* content, which in the unconscious have become connected with the residues of the day. These childhood memories are *screen memories for typical earlier traumatic events,* especially of the oral and oedipal phases. Striking is the preponderant role of the oedipal triad—primal scene, infantile masturbation, and pavor nocturnus.

It is significant that the production represents a *magic reparation of traumatic experiences.* This magic reparation takes the lines either of repetition of the trauma, or of its denial through reversal or overcompensation. It is performed symbolically either upon the image of the traumatic situation or upon the image of the traumatized, impaired body. The painting may, therefore, be the representation of the traumatic situation or of the impaired body image (repetition of the trauma), or a denial of either one (reparation of the trauma). The specific form of the reparation in a particular case corresponds to individual defense mechanisms (oral, anal, phallic, sadistic, masochistic, etc.).

Due to the exclusion of reality-directed ego-function, such pictorial representation follows the principle of the primary process (condensation, displacement, etc.). Therefore the distortions known to occur in dreamwork are also found in free painting. The picture is a condensation of the various tendencies mentioned.

THEORETICAL REMARKS

How can a magic reparation of experienced traumata be achieved through painting?

Elsewhere (24) I have attempted to show that two traumatic phases in human development are of particular influence upon the psychic structure—the phases of the oral and of the oedipal trauma. Both are characterized by the occurrence of excessive stimulation which cannot be adequately discharged, thus leading to physiological shock reactions—namely, the primary shock or neurogenic shock of central origin, a condition which has been extensively investigated from the physiological angle (16), (5), (et al). The shock reactions of the postnatal phase have been described by Ribble (20). They are marked by a clash between the immature, infantile organism and the demands of the external and internal world which the organism is not yet biologically equipped to meet. This constellation which produces the oral shock recurs on a different level in the phallic phase. In the oedipal conflict the organism is overwhelmed by sexual excitations which cannot find discharge in an adequate reaction, that is, in orgasm (10). This leads to the oedipal shock, manifested in pavor nocturnus. Both phases are decisive in the formation of the psychic structure, and especially in the origin of neuroses and psychoses. Since shock actually represents the process of dying, and since any disturbance of the homeostasis is felt as tension on the psychic level, the tendency of the psychic apparatus to relieve tension is a function essential to survival. The relief principle precedes the pleasure principle.

The shock-like reactions of the early infantile period are warded off by means of immediate "discharges into motility"; that is, by crying and restlessness, the original forms of expression. The relief yielded by the discharge through primal expression fixates the magic meaning of expression as a defense against trauma—a meaning which is re-enforced through its real effect, the summoning of the mother who brings help. From now on, the presence of the mother means protection against shock. Later, more organized forms of relief through expression, such as playing in clay or sand, etc., retain the magic meaning attached to the original form. Painting, too, has this meaning. After the first, primitive period of scribbling, when the child has acquired the ability to draw a definite form (14), he paints a loop and calls it the mother. To the child in his phase of magic-thinking this product created by himself means the mother. Quite independently of any pictorial value it may have as a drawing, the loop has become a magic wishfulfillment (symbolic mastery). When, however, the traumatic experience of the situation of "missing the mother" has produced a shock-like reaction (automatic anxiety [9]), then the magic wish fulfillment acquires the meaning of magical mastering of a previously experienced shock situation (reparatory mastery).

Here we recognize a mechanism which brings to the fore a specific category of wishes. Besides the wishes whose fulfillment wards off shock and which are psychically represented by anticipated sensations of pleasure, there are impulses that aim at the reparation of traumatic experiences. The child overcomes the shock experienced in missing the mother through his active re-creation of the needed object, the mother, in a concrete and lasting symbol. The "oh-oh-oh game", described by Freud in *Beyond the Pleasure Principle* (9), is a magic reparatory mastery of this shock experience in several ways: first, in the sense of active repetition of the traumatic situation: the mother disappears, "but I am not helplessly overwhelmed" (by shock); second, through denial of the experienced trauma of helplessness: "I make her disappear, I am active and not overwhelmed"; third, "I make her reappear."

Melanie Klein (11) has demonstrated convincingly that in his play with sand, clay, or blocks, the child seeks to master his traumatic experiences through magic acting. Erikson in his paper "Traumatic Configuration in Child Play" (7), likewise gives highly instructive examples. Actually in the act of painting, the adult patient revives a primitive, infantile way of reparation of traumatic experiences which has been familiar to him since early childhood. It is interesting that the patients in their associations to the paintings very often refer to these childhood games.

The traumata reflected in the paintings are, as already mentioned, primarily the oedipal shock experiences through which earlier—oral—shock experiences are resuscitated. They are specifically manifested in the pavor nocturnus attacks which are typical for the phallic phase (25).

Pavor nocturnus is a shock-like reaction due to the breaking-through, during sleep, of sexual excitation which could be controlled and warded off during the day. Infinitely manifold individual phenomena are experienced in pavor nocturnus, such as oppression, inability to breathe, the feeling of being paralyzed, of a shrinking of the body, of withering, fainting, falling, the feeling of being anesthetized, of going insane, etc. These can by and large be traced to the somatic symptoms of the shock reaction intermingled with the manifestations of a catatonoid defense reaction. They are condensed as hallucinations with a pictorial representation which is conditioned by the content of the dream accompanying the attack. Often they are projected into the external world, in this case represented by the dream content, appearing there as crushing walls and houses, earthquakes, engulfing waves, etc.

In the pavor nocturnus attacks there occurs, as mentioned above, a revival of shock experiences of the oral phase, which mobilizes early, defensive, oral-sadistic trends. Oedipal shock then is conceived as a retaliation for oral destructive wishes, which accounts for the fear of being eaten, swallowed, choked, etc., so common in the pavor nocturnus attacks. Due to the accompanying shock reaction, the sexual stimulation in pavor nocturnus is experienced as a threat to the genitals and very often projected onto the parents, the source of both sexual stimulation and sexual prohibition. This leads to the formation of the castration complex. The castration complex, however, owes its individual structure to the predisposition to the oedipal trauma. This in turn is determined by constitutional as well as experiential factors (such as postnatal shock, reactive aggressive trends, environmental influences, castration threat, and view of female genitals, etc.). In the dreams as well as in the paintings the threat emanating from a parent is frequently represented by animals, such as devouring wolves or biting horses (cf. Wolf Man and Little Hans) or, equally often, by enveloping and swallowing spiders, octopuses, gigantic fishes, etc. (25).

Thus the free paintings in analysis originate from the same tendencies which Freud ascribes to the dream function (9). They represent attempts at a reparatory mastery of previous traumata. In free painting during treatment, the traumatic experiences of the oral and oedipal shock, together with the oral, anal, urethral, and other defense reactions, are repeated and overcome in a magical way, exactly as they are in the play of children (11). Such an act seems to allay enough anxiety to enable the patient to relinquish repression and to live-through the once-experienced traumata. These observations provide the rationale for the therapeutic value of free painting; not only in adult neurotics, but also in children and psychotics. In its application to adult analysands, the primitive infantile mechanism of integration is adapated, through verbalization, to the thinking of the mature ego.

THE PROCESS OF PRODUCTION

The production of the pictures proceeds along the paths of a feed-back reaction, in which the impulses just characterized represent the feeding factor. Under the influence of the primary process they produce overdetermined individual symbols, exactly as in dreams. It is a complex process that gradually gains impetus, according to a principle which I would like to call "inductive resonance." The first strokes are directed by the unconscious impulse. Perception of this first attempt arouses, through empathy and identification, kinesthetic innervations in the patient; these re-activate the complex which had produced the first attempt, thus in turn increasing the impetus of the unconscious impulse.*

"Every action carries with it a specific change in the gnostic function, and every gnostic function carries with it an action" (22). In the analytic session, the same path is retraced in reverse. Perception of the product leads, via the associations given by the patient, to a revival of the unconscious motive.

VALUE OF THE TECHNIQUE

Hence it follows that the picture cannot be interpreted by means of empathy, as suggested by Mosse (17). Whether the picture be clumsily or skilfully executed, it is merely the point of departure for associations leading to the unconscious process which incited the production. This explains why the quality of the patient's draftsmanship has no relevance for the purposes of picture analysis, and thus meets the objection, frequently

---

* This is one reason why the patient often paints several pictures in quick succession; the other is the growing need for mastery of the traumata.

raised, that but few patients possess the necessary degree of artistic skill.

Magic mastery through pictorial representation is a regression to the identical stage of adaptation to reality in which the original traumata, now pressing for reparation, occurred; in most cases to the preverbal phase. The technique used in therapeutic painting is on a level with primitive, pictorial thought. It is of advantage that thus, both as to mode of thinking and of expression, it is on the same plane as the unconscious thought itself. This form of thinking is alien to the ego, and therefore a certain degree of effort and practice is required to overcome ego-resistance, not only in the patient but, judging from my own experience, in the analyst as well. Accordingly, the first attempts are usually vague and timid, and the method attains its full effectiveness only after a little practice.

In deviation from the usual practice in the analytic literature, in some of the examples given here the patients' associations are quoted verbatim. This is done partly to demonstrate the technique, and partly because the sequence of the associations to the details of the picture affords an interesting glimpse into the interplay of forces in the patient during the analytic session, that is, into the struggle between the tendencies which press for repetition of the traumatic experience and those which aim to undo the trauma by means of repression, denial and overcompensation. The scene of this struggle vacillates continually between experiences of the past, actual experiences of the living present, and transference of the revived complexes to the analyst.

CASE MATERIAL

Case A (32 years old, male.)

EXAMPLE NO. 1. I was drunk when I painted that. It was the same as to make a fix on somebody. Womb, drinking, smoking, bed.—(Oral mother fixation.)—As a child I was always cuddling in a hole in my bed, like a bird in a nest, like a womb. Warm security. Joan has left me.—(Occasion for the picture.)—I feel I am *free now, free of mother.* I think of the ocean, of a big wave (in the center of the picture). Sunday we were at the beach. Surf-riding was my chief delight. This here is a penguin, like a dolphin riding the wave.—(Mastering of the trauma of being overwhelmed.)—The penguin is armless. I think of cigarettes, of smoking; it was forbidden. My mother called it a dirty, nasty business. I remember using pillows for masturbation. The snapdragon reminds me of the flower garden of my grandmother. My sister thought that babies came in flowers. I was fascinated by tulips. There was discipline and form in them. Flowers which catch flies.—(Reassurance through perfect geometrical form is denial of imperfection of the female genital, of castration fear stirred up by the memory of masturbation.)

At the age of fourteen, when my father died, I dissected frogs. I remember I made a report about frogs: how frogs grew, how they laid eggs. It was a peculiar time, I was completely involved in that frog business. The frog report reminds me of my mother. After father died, mother clung to me. It was a hotter and closer feeling than before. The stomach is the stomach of my mother.—(Sublimated sadistic attempt to master the fear of being overwhelmed by incestuous wishes: frog=mother=revival of oral-sadistic wishes.)—

I couldn't resist putting in the fence grating; it has dots in it. In new buildings it is used to prevent people from putting their feet through the windows, lest they get injured or jump out and fall.—(Falling represents shock-sensation).—The broken windows, putting your foot in that. Intercourse?—it seems dangerous. To break up a woman, that's fantastic—incest? I am now thinking of wheat on a farm. I remember riding on a reaper, which *cuts the wheat down.* A threshing machine cuts the grain from the wheat. I had a vision of *falling* into it, being swallowed by it, coming out of it at the other end, threshed. I'd like to get the breasts all the way down my throat, breasts and nipples, down my esophagus. Now my throat aches. *Fantasies of slicing up breasts, hanging them up on hooks.*

When I was a boy, a man on the ranch thought a wolf had stolen a sheep; but he caught *a horse eating the lamb.* He even took photos of it. This was terrible, revolting, awful, a gross distortion. *I was revolted by the idea that an animal eats its young.* Now I feel like vomiting. I feel a wish to pinch the breasts of a woman.—(Oral-sadistic impulses as defense against punishment for sadistic incest wishes.)—I can't do it with Joan. I think of Joan, *only of breasts and a stomach.* I was told that as a child, when I first got the bottle, I chewed off the nipple and took the milk wholesale.

I now feel like being a toothless child: nipples at my mother's breasts. I sucked Joan's ears when I made love to her. I always wanted to suck the clitoris. I never did it. When I am with Joan I rather want to satisfy myself on the outside of the stomach. Ejaculation on the outside, and rubbing the sperm on the skin. I am afraid of entering the vagina.

At the bottom, there is a snail. Once mother stepped on a snail; that nauseated me. I identified myself with it and shuddered. The snail, that's me. As a boy I sprinkled salt on them; I enjoyed watching them die.

SUMMARY. The painting was occasioned by the patient's experiences of being left by his girl friend and of going on a sailing trip. To the former he reacted with a revival of his strong, oral-sadistic mother-fixation, which imparts an oral character to the oedipal anxiety; namely, his fear of the devouring, destroying, overwhelming mother. She is represented by the overwhelming wave of the surf, which simultaneously means the mother's stomach (repeated in many of his pictures). The penguin riding the wave is a compensation of his being overwhelmed; at the same time, it is a representation of possessing the mother in masturbation. But the fears break through nevertheless: First, the penguin is armless and castrated; second, he is threatened and dominated by the snapdragon, which again represents the vagina, the flower from which the children come out. The traumatic situation is expressed in the patient's representation of himself as a snail, at the bottom of the picture, crushed by the mother (repeated in many of his pictures; the snail at the same time being identified with penis [body=penis]).

Variations of this situation may be seen in the memories of the devouring and destroying reaper, and of the horse eating a lamb: animals who eat their young. The belly abuts upon the enormous, red vagina, in which the snail (the patient) perishes. In his association to it, the patient reported a symptom which he had previously withheld from the analysis: that he preferred to satisfy himself by ejaculation while rubbing the penis on the woman's belly, rather than to introduce the penis into the dangerous, devouring vagina. A representation of the phallic mother, as of a devouring and gigantic frog or whale spouting a stream of water which serves as a substitute phallus is clearly discernible in the painting, although the patient did not consciously recognize it.

In the picture, the fence, which he obviously conceived as a genital, represents the eye of the animal. The eye, known as a symbol for the genital, here represents the sadistic connotation of entering the vagina, and consequently the fear of being hurt—injured—jumping to death. The geometrical design of the fence (stickers in the grating) is a defense against castration, exactly like the reassuring geometrical form of a tulip (vagina). The choking pain in the throat during the analytic session corresponds to a defense reaction, on an oral level, against being raped.

The picture as a whole represents a magic mastery of traumatic oedipal experiences which revive oral sadistic defenses. It represents in its actual meaning an ambivalent reaction, of relief and hate, to the recent experience of being deserted by his girl.

EXAMPLE NO. 2. (The first of two consecutive paintings.) First I drew a cloud.—Once I was looking through a big telescope. I saw spiral nebulae, dust clouds in the universe, the cloud that lies behind. This makes me think of a dream about a brick house which collapsed:

I was on a hill with Joan; she had painful blisters under her fingernail. We were looking towards a cottage. It had a screen porch. Something happened in the house. A man came out, and I realized that he had killed someone inside. The house was decaying, cracking, the cracks spreading slowly over the face of the wall.

Case A: Example No. 1

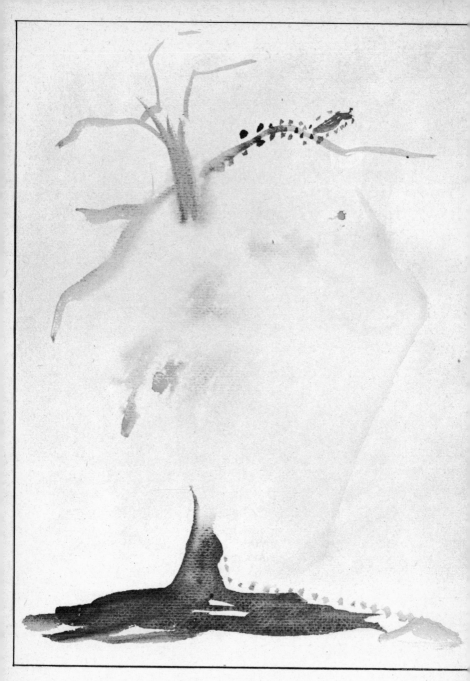

Case A: Example No. 2

Case A: Example No.

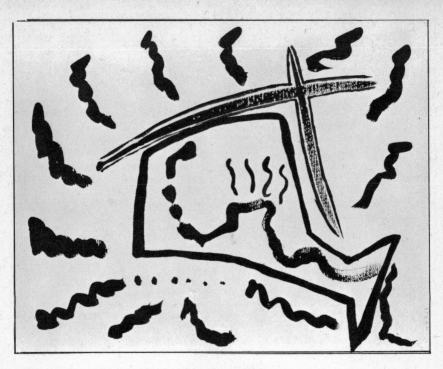

Case B: Example No. 1

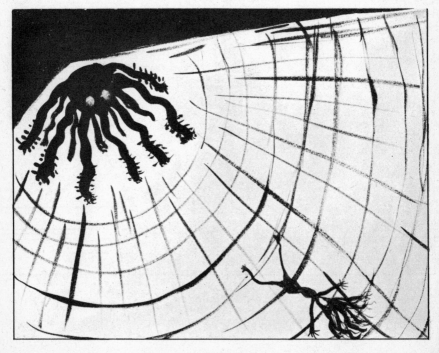

Case B: Example No. 2

Clouds arose, I witnessed the cancerous destruction of a town.
I awoke, frightened.

(Projection of body sensations into the environment in a
pavor nocturnus dream which is connected with the primal
scene and the castrated mother.)

The blue is mother. I lined up the outline red. I now
think of a scar, a disfiguration in the face of my sister.—
I just feel now an urge to scratch my toe. My mother always cut off my toe nail; I then always was crying, she cut
too close, to the quick. I had a tremendous apprehension of
being hurt. An old dream comes into my mind:

I am looking at my foot, and there is a hole instead of the nail;
I see the bone structure. (Castration fears.)

After the cloud, I made a tree. One leaf has berries, red
berries—ants crawling up the tree. Then it's no leaf, but
ants attacking some beast, a bug. Soldier ants chewing off
the legs of a bug—they are coming out of an anthill or a
breast—it will fall down, then they devour it. I am identified with this bug.—(Falling sensation and being eaten up:
well-known manifestations of pavor nocturnus.) (Going
back to the dream): I think of our cottage, with the screen
porches. When you look through a screen, you focus on the
screen and can't look through it well. Inhibition to look at
women.—Barbara; I once saw her on a raft lying in water,
like lying on a woman.—Father and mother lying on
a beach; it was the only occasion when I saw them in bath-
ing suits, playing. I was annoyed by my mother being too
fat. Father seemed much younger than mother. (Screen
memories referring to the primal scene.)

EXAMPLE NO. 3. In the second painting I painted a detail of the first one. I made a bug, a praying mantis, horri-
ble, he holds the prey in his arms, chewing it. An enema is
going into his tail. My mother was always giving me enemas; I had a fear of enemas; I liked them too. The bug is
me. He is pierced by a big blue nail. Blood flows out of
him. Christ comes into my mind. I think of the earthquake
and upheaval when Christ was crucified. "The sun was dark-
ened, and the veil of the temple was rent."—(Masochistic
identification with Christ; hints at primal scene: the rent

veil.)—I have a memory of an earthquake at an early age.
The light dimmed. I was alone and had a feeling of another world. The fear was out of all proportion. In fact,
little had happened—other people had hardly been aware
of it—but for weeks I got hysterics. The fear of earthquakes
terrified me for years. I think now of nightmares, of black
nights, with storm. I feel dizzy, thinking of earthquakes.—
(Revival of nightmare experience in the earthquake fear.)
—When I masturbated, I did it on pillows, I felt dizzy. I
often had a phantasy of being a spider that had legs he
couldn't use, and had to be carried on a pillow.—I am this
bug. There is a tremendous difference between the upheaval and the small meanings of cutting toes and enemas.

SUMMARY. Masochistic fixation on oedipal trauma; feminine identification in primal scene leading to castration fears;
revival of the oral shock complex.

Case B. (24 years old, female.)

EXAMPLE NO. 1.   (Angry.) I don't know what it means.
It has no sense. I'm scared. It is a scorpion. I closed it in a
box, as though I had swallowed it up. The cross in the middle means: "Wipe it out, away with it!" I feel violent, red
and black, it is hate, my father—he is pressing on me, like
worms closing in. I felt much better after I painted it. I get
a cold feeling when I think of him. I can't get at him. I think
of the ritual when I woke up in the night: I had to lie
perfectly still in the middle of the bed, which had to be in
the middle of the room, not to touch anything.—(Touch
ritual as defense against masturbation.)—In the picture,
that's me swallowing a penis, getting like a wooden stick
and being wiped out.—(This corresponds to the sensation
in a nightmare, presumably masochistic masturbation phantasy, including the phantasy of being entered by father's
penis, a libidinized repetition of the oedipal trauma, condensed with a reaction to the oral trauma.)—I remember,
once I had a nightmare based on a story of worms—a scientist found a substance to make things bigger. The worms
grew and grew, crushed a house to death.—(Sensation of
body impairment in pavor nocturnus, projected into the environment—house—determined further by revival of oral

sadistic impulses.)—You heard the noises coming nearer and nearer.—I remember noises on the gravel, outside our house, during the night. I always listened to noises from father and mother. I was anxious when I did this picture. Last week, I had a bad sex life. I didn't want intercourse, it was too much for me. I was afraid. It was pressing in on me too much, like in the picture.—(The occasion for the picture.)—I was afraid of being wiped out. So silly. At one point in intercourse I stop. I feel pressure on my chest. Fear that I have to have an orgasm. All goes into my mind. I think it will be the end of me, it would change me.—(Fear of being changed, going crazy, pressure on chest—typical sensations in pavor nocturnus.)—Fred's noises during intercourse. Father always made noises. Now I remember the baby bed in the corner. When my uncle came, that bothered me. I slept in the baby bed in the same room with my uncle and aunt. I woke up and thought I was going to die. I felt it was inevitable that I must die. My mother came in and reassured me. I didn't want to go to sleep at that time. Father beat me for this. (Primal scene and pavor nocturnus.)

Some sessions later she remembered: "A scorpion phobia began when I was four. While playing in a sandbox I saw a mother scorpion with all the little ones at her back. The little ones ate her up. I never went to a sandbox again. This was shortly after I had my tonsils out. I still remember going under the ether."

EXAMPLE NO. 2. I wanted to draw a spider. When I was ten years old, I stayed with my grandmother in Virginia; there I started the spider phobia. I started to masturbate there. Mother had come and flirted with another man; I had a crush on the same man. There, a spider fell into my hair from the kitchen door. Since then I have this spider phobia. I was always afraid to get a spider in my hair. This picture is revealing—here, it has more to do with my vagina, my vagina is exposed. I always was surprised at the black pubic hair of mother, it looked like a spider. I remember now. I had completely forgotten about her operations. I saw her after an operation on the genitals. I was five

years old. It was awful. She lay just as if dead, she was not
yet out of the ether. I saw her after the operation, in the
nude. She had her pubic hair shaved off. There was always a
neat little triangle; then it was naked. I always wondered
about pubic hair, stiff, curled.—At four years, I had my tonsils out. I remember exactly, going under the ether. I always awakened in the middle of the night, for fear a spider
had fallen into my hair, and screamed. The red eyes—it is
like the inside showing at the outside. Yesterday I swallowed a fly. Last year at Halloween they were "bobbing
for apples"; I couldn't do it; I couldn't bite into the apples.
I was afraid to put my head under water. Mother's breasts
were operated on, brr! When I am not satisfied sexually, I
am furious; my stomach is growling, I am coughing.—The
black widow spiders are fatal. I always thought that spiders
were very big and that they would overpower me. They
would open up their legs and swallow me. Fear of being
choked, like the worms choke, like an octopus chokes. I am
afraid right now, deathly afraid. It scares me. It didn't last
night, when I drew the picture. In the picture I am falling,
falling. A spider looking into my vagina is like looking into
the toilet bowl.

SUMMARY. Spiders as well as octopuses and crabs are
typical nightmare symbols. The nightmare attacks (waking up
at night and screaming with fear) are connected with primal
scene and castration phantasies; they are conceived as a retaliation for defensive oral sadistic urges, mobilized by revival of
earlier oral shock experiences.

EFFECT OF THE METHOD

The effect of this method is to enrich and to activate the
analysis. The intensification achieved by the introduction of this
method into an analysis that is already under way, is often surprising to the analyst and to the patient both as regards the
production of material and the changes resulting from integration of the material. It seems that the effect emanating from a
picture reaches into the unconscious more deeply than does that
of language, due to the fact that pictorial expression is more

adequate to the developmental stage in which the trauma occurred; it has remained more within range of the concrete and phsyical than has the verbal expression.

As this paper is limited to a brief description and explanation of the technique itself, the problems connected with its use in the psychoanalytic process have not been discussed here.

Nevertheless, I should like to emphasize one last, but significant point; namely, that this method can lead toward a more objective science of psychoanalysis. The pictures are objective material, a documentary record of the patient's psychic processes, unchanged and unaffected by any interference on the part of the transmitter. Combined with the patient's associations and the data of his life history, they afford far wider possibilities for scientific control, by comparison and experiment, than have so far been available in the analytic procedure. The same applies conversely to the greater objectivity of interpretation of form elements and its possible use in treatment. The individual composition of the form elements, the distribution of space, the character of strokes, the choice of colors, etc., are expressions of the patient's personality; like his handwriting, they mirror the individual trend of his character (2), (6). Thus the interpretation of form elements through empathy can be replaced by the use of extensive, objective data as controlling factors coupled with the patient's associations, his life history and his psychic structure, as revealed through his analysis.

CONCLUSION

I believe that the results described here call for serious consideration and examination of this method. Its advantages as well as its general applicability justify its recognition as a part of psychoanalytic technique in the treatment of adults, equal in importance to the currently accepted methods.

BIBLIOGRAPHY

1. ABRAHAM, K., Review of O. Pfister, "Der psychologische und biologische Untergrund des Expressionismus." *Imago*, VII, 204–205, 1921.

2. AUERBACH, J. G., "Psychological observations on 'doodling' in neurotics." *J. Nerv. & Ment. Dis.*, III, No. 4, 304–332, 1950.

3. BERTSCHINGER, H., "*Illustrierte Halluzinationen.*" *Jahrb. f. psychoanal. und psychopathol. Forsch.*, III, 69–100, 1911.

4. BYCHOWSKI, G., "The rebirth of a woman: a psychoanalytic study of artistic expression and sublimation." *Psychoanal. Rev.*, XXXIV, No. 1, 32–57, 1947.

5. DAVIS, H. A., *Shock and Allied Forms of Failure of the Circulation.* New York, Grune & Stratton, 1949.

6. ELKISCH, P., "Children's drawings in a projective technique." *Psychological Monographs,* LVIII, No. 1, 1945.

7. ERIKSON-HOMBURGER, E., "Traumatic configuration in child play." *Psychoanal. Quart.*, VI, 139–214, 1937.

8. FREUD, S., "The Interpretation of Dreams." *The Basic Writings.* A. A. Brill, trans. New York, Random House, 1938.

9. ———, *Beyond the Pleasure Principle.* C. J. M. Hubback, trans. London, Hogarth Press, 1948.

10. ———, "Schriften aus dem Nachlass." *Gesammelte Werke.* XVII, 152. London, Imago Publ. Co., 1946.

11. KLEIN, M., *The Psycho-Analysis of Children.* A. Strachey, trans. London, Hogarth Press, 1937.

12. KRIS, E., "Bemerkungen zur Bildnerei der Geisteskranken." *Imago,* XXII, H. 3, 1936.

13. LEWIS, N. D. C., "The practical value of graphic art in personality studies." (I. An introductory presentation of the possibilities.) *Psychoanal. Rev.*, XII, No. 3, 316–322, 1925.

14. LOWENFELD, V., *Creative and Mental Growth.* New York, Macmillan, 1949.

15. MARCINOWSKI, J., "Gezeichnete Traeume." *Zentralbl. f. Psychoanal.*, I, 575, 1911.

16. MOON, V. H., *Shock.* Philadelphia, Lea and Febiger, 1942.

17. MOSSE, E. P., "Painting-analysis in the treatment of neuroses." *Psychoanal. Rev.*, XXVII, No. 1, 65–82, 1940.

18. NAUMBURG, M., *Schizophrenic Art; Its Meaning in Psychotherapy.* New York, Grune & Stratton, 1950.

19. PFISTER, O., *Der psychologische und biologische Untergrund des Expressionismus.* Bern, Ernst Bircher, 1920.

20. RIBBLE, M. A., "Disorganizing factors of infant personality." *Am. J. Psychiat.,* XCVIII, No. 3, 459–463, 1941.

21. RORSCHACH, H., "Analytische Bemerkungen ueber die Gemaelde eines Schizophrenen." *Zentralbl. f. Psychoanal. und Psychother.,* IV, 1914.

22. SCHILDER, P., *Mind: Perception and Thought in their Constructive Aspects.* New York, Columbia Univ. Press, 1942.

23. SPITZ, R. A., "Anxiety in infancy: a study of its manifestations in the first year of life." *Intern. J. Psycho-Anal.,* XXXI, 1/2, 138–143, 1950.

24. STERN, M. M., "Anxiety, trauma and shock." *Psychoanal. Quart.,* XX, No. 2, 179–200, 1951.

25. ———, "Pavor nocturnus." *Intern. J. Psycho-Anal.,* XXXIII, No. 4, 1951.

► GROUP THERAPY AS A SPECIALIZED PSYCHOTHERAPEUTIC TECHNIQUE

*By Hyman Spotnitz, M.D.**

INTRODUCTION

In contrast to the other methods of therapy presented in this volume, this paper describes a method of therapy directed particularly to the simultaneous treatment of two or more individuals. The individual psychotherapeutic procedures have as their aim the treatment of one individual at a time. Group psychotherapy has as its purpose the treatment of two or more persons at the same time. In one sense, individual and group psychotherapy are not so far apart. It has been observed frequently that individual psychotherapy can be beneficial not only for the patient, but also for the therapist. In this sense, then, individual therapy too is group therapy. However, the conscious purpose of the therapy is the treatment of a single individual. Group therapy, on the other hand, attempts to have therapeutic effects on several individuals simultaneously. Some forms of group therapy aim at the therapeutic influencing of only one individual in the group; in these forms the group is used as an aid in treating that individual. There may be a concentration on one individual over a long period of time, or there may be concentration on single individuals in rotation. Thus, the therapist may find in other individuals of a group, assistants to aid in the treatment of each separate individual in the group.

---

* Consulting Psychiatrist to Jewish Board of Guardians, New York City; Assistant Neurologist, Vanderbilt Clinic, New York City; Assistant Neurologist, Neurological Institute, New York City.

Depending upon whether group treatment is directed to the treatment of several individuals simultaneously or one individual at a time, different methods are used for the selection of patients in a particular group.

HISTORY OF GROUP THERAPY

As far as is known, group therapy began as a reported method of treatment in 1905. Pratt attempted in a classroom setting to treat groups of somatically ill patients with inspirational talks. He and his associates also introduced class instruction with psychotic patients. Later this method was developed by Hadden. Since that time many different group methods with which to treat individuals have been used. Early experimenters with group therapy for psychotic and non-psychotic patients were Wender and Schilder. Group therapy with children was introduced in 1934 at the Jewish Board of Guardians in New York City by Slavson. In 1937, at the same institution, Gabriel was the first to work with interview groups of children. Later, activity groups, interview group therapy, analytic group therapy and guidance groups were developed under the direction of Slavson.

Many different types of group therapy have been developed in recent years for various conditions in and outside of institutions. Excellent annual reviews summarizing the literature have been appearing since 1946 in the volume edited by Spiegel, entitled, *Progress in Neurology and Psychiatry*. Articles presented under the heading of "Group Therapy" have been prepared by Slavson and his collaborators, Scheidlinger and Hallowitz. The number of reports dealing with group therapy has been increasing each year. Considerable attention has been devoted to play group therapy with children, activity group therapy with children, combinations of activity and interview group therapy with adolescents, psycho-drama (10) and analytic group therapy with adults.

To minimize the emotional trials associated with deep analytic therapy, there has been a definite trend toward the formation of discussion groups with therapeutic intent. Sometimes the

aim has been to benefit the individuals in the group and sometimes the aim has been to benefit the children of the parents in
the group.

Recently interest has been developing in the relationship
of group therapy to the organization of society and sociology.
Also attempts have been made to differentiate between the dynamics of individual therapy and of group therapy. The idea is
also being investigated of using individual therapy part of the
time, and group therapy part of the time in the treatment of
certain individuals, and of studying the different effects on the
same individuals.

CRITERIA FOR SELECTION OF PATIENTS

In the selection of patients for groups there are several important principles to be considered. It is obvious that in a group
setting, individuals of varying social-economic backgrounds and
various emotional and intellectual capacities will tend to have
different effects upon each other.

Different patterns of behavior will tend to arouse either positive or negative feelings in the individuals in a group. Depending
upon whether or not the group therapist desires to stimulate
different patterns, or maintain the same patterns in the individuals who are to receive group therapy, it can be decided whether
or not to select different or similar types of individuals. The use
of similar persons with the same type of problems, tends to stimulate the suppression of different behavior patterns. The use of
different persons, those with contrasting problems, tends to
develop maximum stimulation and acts in the direction of stimulating the discharge of tension in the group setting. The use of
indifferent persons, those without similar or contrasting problems,
favors the development of transference patterns that makes it
comparatively easy to recognize the transference patterns. A good
balance is desirable in treating individuals in groups. A balancing
of similar, contrasting and indifferent (people without contrasting
or similar problems) types of individuals tends to favor the
smooth development of the therapeutic process.

Some individuals would do well in group therapy, but would

be extremely resistive to individual therapy. This is true especially of people who do not have much opportunity to socialize or to have developed interests outside their own families. The group therapeutic situation is an ideal setting in which one individual can compare his own problems with those of others. It favors an objective evaluation of oneself. Obviously, individuals who have a particular need for this type of experience will do well in groups.

The number of patients available for treatment is an important factor in making selections. The personality of the therapist is a factor. He may find it easier to work with certain types of personalities rather than with others. The economic factor also comes into consideration, as it is easier for several people receiving treatment to meet the cost of the interview sessions, than it is for an individual to defray the expenses of individual sessions.

If we assume that the individuals who are to form the group to be treated have been selected, there is the problem of deciding upon the frequency of visits, the type of treatment to be used, and how the group will work. As has been stated, under the heading of group therapy may be found activity groups, relationship groups, authoritative groups, educational groups, interview groups, analytic groups. Furthermore, there is the question as to whether the individuals to be treated in the groups are to be consulted as to their ideas of the procedure of treatment or whether treatment is to be carried out according to principles and procedures determined by the therapist. The details of various methods and procedures used for different types of groups have been described by many therapists.

Originally the hope was that through group psychotherapy rather than by individual therapy, special results could be obtained. Further research however has indicated that the unique benefits are offset partly by the fact that special requirements exist. If emotionally disturbed people are to be treated competently with group therapy, the highest form of specialization is desirable. The group therapist should be trained in the following disciplines: general medicine, psychiatry, psychoanalysis, and group therapy. This does not mean that any particular individual may not be successful even without these qualifications. Here as elsewhere, the essential element in therapy is the capacity to develop an emotionally understanding relationship between the therapist and the individual or individuals whom he is treating.

Exceptionally gifted lay individuals, psychologists, or social workers may do much better with certain groups than a physician who may lack intuitive understanding of the individuals in the group and of group dynamics. In view of the great need that exists today for emotional therapy, it cannot be made an essential requirement that all people who engage in the practice of individual or group therapy should be physicians. On the contrary, the aim of many of those interested in training therapists, is that many types of institutions should be organized for the development of both individual and group therapists. These institutions eventually should develop increasingly high standards for practitioners, so that in time there will be better trained therapists available for the difficult tasks of treating successfully groups organized for therapeutic purposes.

THE SPECIAL VALUE OF THE GROUP SETTING

There has been an increasing trend toward the application of psychoanalytic principles to the treatment of several individuals in a group. The great danger of individual analytic treatment of a patient with a relatively defenseless ego, is that he may be exposed to the damaging influence of a practitioner who may have little sympathetic understanding and may do more harm than good.* The group is collectively more powerful than the individual who is the group therapist and relatively less helpless in relationship to him. This fact makes the group of patients less fearful; they therefore have little need to utilize the extreme defensive measures to prevent the discharge of their instinctual impulses found in patients being treated individually.

---

* It would appear that training in the psychoanalysis of groups might well in the future be made a requirement for the psychoanalyst. In the group setting, any human tendency of the analyst to make errors would be less costly to the individuals whom he is treating.

The essential problem of the treatment of emotional disturbances is to regulate the discharge of instinctual impulses so that the individual is capable of perceiving his own instinctual impulses in the form of feelings, and of organizing them into thoughts and language to the end that he may be able to function properly in relationship to his environment.

Psychoanalysis has revealed that unconscious compulsory patterns of behavior may lead an individual to behave in a way that is not to his immediate or ultimate advantage. One of the desirable aims of psychoanalytic therapy is to make the analysand conscious of these unconscious compulsory patterns of behavior. It is one of the tasks of the analyst to help the patient to the point where he can recognize his own formerly unconscious patterns of behavior. It is desirable that the formerly unconscious patterns of behavior become conscious and capable of being used in a voluntary way. Formerly compulsory patterns of behavior are no longer compulsory if the individual is aware of them and has a genuine feeling of freedom and choice in connection with using them. The healthy ego is the one that has the capacity to be aware of external and internal stimuli and of all sorts of patterns of behavior and tendencies for reaction within the self. Such a healthy ego can select and act in harmony with the behavior patterns that are most in accord with its immediate and long-range objectives.

The understanding of resistances, transference phenomena, the repetition compulsion, together with the technique of imparting this knowledge to the patient in a palatable form, makes it possible for the analyst to develop a relatively healthier ego in the analysand.

PSYCHOANALYSIS OF GROUPS

To a large extent, group psychotherapy has been evolving into the psychoanalysis of groups. How has the application of psychoanalytic principles to group therapy served to help this vigorous and rapidly developing and expanding form of therapy? The earliest form of group psychotherapy attempted to appeal primarily to the conscious aspects of the personality. People in groups have been treated by intellectual instruction, commands, attempts to exhort and to impose upon the individual, in order to get him to exert his conscious will to improve himself. With the application of psychoanalytic principles, group therapists have attempted to work with the unconscious of the individual in the group. They have studied transference phenomena as they have appeared in the group, and recently there has been increasing focus on resistances as they appear in the group setting. Slavson is largely responsible for the recent application of principles of analytic theory to therapeutic groups. Considerable work in this direction has also been done by Ackerman and Wolf. In England, Foulkes has been the impetus for considerable interest and application of analytic principles to group therapy.

The result of the application of psychoanalytic principles to group therapy is that analytic group therapy has been developing as a therapeutic process based upon a definite understanding of how the basic unconscious patterns of the individual influence the unconscious patterns of group functioning. All sorts of interactions have been discovered, many of which have been described in terms of therapeutic usefulness. The most important discoveries are that the ego-functioning of the individual is improved in the group setting. The resistances of the individual patient are strengthened in a group setting in which people are selected for a group on the basis of the principle that a therapeutically functioning group requires the presence of instigators, neutralizers, and pacifiers. Such a setting tends to nullify the need for the increased utilization by the individual patients of regression as a method of defense. Instead, less pathological and less dangerous defense mechanisms are adequate for the functioning of the individual, and these can be studied and understood at a more leisurely pace, with less danger to the health of the individual patient.

In addition, there is the important fact that there is an unconscious trend in the group to unite and to function in an organized way relative to the group analyst. The common libidinal strivings of the individual members serve to stimulate them to help each other and to attempt to understand each other; this libidinal component is of considerable help to the group analyst, since through it part of his task is made easier. Certain resistances, especially those that are not shared in common by the individual members of the group, tend to become the object of study. Attempts are made by other members of the group to overcome such resistances, so that eventually each member of the group may tend to have similar libidinal strivings and to develop similar patterns of an organization which they can utilize jointly in relationship to the group analyst. The main task, then, confronting the group analyst is how to deal with the resistances that are common to all members of the group and with the types of transference that are common to all members of the group in their relationship to him, the group analyst.

The fact that many individual resistances are handled early by the members of the group, results in early and rapid symptomatic improvement in many properly organized therapeutic groups. This rapid and early improvement is inspiring to both patient and therapist and tends to keep the group together and to stimulate the hope that ultimately the group therapeutic experience will help the various group patients realize their goals. It makes them more willing to work and to exert efforts in order to obtain good results.

The task of the group analyst is made easier by the assistance of the group members in handling the individual problems of members of the group. Thus, to the extent to which individuals have different problems which they help each other to resolve successfully, the work of a group analyst, in conducting a group, is done with the expenditure of relatively little energy on his part. In the beginning, it is relatively easier to obtain improvement in the treatment of a group of individuals than it is in individual treatment. What happens later in the course of group therapy is the opposite. Then the intensity of the libidinal strivings and the powerful resistances of the group make the task of the group analyst much more difficult than the task that he may have to face in individual analysis.

LIMITATIONS OF THE GROUP SETTING

The fact that several individuals are receiving therapy at the same time means that each individual receives less attention than he would receive if he were being treated alone. Furthermore, those problems that he has which are different from those of other members of the group, are found to be sources of annoyance and irritation. Any one individual may be subjected at any time to the combined hostility of the group. The guidance of the group in a therapeutic direction demands on the part of the therapist more skill and the capacity to utilize more thought, care, and energy at one time than is the case in the individual therapeutic setting.

The pre-verbal period in the life history of the individual is one that involves his relationship primarily with one person at a time, that is, his mother. As the child enters the oedipal period, he becomes able to distinguish emotionally between father, mother, and other members of the family. For those oedipal problems that involve several members of the family at the same time, the group setting can serve as a substitute stage, and transference phenomena may facilitate the dealing with such oedipal problems. However, when pre-oedipal problems or unipersonal problems (those involving a relationship with one person at a time) are a factor in the problems of the individuals, the group setting tends to inhibit the presentation of these problems. Thus it becomes more difficult for unipersonal problems of the anal and oral type as they occurred between individuals and their separate parents to be remembered, verbalized, and understood. This type of material tends to be inhibited, and it is generally regarded that this factor may make it more difficult to treat unipersonal problems in the group setting than in the individual setting. However, even in the individual setting, this type of material requires several years of analytic work to be thoroughly understood. It is still a subject for further investigation to determine whether therapeutic groups which are held together over periods of three or more years will not also pre-

sent such unipersonal material with sufficient clarity for satisfactory treatment.

EMOTIONAL CURRENTS IN
THE GROUP SETTING

Studies of the group therapeutic process have revealed that
the instinctual forces at work in the group setting can be understood in terms of the life and death instincts as described by
Freud. However, in view of the fact that in the group setting
instinctual impulses appear regularly in the form of certain ego
organizations, it has been found desirable to categorize the organizations in the form of certain constellations of forces.
These constellations of forces have been called the "reproductive constellation of forces" and the "inadequacy constellation of
forces" (17). More recently there has been evidence for another
grouping of forces: the "negative reproductive constellation of
forces" (19). These constellations of forces make it easier to
comprehend the complex phenomenology of the group therapeutic process. By the "the positive reproduction constellation
of forces" is understood those forces that make themselves felt
in the desire to have sexual congress, to cause pregnancy, to
produce a healthy normal adult, better in every respect than
the parent. By the "inadequacy constellation of forces" is understood the physical, emotional and integrational inadequacies
which deter individuals from the realization of the ultimate goal
set by the reproduction constellation, that is, the production of
a child who is to become a better adult than the parent. By the
"negative reproduction constellation of forces" is understood
those forces that make themselves felt in the desire to prevent
sexual congress, to prevent pregnancy, to produce defective
and unhealthy children, to deter them in every way from a
healthy development so that they will die at an early age or
never become superior in any respect to the parent and/or parents. Depending upon the state of organization of the individual
ego, each person is more or less aware of these forces in the form
of thoughts, feelings, and behavior.

It has been observed that when the driving force of the reproduction constellation of emotions was stimulated and the misdirecting force of the inadequacy constellation was diminished by the group therapeutic process, the two forces served as binding energies and tended to hold the group together. On the other hand, when the directing force of the reproduction constellation was diminished, or the misdirecting force of the inadequacy constellation was increased by the group process, then the two forces served as disruptive energies and tended to break up the group. Whether the constructive or destructive process dominated, depended upon whether the group situation permitted either partial and immediate or delayed gratification of the instinctual energy of these constellations of forces. What is significant is that the disruptive forces took the form of the negative reproduction constellation of forces and that these operated in a non-therapeutic way unless they were discharged in the form of language with feeling (anger, resentment, etc.) in the group setting.

The instinctual energy which supplies the forces for the constellations of forces here described, when blocked from discharge into consciousness, ordinarily makes its appearance as symptoms of neurosis, or psychosomatic and allied disorders. The presence of the group setting tends to facilitate the discharge of impulses into consciousness in the form of feelings. Thus it is possible to recognize more easily in the group setting that there is an emotional current present, and to recognize at any given time which of the constellations of emotions described above, or any combination of them, dominates the current.

RESISTANCE IN ANALYTIC GROUP THERAPY

When individuals are gathered in a group for therapeutic purposes and are directed to give an account of their life histories, feelings, and thoughts in a spontaneous emotionally significant way, it is natural that they will find it difficult to do so, and the voluntary and involuntary methods which they use to avoid presenting the desired material are considered the "resistances" (18). It has been observed that the resistances of the inadequacy constellation are based upon the infantile needs of individuals in the group setting—needs which had not been supplied by the parents. The resistances of the reproduction constellation are evidently the result of the instinctual urge toward genital gratification. It is evident that both types of resistances obtain their energies from drives at work in the child-parent relationship. Resistances help both the individuals in the group and the group therapist to adjust to the immediate stresses produced by the functioning of the group. The utilization of resistances serves to preserve the status quo and to maintain the existing relationships in the group.

It must be borne in mind that the resistances can be given up in a voluntary and satisfactory way only when the mobilized energy does not threaten the therapeutic situation and relationships. Too much pressure for the resolution of the superficial resistances may lead to the too early utilization of deeper resistances, and by their action may be dangerous to the preservation of a healthy equilibrium of the individual personalities. The success or failure of the group therapy, in a large measure, appears to depend upon whether or not the group therapist is successful in helping the group members to a gradual understanding of their resistances in terms of the history, origin, and meaning of these resistances. To the extent to which the resistances are thoroughly understood, an emotional evolution occurs in the group setting. It is possible that the emotionally intensified forces of the group situation may be channelized into a process that is therapeutic for both the individual members of the group and the group therapist, if they can be directed toward the gradual resolution of all types of resistances: the individual resistances, which are the distinct resistances of the individual members of the group; the common resistances, which are the resistances that are common to all members of the group; and the induced resistances, those that are induced in the group therapist by the group.

DIFFERENCES BETWEEN INDIVIDUAL
AND ANALYTIC GROUP THERAPY

In individual therapy the immediate problems with which the therapist has to deal are those that are part of the personality of the individual, as the result of his past experiences as they are re-activated in the presence of the therapist. In group therapy where there are several individuals present at the same time, there is a more complicated interaction going on between the individuals and the group therapist. The capacity of the group therapist to control the amount of stimulation to which each individual is to be exposed, is extremely restricted. Therefore, the subjects receiving treatment are called upon to adapt more or less continuously to a relatively more complicated and less controlled environment. In individual treatment the therapist can control exquisitely the amount of stimulation to which the patient is exposed at all times during treatment by his silence or by speaking for longer or shorter periods of time. Furthermore, there the therapist can control his own thoughts and feelings and study the extent to which he is being influenced by the patient, or vice versa.

In the group setting it is rare that such a simple adaptation problem is present for study. Instead, we have several individuals of different states of adaptation to each other, and, in turn, the therapist who is adapting to several individuals at the same time. Thus it follows that the individual situation favors the concentrated study of the patterns of behavior of one individual; these can be highlighted by the control of the therapist's behavior in such a way as to bring to the patient's attention some particular aspect of his personality. Since this is more difficult in the group setting, the therapeutic experience tends to become one of emotional learning of adaptive behavior, rather than a step-by-step learning of individual patterns of behavior and how to change them. Thus in the group, where the problems of the adaptation of one individual to several others at a time are involved, the learning experience of necessity must be more through emotional impact than through insight.

There is no substitute for individual treatment, with regard to the intense feeling and experience of understanding which is possible only between two individuals.

However, the intense emotional relationship between two individuals has many disadvantages that tend to be neutralized in the group setting. Excessive dependence upon one individual tends to be discouraged. Irrational expectations are held in check. The emotions of the individual tend to be less important, so that magical expectations and strivings for omnipotence are curbed. Also it is found that feelings of security and gratification can be obtained from several different members of the group. Instead of the tendency toward free association with its disadvantages in human relations, there is consistently the experience of spontaneous emotional interactions which tend to help the individual to become a more social human being.

The group setting tends to encourage the "feeling-out" of conflicts rather than putting them into language and controlling them. Individuals learn to control their impulses as a result of emotional interactions, rather than as the result of the conscious recognition of their impulses. Thus there is a marked tendency in the group setting to assuage intense feelings which tend to disorganized behavior. There is an improvement in functioning, yet certain impulses remain bound to certain feeling-patterns, and there is less driving force for individuality. By way of compensation, there is a greater readiness to respond to the needs of the group and to operate in harmony with the principles of the group. The repeated experience of clashing with group members and eventually adjusting to this continuously changing social reality, which becomes more familiar and more understanding as time goes by, tends to promote the growth of feelings of self-confidence and self-esteem with a resulting improvement in general functioning.

THE FUTURE OF GROUP THERAPY

Since the time when the first therapeutic groups were reported by Pratt, there has been a profound change in group therapy. The initially reported groups were "classes" for tubercular patients. Later the groups became more organized; the therapist used the group setting purposefully to obtain special therapeutic effects. For example, Slavson organized and reported upon activity groups: children as a group were permitted to release impulses in activity which would be mutually beneficial. Gabriel reported upon the effects of psychotherapeutic groups whose primary activity was speech: these were called "interview groups." As has been stated, the more recent trend has been toward psychoanalytic groups. The aim has been developing to attempt to make the group experience approximate as closely as possible, the experience of an individual psychoanalysis, with the additional factor that several people are being treated at the same time. One of the handicaps that has retarded the development of group therapy, has been that the emphasis has been primarily on therapy in the group. It is hoped that with the increasing interest of trained psychoanalysts in the functioning of groups, there will develop more interest in the analysis of groups. It is desirable for groups to be studied not only for the operation of therapeutic factors, but also to increase our understanding of the functioning of different types of individuals in the group setting.

There is practically an untouched field for investigation in the group evolutionary process. When individuals meet in a therapeutic group, they have certain distinct characteristics that distinguish them as individuals. In addition, they have certain characteristics in common that are more or less unconscious: their common resistances and common transferences. It is perhaps not too farfetched to anticipate that there are certain types of social organization toward which mankind is evolving, and that considerable information about these trends might be obtained from the study of the simultaneous emotional evolution of different types of individuals.

One of the frequently justified attacks on psychoanalysts has been that their occupation tends to isolate them from society, so that they may protect the certain degree of anonymity which is important to the practice of their profession. The advent of group analysis promises to do away with this trend.

The treatment of groups of individuals requires that the group analyst frequently adjusts himself to all sorts of individuals, sometimes in a more active, sometimes in a more passive way. Thus the analyst receives constant training in different types of social roles. He is called upon continually to expand and to develop his social ego. In this way, whatever latent qualities for group leadership are present can develop, and thus the analyst can do his part to assist society by helping provide better patterns of leadership.

SUMMARY

In summary, one may expect that the rapidly expanding field of group therapy will provide us not only with healthier citizens, as a result of their own group experience, but also with a vast knowledge as to how different types of individuals behave in various groups. In addition, one may anticipate that the role of society in producing group hostilities may be elucidated further. How society contributes to personality disorders, and how the pathological patterns of individuals contribute to social deterioration, may be studied under controlled conditions. Finally, group therapy may develop leaders who will guide society on its path with increasingly less mass and individual destruction.

BIBLIOGRAPHY

1. ACKERMAN, N. W., "Group therapy from the viewpoint of a psychiatrist." *Am. J. Orthopsychiat.*, XXXI, 667–681, 1943.
2. ———, "Dynamic patterns in group therapy." *Psychiat.*, VII, 341, 1944.
3. ———, "Psychoanalysis and group psychotherapy." *Group Psychotherapy*, III, 204–215, 1950.
4. FOULKES, S. H., *Introduction to Group-Analytic Psychotherapy*. London, Wm. Heineman, 1948; New York, Grune and Stratton, 1948.
5. GABRIEL, B., "An experiment in group therapy." *Am. J. Orthopsychiat.*, IX, 146, 1939.

6. ———, "Interview group therapy for adolescent girls." *Am. J. Orthopsychiat.*, XII, 593, 1944.

7. GREENE, J. S., "Speech and voice disorders." *The Medical World*, LVII, 719, 1939.

8. HADDEN, S. B., "Treatment of the neuroses by class technic." *Ann. Int. Med.*, XVI, 33, 1942.

9. KOLODNEY, E., "Treatment of mothers in groups as a supplement to child psychotherapy." *Ment. Hyg.*, XXVIII, 437, 1944.

10. MORENO, J. L., "Psychodrama and group psychotherapy." *Ann. N. Y. Acad. Sci.*, LXIX, 902, 1948.

11. PRATT, J. H., "The home sanatorium treatment of consumption." *Johns Hopkins Hosp. Bull.*, XVII, 140, 1906.

12. SCHILDER, P., "The analysis of ideologies as a psychotherapeutic method, especially in group treatment." *Am. J. Psychiat.*, XCIII, 601, 1936.

13. SLAVSON, S. R., "Group therapy." *Ment. Hyg.*, XXIV, 36, 1940.

14. ———, *An Introduction to Group Therapy.* New York, The Commonwealth Fund, 1943.

15. ———, *The Practice of Group Therapy.* New York, Intern. Univ. Press, 1947.

16. ———, *Analytic Group Psychotherapy.* New York, Columbia Univ. Press, 1950.

17. SPOTNITZ, H., "Observations of emotional currents in interview group therapy with adolescent girls." *J. Nerv. & Ment. Dis.*, CVI, 565–582, 1947.

18. ——— AND GABRIEL, B., "Resistance in analytic group therapy." *Quart. J. Child Behav.*, II, 71–85, 1950.

19. ——— AND SIBULKIN, L., "The negative reproduction constellation in an adolescent girl." (In preparation.)

20. WENDER, L., "Dynamics of group psychotherapy and its application." *J. Nerv. & Ment. Dis.*, LXXXIV, 54, 1936.

21. WOLF, A., "The psychoanalysis of groups." *Am. J. Psychother.*, III, 4, 1949; IV, 1, 1950.

► SIMULTANEOUS TREATMENT OF BOTH PARENTS AND THEIR CHILD

*By Bela Mittelmann, M.D.**

INTRODUCTION

It will be shown in this paper that the simultaneous treatment of husband and wife and child by the same therapist is not only of advantage in some instances, but may be indispensable for full therapeutic results; and that any situation that is beyond the patient's resources to cope with (his ego-strength), should be handled if possible directly or indirectly by the analyst—otherwise new insight and unconscious material remain inaccessible. The simultaneous treatment of members of the family furnishes material about such situations and enables the therapist to cope with them. It will be shown further that the patient's neurosis forms a complex complementary pattern with the members of society in his enviroment, particularly with members of his family.

THE HUSBAND AND THE WIFE

I shall here present the case history of a wife, her husband, and their child: **

> The woman is now thirty-six, the man forty, and the child eight. The man and the woman have been married for seventeen years, and are compatible in their interests and activities. The history begins ten years ago, several years before their treatment was started. The wife saw a child being run over by a trolley car and became so "hysterical"

---

* Associate Visiting Neuropsychiatrist, New York University-Bellevue Medical Center.
** Some aspects of the analyses of these three patients have been presented in previous communications (3), (4), (5).

that people on the street thought it was her child who had been killed. Two nights later she had a nightmare in which she saw her husband with his genitals cut off. She became anxious and depressed and the family physician suggested that she have a child. During her pregnancy her depression and anxiety disappeared.

The child, at the age of one month, developed eczema which lasted for a year. The mother was quite upset by this, as well as by the child's later gastro-intestinal symptoms of vomiting and diarrhea, caused by allergy. The child turned out to be a feeding problem and when he was a year-and-a-half old the mother developed obsessional thoughts of cutting her child's throat. About a year later (that is, about five and a half years ago), she started analytic treatment. In addition to her obsessional thoughts, arousing profound guilt, she had another complaint, this one deeply injurious to her self-esteem, namely, frigidity. Soon after the beginning of her analysis she staked the success of the treatment on the cure of her frigidity.

It took this patient six months finally to inform me that she thought her husband suffered from premature ejaculation, an assumption which proved to be correct. He reached orgasm within half a minute after the beginning of intercourse. After this had been discussed with both partners, he too started analytic treatment. After another month the woman asked, "How do you know that if my husband were adequately potent I wouldn't be sexually responsive and wouldn't be free of all symptoms?" On the basis of my knowledge of psychopathology I was convinced that she would not be well. However, she chose this issue as the incontestable battleground for her resistance, and I agreed to stop her treatment until her husband's potency improved.

Within ten months his sexual performance improved so much that the wife had to agree that she ought to be able to reach orgasm. This she was not able to do, and she resumed treatment in a most disappointed mood. She was disappointed despite the fact that her husband's improvement gave tangible evidence of what analysis can accomplish in correcting sexual difficulties.

Let us now skip two-and-a-half years of analysis. The wife

has her first analytic hour after two months' vacation. She relates that in the course of the summer the potency of her husband declined again and that the situation was pretty hopeless: if after two years of treatment her husband's potency was still poor, how on earth could she ever achieve orgasm? (She had had two very faint orgasms during intercourse before the vacation.) Later in the day, during his hour the husband told me the same story, but he mentioned the fact that they had had intercourse only three times in two months. I expressed surprise, reminding him that his usual frequency was three to four times a week. "Well, our son," (at that time six years old) "was sleeping in the same room even on those three occasions, and my wife was afraid he might observe us. She did not want intercourse at all at any other time." I asked him what was wrong with daytime. "Well," he said, "I suggested it but my wife won't hear of having intercourse in daylight."

Now here was this patient, who was staking her whole treatment on the correction of her vaginal frigidity, failing to mention the two significant facts that the child slept in the same room, and that she refused to have intercourse during the day. Up to this point in her treatment I had utilized crucial information obtained from her husband only indirectly for getting the same information from her through casual but skillful questions (4). However, indirect questions in the next analytic hour did not lead her to add the omitted information to her hopeless story of the summer. I then decided to confront her directly with the information, and she confirmed it. I pointed out to her that the reason she had omitted this information was because she had to put the blame on her husband, even at the cost of a hopeless outlook; to her it meant catastrophic failure and humiliation to admit that she had any fundamental problems.

From that point on I started to use directly, in the wife's treatment, information obtained from the husband. The information was quite remarkable. She never prepared the vaginal diaphragm herself; it was always the husband who did it. Even this she would not allow in advance. They would start the preliminaries and she would get interested;

then the husband would get up, apply the lubricant on the vaginal diaphragm, and bring it to her. She would not discuss anything sexual with the husband. She would get hurt and angry if he asked her whether she preferred any particular preliminaries or whether she had reached orgasm. None of this had she ever reported spontaneously in the analysis. In fact, she was reluctant to use the word "orgasm" even in the analytic hour. Not that she objected to the word. She would simply report that she had had intercourse the previous night. I would ask how it went. She would reply, "Well . . . all right." I would say, "What do you mean 'all right'?" She would reply, "I had a fair reaction." "What do you mean, you had a fair reaction?" "Well, I reacted more or less adquately." "Do you mean you had an orgasm?" "Yes, I had an orgasm." "Why did you not tell me?" "Because it was only fifty per cent." The information obtained from the husband was now being consistently utilized in her treatment, and her behavior was being interpreted to her.

The husband's analysis likewise needed supplementary information. During this period he would start the hour in a slow, somewhat monotonous manner and would reply to the question whether he felt depressed in the affirmative. He was able to tell when he got depressed but was uncertain what he felt depressed about. I usually knew from the wife that intercourse had taken place at the time from which the husband dated his depression. Then some such conversation would take place in the hour: "Didn't you have intercourse at the time you say you got depressed?" "Yes, I guess so." "Why didn't you mention it?" "I guess I forgot." "What made you depressed?" "Because my wife had no orgasm." This had two opposite meanings to him simultaneously: one, that he was sexually inadequate; two, and this was accompanied by quickly repressed bitterness, that no matter how he performed there was no way of getting his wife's approval. The latter meaning confirmed his unconscious conviction of an unfriendly, depriving fate, built up since the age of five when his father died and his mother sent him to an orphan asylum. The fact was, of course, that his wife had reached a "fifty per cent or seventy per cent orgasm" but would not talk about it to her husband.

In the past, if his depression lasted a while, his potency declined. This then confirmed the wife in her false conviction that her difficulty was to be blamed on him. The recovery of his potency in a week or two would not eradicate this effect, and soon the wife's behavior would lead to another temporary decline in his potency. This vicious circle was first broken when the causes of the husband's depression were immediately recognized and analyzed with him and thus a decline in his potency prevented; second, when the wife was confronted with the nature and analysis of her behavior and its effects on her husband. Within four months the wife had adequate orgasms during intercourse.

THE CHILD

Let us now skip another year and point up certain aspects of the child's relationship with his parents, particularly with the mother.

The boy is now seven-and-a-half years old and has been suffering, among other symptoms, from nightmares since the age of three. For the last six months the nightmares have become more severe and have the usual content that he is being chased by a monster. When he is awakened by a nightmare, he goes to his parents' bed where he quiets down, and then goes back to his own bed.

In the course of the treatment he had a simple nightmare: he lost his bicycle. Actually he had lost not his bicycle but a book that he had borrowed from the school library. If we look further into the dream, we have a beautiful illustration of condensation. The dream occurred at the time when the family moved to a new place. The child was worried that he would not have new friends, and used to go back to the old street to play with his old friends. He had his mother take his bicycle in the car to the old place so that he could ride the bicycle with the old friends, and his mother would drive over some hours later to bring him and his bicycle home. He would get upset if the mother was reluctant to make the trip. The child himself had told me earlier in his treatment that his more severe nightmares had started when he got a domineering, strict, new teacher. We can now see a fusion of five anxieties in this simple dream: the child is afraid of failure and disapproval in school; he is afraid of abandonment by his mother; he is afraid of abandonment by his friends; the bicycle being a male symbol, very likely he is afraid of not being a boy, and of being completely helpless and immobilized. It should be mentioned in connection with the latter point that when he had infantile eczema, his hands were at times tied to the sides of the bed to prevent scratching. While enacting the bicycle dream in the subsequent session, the child played walking in his sleep, then his bicycle was stolen and then somebody knocked him on the head, somebody knocked somebody else on the head, and there was a general fight. Thus we may add to the previous list of fears that of counter-attack for aggression (5).

Circular Reactions Between Both Parents and the Child

We can now establish one link, out of the many, between the behavior patterns of the mother and the child. The mother, in the attempt to remedy her deep feeling of being a failure in all significant aspects of life, had been perfectionistic since the age of five. One expression of this perfectionism was her inability, in the course of her treatment, to acknowledge problems without putting the blame on her husband. Of course her child became the victim of her perfectionism in two ways: through her expectation that he be perfect according to her standards, and through her hostility if he was not. The latter reaction was one of the determinants of her obsessional thoughts of cutting her child's throat. (Another determinant was her displaced hostility, including her castration wish against her husband.) In response, the child himself became perfectionistic as well as hostile. The mother and father were fairly permissive in the home. However, in school his hostility was thwarted and loomed hopelessly dangerous; from this resulted increasing anxiety and the nightmares. The drawings made by this child showed his intense aggression and anxiety. They were crowded, fairly disorganized, and at first glance seemed to represent hardly anything except a confusion of lines. The content, however, was telling: The school is on fire; there is a fight between gunmen; there is a battle between Japanese and American planes, etc.

The child's symptoms made the mother feel all the more that she had failed in her maternal role, re-enforcing her feeling of failure as a wife. This in turn led to sexual disinterest and refusal, which re-enforced the husband's potency disturbance. This aroused the wife's hostility and castration-wish because of the resultant frustration, which then was again displaced on to the child. In the simultaneous treatment of the parents (particularly of the mother) and the child, this vicious circle was broken. After I saw the child once, I told the mother that her panicky anxieties about him were unfounded, that he had a moderate emotional disturbance which, of course, was curable. To this she replied, "Well then, why don't I send him to camp for the summer?" This she did two months later. The child had a wonderful time and was one of the leaders in the group. When the child came back from camp, the mother said, "Well, why have I been so worried that he would not get along with other children?" These remarks are given to illustrate the decrease in the anxiety of the mother. Her handling of the child improved markedly. For example, if the child would become unruly, begin to complain of headache and get fussy over his food, the mother, instead of scolding, would ask the child whether he was worried about his school work. It usually turned out that this was the case, and with attention to his school work the essential behavior difficulty would disappear.

For the mother the concurrent treatment of herself and the child by the same therapist had the advantage that her anxiety reactions were resolved as soon as they arose, and that she could not misquote, as such anxious mothers often do, the child's therapist to her own analyst. Furthermore, she could utilize the information gained in the handling of her child. The third advantage was perhaps most impressive. I mentioned that because of her fear of failure she did not approach any of her problems voluntarily but had to be forced up against them by the analyst, as for example, by his utilization of the information gained from her husband. This was necessary not only in connection with her sexual problems but also in her relationship with her friends, her mother, and her art work which she took up during her analysis. The one area in which she took the initiative in the recognition and correction of her emotional problems was that of her relationship with her child; this she did as soon as his treatment started. Her handling of this field could then be utilized to convince her of the reluctance with which she faced her problems in the other fields, and to correct that reluctance.

For the child the advantages of concurrent treatment were the following: more complete information gained by the analyst of the events of the child's daily life because of his (the analyst's) intimate knowledge of the mother, less exposure of the child to the mother's anxieties and aggression, and better handling of the child by the mother through her making use of knowledge imparted to her by the analyst.

RESULT OF TREATMENTS

Excellent therapeutic results were obtained with both parents and with the child. The mother lost her obsessional symptoms, has adequate vaginal orgastic responses, has developed her art work successfully, treats her child well and has become self-assertive with her mother and her friends. The husband developed adequate potency, lost his spells of depression, and is self-assertive with family, friends, and colleagues. The child lost his anxiety and is well adjusted in work and play situations. The results could not have been attained with the parents without their being treated simultaneously by the same analyst since both of them, largely unconsciously, excluded crucial information from the treatment. This excluded information could gradually be collected from the mate and utilized in the treatment. The simultaneous treatment of the child by the same therapist was not indispensable, but was of advantage in the treatment of the child as well as of the parents.

DISCUSSION

In two previous communications (3), (4) the author has presented evidence that the patient's reactions form a complementary neurotic pattern with those individuals with whom he has intimate relationships, such as mate and siblings. In the present communication a similar problem between parents and child has been presented. This picture can be extended to relationships with superiors, workers of equal rank, those under the patient's jurisdiction, and friends. An important difference, although one only of degree, between these latter situations and intrafamily relations is that a greater mobility obtains as a rule in the extrafamily relationship. The patient can quit one job and look for another; divorce entails a much more radical realignment. Furthermore, the intimacy of the relationship in the intrafamily setup leads to more intense expectations and to the lack of certain inhibitions. Therefore they are apt to represent more intense and more complex complementary patterns.

A general formulation is this: genetic as well as current patterns comprise attitudes (sentimental and erotic attachment, hostility, anxiety, esteem and guilt, striving for safety) toward parts and the whole of the self, and toward others. To a considerable extent these complex patterns are intrapsychically self-perpetuating. They appear in the form of constructive and vicious circles or combinations of both. In addition to these internal circles there is a complementary series of interactions, also self-perpetuating to a large extent, with family members, intimates, and work mates. Personality as a whole as well as its neurotic aspects are an integrated system of such genetic and current internal and external complementary patterns.

Many patients show a definite limitation in their ability to cope with certain aspects of internal or external problems in the course of their treatment. Such limitation of integrative and coping ability (ego-strength) is generally assumed in adult psychotics and addicts and in children, and the treatment is expected to succeed only if provisions are made to supplement

the internal work with external measures, such as hospitalization of the psychotic, and direct contact with the parents of the
child (1). In more limited areas many adult patients suffering
from neuroses have similar limitations in coping-strength. No
one will doubt that vaginal frigidity cannot be cured if the
patient's mate suffers from a serious potency disturbance. Likewise many analysts recognize the therapeutic limitations unless
the mate's whole emotional life, apart from the patent sexual
aspects, is remedied. There is more disagreement about the
technical propriety of any guidance in the course of psychoanalytic treatment of relatively helpless patients. In the opinion
of some, such procedure interferes with the analytic process.

My experience has been that any measure that is warranted by the limitations of the patient's coping-ability not only
does not interfere with analytic progress, but is actually indispensable to it and leads to increased presentation of utilizable
unconscious material. Concurrent analysis of family members
by the same therapist proves to be such an indispensable measure if the respective patients cannot help but keep out of
their individual analyses crucial behavioral information. In discussing the problem of handling the mother-child relationship
in a recent article, Burlingham comes to the conclusion that it
is more effective therapeutically for both mother and child to
be treated concurrently by the same therapist.

> One may raise the question in the case of this husband
> and wife of whether it was the fault of the analyst's tech-
> nique that certain crucial information concerning them-
> selves was not forthcoming, particularly from the wife, but
> also from the husband. Or one might further add the ques-
> tion whether it was not the very fact of their going to the
> same analyst that was responsible for this limitation of in-
> formation.
> To dispose of this latter point first, this could certainly
> not have been the case with the husband. For he actually
> forgot that his depressive moods started with the occasion of
> sexual intercourse when he could not discuss with his wife
> the question of whether she did or did not reach an orgasm.

He never felt that the analyst was his wife's ally ranged against him. The trouble with him was that self-assertion and criticism and hostility toward his wife aroused an amount of guilt, fear of abandonment and of retribution, and that it was insurmountable by free association even when he assumed the therapist was on his side.

The wife at times had the feeling that the therapist was her husband's ally ranged against her, but it should be emphasized that she subjected to the same distortion the material relating to her mother, her child, her ambitions, as she did the material relating to her husband. It was impossible to get an adequate and accurate picture of how she was handling these issues and how she was reacting to them except if one also took into consideration her husband's account of it. For example, when it was clearly advisable and financially easily manageable for them not to continue to live with her mother, she would say that moving to a different apartment was reprehensible and impossible. It was reprehensible because it meant abandoning an old woman who had no money of her own and who was therefore being deprived of the emotional and financial support that she deserved; that therefore she, the patient, was an ungrateful daughter. She would then attack her husband for being inconsiderate and not understanding the moral obligations in the situation. She presented an airtight picture in this respect. However the husband brought out the fact, in his own therapeutic hour, that they had already given her mother $5,000 as a gift and that separate apartments were available for which the total rent for both would hardly be more than the rent for the present one. Besides, the mother would not be living alone but with a willing unmarried daughter. When confronted by the therapist with these statements, the wife agreed although in a stormy fashion. The point about this patient was that she, like her husband, had conflicts about self-assertion and hostility but, in addition, she had the need to be flawless and therefore the idea of having any problems was unbearable to her. These were difficulties which were insurmountable by free association or even by direct questions unless one was in actual possession of the correct information.

As regards the other point, namely the concurrence of the two analyses being responsible for the deficiency of information, the author recalls and even now has patients in individual analysis where he experiences the same difficulty and puzzlement as he did with this husband and wife; according to customarily valid criteria—namely the nature of their pathology, the possibility of seeing connections, their responsiveness to interpretations—they should make therapeutically good analytical patients, and yet the therapeutic effect is not up to expectation. Repeatedly it looks as if crucial difficulties were overcome and yet, fairly soon, one is up against the same obstacles and symptoms without clear evidence as to why. In the case of this couple, it was only after the analyst began to obtain and use information from the other mate that this puzzle was solved. The answer to the puzzle was that crucial material was missing from the patient's free associations and could not be obtained from the patient through indirect questions either, even when the therapist knew the answer. The straight reply was forthcoming only when the analyst had the information and asked the patient point-blank whether the situation was as it had been reported to him. It may be added that when either mate had to be absent from his (or her) respective treatment for several weeks, either because of some urgent family affair or business engagement or illness, the same obscurity returned to the other mate's analysis.

It is just a simple fact that some patients suffering from character neurosis and/or psychoneurosis are not able to furnish all significant crucial information spontaneously in the analytic hour. One would never expect a psychotic or a child to be able to do this, but one does assume that neurotics can. This seems to be a wrong assumption, and one is asking the impossible of many neurotics. The material furnished by all patients in psychotherapy is for a long time slanted consciously or unconsciously and has many gaps. The majority of psychoneurotics and character neurotics correct the slant and fill in the gaps gradually, often by giving unwitting clues. Some patients, however, never do. This one finds out when one concurrently analyzes family members. There are, of course, all gradations between adequate correction of the initial slanting and gaps, and the maintenance of the entirely uncorrected distortions. If it reaches a certain degree then the therapy involving the patient alone suffers from a serious deficiency. Returning to the question of whether the analyst's technique was faulty with the husband and wife, the author's impression is that the method of dealing with the patients alone and the method of free association have their therapeutic limitations in some instances, and he suggests that those who are strongly inclined to doubt this try concurrent analysis of husband and wife in cases where they have the perplexity referred to earlier, namely that according to the customary criteria, the individual patient should have been making better progress than he is making.

One question remains open, namely, to what extent contact between the respective analysts of husband and wife can remedy the uncorrected slants and gaps. The author has no answer to this question because he knows of no published study on the topic.* Probably such a procedure would take care of most instances of uncorrected distortions. It seems probable, however, that with a husband and wife of the types here described, the contact between the two analysts would have to be continuous, certainly weekly, and at times daily. For example, one analyst would have to get the information from the other that the couple had intercourse on a night which the husband had forgotten and which had started his depressive reaction—otherwise the husband's analyst could not cope with this problem, the husband's potency disturbance would appear sooner or later, and the wife would again be in the position to project her problems out onto the husband. It certainly seems more efficient and effective if they are treated by the same analyst.

We may add an obvious comment: The fact that a patient does not correct distortions in the course of the treatment even

---

* The value of such a procedure is demonstrated in the forthcoming article of Drs. Peter A. Martin and H. Waldo Bird, "The Stereoscopic Technique: An Approach to the Treatment of Marriage Partners," to be presented at the 1952 Annual Convention of the American Psychiatric Association.

by clues, can be found out only if one has an additional source of information. It is precisely this fact that is revealed strikingly in the concurrent analyses of some couples. In other analyses there is no noticeable difference in this respect, whether the analyses of husband and wife are conducted by the same analyst concurrently or entirely individually. It is possible that there are analyses in which concurrent treatment is disadvantageous although the author has so far not observed this.

The crucial information omitted is either current behavior or events that have taken place in the course of the relationship of the two individuals. The omission is either some defensive maneuver or some form of gratification, either of which cancel out in large measure the effectiveness of other material brought into the analysis. Obviously in the adult it is never infantile material, although, as shown in a previous publication (4), crucially significant infantile material may be spontaneously revealed by the patient only after the use of information obtained from the mate.

In the analyst's handling of concurrent analyses two points become of paramount importance: he must have a reliable enough memory so that he is never in doubt from which of the mates he received a piece of information. If he utilizes information obtained from the other mate, he must be aware of it and (usually) must say so. Secondly, if he becomes the target of the mates' rivalling contentions and hears heated declarations of the unbearable behavior of the other mate, he must realize that there is ample time to single out and interpret each mate's complementary problem. One of the most useful slogans to give to the patient in such situations is, "Two wrongs do not make one right."

Some of the complexities of the effect of concurrent treatment of family members on the patients' attitudes toward the analyst have been discussed in previous publications (3), (4). The following additions seem important: the patient takes the fact of the analyst's changing his environment by treating the other member of the family as an extension of his own strength, particularly at points at which such strength is lacking. One could say that at those points the analyst becomes to the patient an extension of his own ego. To put it differently, in these problems the patient considers the analyst as an active helper, perhaps of magic power. There is a similarity between these two coexisting attitudes and the attitude of the child toward the benevolent parent. Both of these elements might entail the risk of permanently tying the patient to the therapist and strengthening his dependency and magic expectations. There are, however, two factors which invariably counteract this: one is the patient's realization that the external help appears at points where it is indispensable. Thus, the patient obviously cannot cope with some of the neurotic behavior of the mate, whereas the analyst can. The second point is that as soon as the situation changes, and the patient still wants to follow the old mode of behavior, the analyst can interpret very actively and thus exert pressure on the patient to move forward with his problems. Perhaps in this respect too there is a parallel between the analytic situation and the child's relationship with the benevolent parent who is not unqualifiedly permissive at all times. Through this pressure, reality-testing and clarification of remaining unconscious problems finally lead to adequate integration and independence.

SUMMARY

Concurrent treatment of family members (of both mates or of parents and children) by the same therapist is not only feasible in most instances but is frequently advantageous and at times indispensable for the best therapeutic results. The latter is the case if the respective patients cannot help but exclude from their treatment crucial behavioral information.

Close contact with some key members of the family, guidance, and supportive procedures are considered routine in the analysis of adult psychotics and addicts, and of children. Often there are also areas of restriction of integrative and coping-ability (ego-strength) in adult patients suffering from neurosis. The application of external measures in such areas not only does not interfere with the analysis but increases the flow of unconscious material.

The total personality as well as its neurotic aspects can be viewed as an integrated system of current and of genetic self-perpetuating circular patterns of intrapsychic and interpersonal strivings.

The patient evaluates the analyst's activity in changing other members of the family, as well as his limited guidance, as an extension of his own functioning self and as the support of a magic helper. The coexistence of these attitudes is paralleled by that of the child toward the benevolent parent. The magic dependence, however, is counteracted by the pressure toward change exerted on the patient by the analyst's interpretations, if the patient wants to retain the old adaptation after favorable changes have occurred in the environment. This also parallels the attitudes of the child toward the benevolent parent who, however, is not unqualifiedly permissive. The pressure, together with reality-testing (the realization that supplementary help was indispensable and that the actual situation has changed), eventually leads to adequate integration and independence.

BIBLIOGRAPHY

1. BURLINGHAM, D. T., "Present trends in handling the mother-child relationship during the therapeutic process." *The Psychoanalytic Study of the Child*, Vol. VI. 31–37. New York, Internat. Univ. Press, 1951.

2. FREUD, A., *Introduction to the Technique of Child Analysis*. New York, Nerv. & Ment. Dis. Publ. Co., 1928.

3. MITTELMANN, B., "Complementary neurotic reactions in intimate relationships." *Psychoanal. Quart.*, XIII, 479–491, 1944.

4. ———, "The concurrent analysis of married couples." *Psychoanal. Quart.*, XVII, 182–197, 1948.

5. ———, *Ego Functions and Dreams*. (In press.)

ADAPTATION OF THE PSYCHOANALYTIC TECHNIQUE FOR THE TREATMENT OF YOUNG CHILDREN WITH ATYPICAL DEVELOPMENT*

*By Beata Rank***

INTRODUCTION

Adaptations and modifications of the psychoanalytic technique have depended largely on the advances made in psychoanalytic theory. The changes that have taken place within the framework of the "orthodox" school have been principally due to our better understanding of ego formation and ego function, that is, "ego psychology." Further changes have evolved in the course of the development of psychoanalytic treatment of children and psychotics (5), (6), (9), (15).

Our aim here is to describe the method of analytic treatment of very young children, especially those whose development has been arrested at a very primitive, infantile level, and who have generally been considered feebleminded or psychotic. Because of the very pessimistic prognosis, no clearly defined method of psychotherapy had been devised for such children. The techniques we are utilizing at The James Jackson Putnam Children's

* Reprinted with the permission of *The American Journal of Orthopsychiatry*, XIX, No. 1, 130–139, 1949.
** Co-Director of The James Jackson Putnam Children's Center, Boston, Massachusetts.

Center represent an attempt to apply the psychoanalytic approach to this type of problem in a clinic setting.

EMOTIONAL DEPRIVATION IN INFANCY AND CHILDHOOD

Our investigation of these young children is based upon the hypothesis that they have suffered gross emotional deprivation. This assumption in turn was derived from Freud's concept of neurosis. We understand that present-day culture makes demands for deprivation and frustrations in terms of mastery of the instinctual drives—both sexual and aggressive—beyond the average individual's capacity for tolerance. The question arises: Are these demands made early in infancy exaggerated and should we revert to primitive ways of freedom with no restraint? Certainly not, if one really understands the formation of the psychic structure. But there is plenty of room for finer understanding of the infant's formation of self and a great deal more clarification is needed of the interrelationship between infant and mother.

In recent years a number of analysts have devoted themselves to the study of the early manifestations of emotional life in infancy and in childhood through direct clinical observation (7), (8), (10), (17), (18), (20). Others (2), (11), (14), and recently Hartmann, Kris, and Loewenstein (12) have attempted to clarify Freud's concepts from the genetic point of view. Deprivation is necessary, they state, in order to achieve the distinction between the self and the outside world. Differentiation cannot occur before the maturation of the cognitive and perceptual equipment. And "as the child learns to distinguish between himself and the mother, he develops understanding for her communications. Little is known about the detailed processes by which this understanding is established" (13). This bond is gradually replaced by the child's identification with the mother's attitudes, and this identification in turn furthers the development of the reality principle, that is, the capacity to postpone immediate gratification for later goals.

Personality of the Child's Mother

For the causes of gross emotional deprivation we must examine the personality of the mother, who is the medium through which the primitive infant transforms himself into a socialized human being.

We can roughly divide the mothers of our children with arrested or fragmented development as follows: First, those with diagnosed psychoses: mainly manic-depressives who have had repeated hospitalizations and/or depressive episodes shortly after the birth of the child; or schizophrenics with remissions. Second, extremely immature individuals with narcissistic cathexes, incapable of mature emotional relationships.

The latter group is predominant and offers an intriguing challenge for therapy. On the surface these mothers may give the impression of being well-adjusted; not too rarely they are highly intellectual, highly placed individuals. Close investigation reveals that the majority of them are immature and narcissistic, with precarious social contact, akin to the type known as "As If" described by Helene Deutsch (4), who have struggled heroically to build and maintain the image they have created of a fine woman, wife, and mother. The nearer to perfection the success of their efforts, the stronger their belief in magic—their own magic (impenetrable defenses). In their background we find almost without exception an extremely strong but ambivalent bond to their own mothers, which resulted not in identification which would lead to emancipation and maturity, but in hateful dependency. The urgency to flee this dependency, the need for an "own" life and personality, even if only a vestige, makes it possible for them to enter matrimony rather early (in their twenties). Their husbands are outstanding for their passivity. Often they are scientists with variable professional success, but aloof and inadequate as family members. The forebears of both parents include an unusual number of eccentric and psychotic individuals, suggesting poor heredity as an important etiological factor in the development of atypical behavior in the child. Awareness of the hereditary factor should not, however, block us from further investigation. The question still remains as to the influence of the "quasi-mystical" union of the mother and the child in infancy.

We have mentioned before that this type of mother has a very definite picture of what a good mother should be. The need to be a mother, the hope and expectation that through this experience she may become a real person capable of true emotions, is so desperate that of itself it may create anxiety, ambivalence, fear of failure. Because she is so barren of spontaneous manifestation of maternal feelings, she studies vigilantly all the new methods of upbringing and reads treatises about physical and mental hygiene. Her greatest fear is of "spoiling" her child. Frequently she insists on an aseptic environment, and the child grows in an orderly, scientific atmosphere where routine and dietary prescriptions prevail. The sunshine which is radiated by the spontaneous, tenderly devoted mother is missing. The result may be passive inertia of the infant or at the other extreme, restlessness and sleeplessness. The passive child is less of a threat because he does not make exaggerated demands on the mother, who feels constantly in danger of revealing that emotionally she has little or nothing to offer, that she is a fraud. Parallel with this or independently, we may find in her personality structure the "messianic idea," not in the psychotic sense, but as a symbol of hope that through identification with the child, her own flesh and blood, she may experience vicariously the joys of real living, of genuine feeling.

Child's Reaction to Mother's Unconscious Feelings

If then, as frequently occurs, the mother becomes aware that this is not the case, she is compelled to face the fact that she is really without magic. She fights desperately for control, no longer of herself perhaps but of the child. The struggles over weaning and toilet-training are generally battles in which she tries to redeem herself. The child becomes the real victim— victim of the mother's helplessness which in turn creates an aggression in her that mounts to destruction. The only way for the child to survive is to retreat, to withdraw not only from the dangerous mother but from the whole world as well. A world of his own is created, a world of fantasy, but of fantasy so primary, so repetitious, so remote from our own feelings and experiences that he appears to us odd, bizarre, and dull intellectually and emotionally. He may then remain arrested in this stage, showing a scattered development, or regress even further to a complete breakdown of all social patterns. He becomes a restless wanderer in search of no one and no place, weaving about the room, swaying back and forth, circling the walls as if they were bars he would escape through; and he frequently does escape into the neighboring yard or the street, unconcerned with danger, absorbed in his own world. Unaware of the people he encounters, he stumbles over their feet or their most precious possessions. But all at once he may get panicky and in his fury and anguish throw himself to the ground when suddenly aware that his mother or mother-substitute is not at his side. It is as if he had been running away from her only to be able to return to her over and over. This special quality of pulling away from and yet leaning on an individual, is one of his many enigmatic characteristics. Because he tries so desperately to be invulnerable in his own world, he is pathetically helpless at the same time. This unique quality makes for his "charm," which exists alongside of, above, and beneath all the other odd characteristics. For us he offers a challenge similar to that recounted in myths and legends, where the hero (now therapist) conquers monsters and dragons and undoes the curse bestowed by evil spirits, thereby freeing the beautiful prince or princess (cf. Sleeping Beauty). In the same way, we hope that behind the thick walls built out of hatred and fear lie potentialities for a happier, even normal childhood.

CASE MATERIAL

CASE NO. 1.   Anne G. is a striking example of this group. When first seen at the Children's Center, her appearance and behavior were recorded by Dr. Eveoleen Rexford as follows: "Anne was a curious looking child: tall, thin, with a long, narrow skull and straggly black hair. She moved constantly, walked in a jerky, awkward fashion, or swayed rhythmically from one foot to the other. When she sat down for short periods, she rocked back and forth in her chair, leaving it abruptly, usually to tip it over. Her hands twisted and turned in midair, with the upper arms abducted, elbows flexed, and hands moving in fleeting, athetoidlike motions. Except for an occasional slight, mechanical smile, her face remained impassive, and she ignored or chewed the hair which fell frequently over her mouth. Her voice was high-pitched, insistent, and hoarse, and whatever she said was repeated several times.

"Anne wanted all activities carried out in the same way each time, went to the same chair, and played repetitively what she had played before. Her use of language was striking, and she spoke constantly during our early contact. Catching sight of the toy telephone, she asked: 'Is this a dial? Is this the way to do it? Is this a 'phone? This is a 'phone. This is a black 'phone. It has a yellow dial.' She named toys endlessly, picking one from the toy drawer or the table, carrying it from one place to another, saying repetitiously: 'Is this a basket? This is a basket. Is this a basket?' putting it down and choosing another, over which she would rapidly intone: 'Table. Is this a table? This is a table. Is this a table?' She referred to herself constantly as 'you': 'You want me to unbutton your coat,' or 'You don't want to cry.'"

CASE NO. 2.   The first impressions of Dr. Eleanor Pavenstedt, who is in charge of Henry C., are so identical with the picture of Dr. Rexford's Anne G. that at first one gets quite an uncanny feeling. Here are but a few lines from Dr. Pavenstedt's report to illustrate this point: "After a while Henry moved out into the big room. He headed for the piano and for the next fifteen minutes was completely absorbed in it. He would strike the keys at random and watch the hammers behind the music rack. His hands were waving all the while. Frequently he went and looked behind the piano and wanted to know what was there. He also spoke of 'piano,' 'radio,' 'phonograph,' waving his right hand circularly. He said: 'You strike it and movement (mother said "music") comes out.' He became so deeply absorbed in the piano that no one could have watched him without feeling that this piano was a part of himself. Pointing to the two-way screen, he kept saying: 'Play the radio. Is that a radio? Play the radio.' Once he said: 'Henry is a radio,' which mother promptly corrected. When it was time to go, we said goodbye to Henry, and he became very upset. 'You don't want to say goodbye.' He remained distressed until we sat down again. A few minutes later we left, saying we would see him tomorrow, and all was tranquil."

CASE NO. 3. Billy M., at present in his third year of treatment and close to recovery, is another example of this type of problem. He was, however, somewhat younger when first seen and had no speech. Let us glance at Dr. Marian Putnam's report, as she records her first observation: "On the first few visits Billy, who was then two years and eight months, paid absolutely no attention to children or adults but busied himself for the most part with the blinds and doors of the house, opening and shutting them, examining and manipulating the latches, peering first on one side and then on the other. Or he roamed about the yard with a curious propulsive gait with head and shoulders well forward, a posture which mother assured us was not his usual one. Occasionally he paused to stand doubled over with his head on ground, quite motionless. He was in general so removed and unresponsive that it was difficult to interpret his mood and behavior."

CASE NO. 4. Polly P., with her birdlike quality, belongs here, too. Following is an excerpt from Dr. Dorothy Macnaughton's observation: "In our room Polly instantly drops her toys and runs about inspecting everything. Her interest in 'little things' is apparent, and she tends to collect them and attach them to herself. Her body is beautifully made, and she shows unusual coordination in all she does. She moves so quickly that one has the impression suggested by her pet name 'Birdie' that she has flown rather than walked. Even in the odd postures which she assumes, of sudden squatting on the floor, bending archwise over the objects she is examining, or the still more bizarre one of lying full-length on her side on the floor, head almost touching heels, her lips moving in inaudible maunderings, she shows agility and grace. Although there is considerable movement of the muscles of the face, it does not contribute to her expression. The total impression is one of impassivity and aloofness. True, she looks at us squarely from time to time but with a sort of staring unresponsiveness. Her attention and contact with us vary in the same way. One time she will respond to a remark in an apparently appropriate way but at other times will repeat what we have said so that she seems to be referring to herself as 'you.' This intermittent echolalia gives the impression that what she says or what is said to her remains separate and apart from herself."

ARREST IN CHILD'S DEVELOPMENT

As we have seen, each one of these children is an individual in his own right and represents his own entity. However, they show many definable similarities which together constitute the typical picture of this group of children.

Lack of Contact with Reality

The most significant characteristic is that they are out of contact with reality and apparently without need for communication with others. They may or may not be in possession of speech. Language is used for other purposes, chiefly as a powerful magic weapon against the dreaded world. Magical gestures are frequently seen, as well as stereotyped behavior, rituals, tics, grimaces, monotonously repeated mannerisms, appearing without external provocation but prompted from within. The quality of voice is peculiar. It varies from rasping, squawking, and hollow sounds to a melodious, normal-sounding child's voice. They use their eyes to detect or to explore some object intently. At persons they glance only fleetingly, looking through one as a rule rather than at one. Their eyes seem not to focus.

Motor development is often above average; their grace and agility are frequently outstanding; or, at the other end of the scale, they may show extreme awkwardness, stiffness, and rigidity. In the body build, too, we find extremes: husky, well-proportioned bodies, or frail, sickly-looking ones with or without some congenital stigmata (1). These children move either constantly, aimlessly (perpetual motion), or are so passive that they slide into their seats like lumps, heavy to remove. Their play is mostly repetitious, compulsive; they do not derive from it real enjoyment, but rather frequently, excitement and at times sudden panic. Rocking in a rocking boat or moving cars, ritualistic touching, handling of mechanical gadgets, swinging, spinning, balancing objects, or mouthing them are the most frequent activities, which in turn remove these children even further from external contact. Except for play with water, which many of them enjoy, none of their playful activities resemble those of an average child. They are extremely finicky or eccentric eaters. Some only accept two or three items, always the same (usually bread). Others are gluttonous and devour tremendous quantities of food like an animal. Many drink enormous quantities of water, sometimes juice or milk. Their sleep, too, shows the same extremes. They either fall into a deep sleep, remaining immobile in the same spot from the moment they are put to bed to the moment of awakening, or they are restless wanderers, frequent visitors in their parents' bedroom. They at first undoubtedly identify with inanimate objects (cars, radios, etc.) and in the next stage with animals (pigs, dogs, cats, lions, giraffes, etc.) before they are able to make an identification with the mother or mother-figure. Each one of them has a special talent or ability. Whether it be music (this seems frequently to be the case), or an extraordinary ability to construct or build, or a special volubility and refinement of vocabulary, or whether it be simply their acrobatic agility, it amazes us and has a definite personal appeal regardless of what the specific characteristic indicates in the evaluation of the child's potentialities.

Development of a Fragmented Personality

To undo or release an arrest in the development of the emotional life of a child thus described is to transform a static state into a dynamic process. Such an artificial, early arrest in development occurs, we believe, because of the frailty of the ego which could not cope successfully with the onslaught of the instinctual drives. We say that such a child was raised in an emotional climate which was not favorable for the development of a clear-cut distinction between the self and the outside world, thus crippling the capacity for identification with the mother and her attitudes and thereby interfering with the development of both a unified personality and the reality principle. What characterizes them, however, is the coexistence of various achievements on different levels of development. We may say that these children present the picture of a scattered and fragmented personality rather than a uniformly infantile one. The tenuous relationship with an emotionally disturbed mother we recognize as the chief source of this condition. We recognize further the traumatic influence of events which ordinarily, in a different milieu, would not have the same significance. We have in mind the sudden separation of mother and child, chronic illness such as prolonged upper respiratory infection or gastro-intestinal disturbances, particularly diarrhea. In other words, the deprivation involved was poorly "planned" in terms of the how, when, and how much.

THE THERAPEUTIC APPROACH

In order to establish a relationship with a child who escapes from an imaginary or actual danger in reality by exclusion of people from his own world of magic and fantasy, we must provide by way of restitution: an environment with the right emotional climate; a temporary mother-substitute; and help for the real mother so that she may eventually be able to take over and herself meet her child's need. In brief, we have a three-fold approach: individual therapy with the child, individual therapy with the mother, and nursery school.

Providing the Right Emotional Climate

First of all, the child analyst who undertakes the treatment must have the capacity for an unconditional acceptance of the child as he presents himself, making no demands which he is not ready to meet and trying only to understand the meaning of all his odd behavior.

The difficulty which the analyst encounters in meeting a child of this sort on his (the child's) own level is considerable, not only because the child's mode of thinking, feeling, and behaving are so remote from the analyst's but also because the primitiveness of his drives frequently threatens our need for maintaining our own defenses such as our socially useful reaction-formations. Even among analysts few can accept without a shudder the offer of a prechewed raisin bathed in urine, which for the child may represent a demonstration of confidence and love. For many of our children go through a stage in which they explore and experiment with food by stuffing it into the mouth of the therapist inviting him to prechew it or vice versa. Indeed, his very primitive ways of getting close to people may sometimes be not only emotionally painful but physically so. Many of these children express their desire to enter into personal contact after an initial period of isolation by biting one, urinating on or at one, or soiling while sitting on one's lap; or they may fling some dangerously heavy object. And there is no use trying to conceal one's fear or anger. With an animal flair they detect the most clever disguise.

A further difficulty in understanding these children lies not only in the fact that their use of language or gesture is magical and symbolic, but also that a symbolic expression varies in its meaning according to the autistic representation of the child's inner experience into which the therapist has no entry. Louise Despert (3) stresses this element of condensation which makes so many of the child's manifestations at first unintelligible. In spite of all the handicaps which such a problem offers, the therapeutic task can be clearly defined by stressing again the importance of keeping in mind the different levels of emotional development attained by the child, which in these cases we define as the undeveloped self or the fragmented ego and for which we must create conditions favorable for growth.

Providing a Mother-Substitute

When we stress the need for an accepting mother-substitute for a child of such scattered levels of development, we must have a definite notion of what we mean. We shall not try to embark upon a theoretical or microscopic investigation of this relationship but rather aim to convey a clear picture of clinically observed behavior. Many of these children demand that we faithfully repeat right after them whatever they are doing, or we ourselves respond in this way intuitively in the so-called play situation. A reciprocal identical response to each other's activities is established. It is as if we were offering to the child a mirror in which to look at himself without fear or shame. If we introduce any change or variation of the theme, it will be a slight and subtle one. The play becomes, one might say, an exercise in projection and introjection, to enable the child to learn to differentiate between himself and the outside world. The insistence of some children that the analyst continually repeat their actions and verbal productions makes one understand that what they want is that one should feel as they have felt or feel. By creating an opportunity for them to repeat and relearn earlier, not-assimilated situations, one is able to help the child to establish or find himself on a given infantile level and to experiment with the next stage of development. When the ego of the child acquires a certain strength and integration as evidenced by his taking us as a love object, only then can we act as the mother-substitute who not only accepts but educates by sharing reality-experiences, giving concrete knowledge while at the same time recognizing fears and conflicts as they come to expression in the course of treatment. But until the child is established as a person who seeks out our approval and support, the resolution of conflicts is at a minimum. This introductory phase in the treatment of these children sometimes lasts for over two years.

Providing Help for the Mother

The younger the child, the more important for us is the task of modifying the mother's personality and of giving her awareness of her many entanglements and identifications with the child. Many of the children become involved in their mother's unconscious fantasies and may represent a replica of her neurosis. By allaying the mother's anxiety and guilt, we gradually enable her to gain the capacity to further her child's growth without too many interferences on her part. This is by no means an easy task for the analyst who treats both mother and child at the same time. This procedure undoubtedly has many advantages since it allows the analyst to investigate and compare at first hand the parallel conflicts in mother and child, but it also offers disadvantages. Frequently one can delegate the work with the mother, especially in a clinical setup, to a qualified social worker, who because of her training and her own psychoanalysis, can carry on the task successfully with the support of frequent discussions with the child's analyst. An excellent example of this kind of cooperation is to be found in the case of Peter M. (16). In some instances we have been able to divide the analytical work with mother and child between two analysts. But even then it is important for the child analyst to have an appointment with the mother at least once a week. Here the work would be on a somewhat different level. Experience will teach us whether the simultaneous analysis of parent and child represents the ideal solution.

To supplement individual therapy and offer an opportunity for homelike activities throughout the day, we have established a nursery school as a part of our setup at The James Jackson Putnam Children's Center. The teacher, too, acts as a mother-substitute accepting the child on his actual emotional level, regardless of his chronological age. Bottle-feeding is offered whenever indicated, elimination tolerated when and how the child chooses, as well as other instinctual manifestations, sexual or aggressive. This means that the teacher meets the child's need regardless of prejudice or established conventions if in her consultation with the child analyst the indication for it is established. In this aspect the nursery school and the teacher act as a continuation of therapy, "as the outstretched arm of the psychiatrist." Demands for control of instinctual manifestations are made step by step, simultaneously with the offer to the child of equipment and opportunity to sublimate these drives in a more socially acceptable way. The presence of other children, though initially ignored, constitutes an important positive factor for identification and socialization once the child is ready for it.

SUMMARY

An attempt has been made to indicate that the personality of certain children with arrested emotional development is a result of a special family constellation in which an immature, narcissistic mother was not able to offer the infant in his early stages an environment with an emotional climate favorable for the formation and differentiation of the self and the establishment of the reality principle. The fragmented, scattered personality of such children is considered to be the result. Their retreat and withdrawal are understood as an escape from a dangerous world. The three-fold approach based on our psychoanalytic understanding was described. We emphasized the necessary element of restitution through acceptance of the child on whatever level or levels of emotional development he may be, regardless of chronological age. It was shown that gradual education and therapy directed toward the resolution of conflicts, similar to other psychoanalytic technique for childhood neurosis, can then be instituted. The necessity for simultaneous work with the mother to allay her guilt and anxiety and to mobilize the warmth of the mother-child relationship was stressed.

BIBLIOGRAPHY

1. BENDER, L., "Childhood schizophrenia." *Am. J. Orthopsychiat.*, XVII, 68–79, 1947.
2. BIBRING, E., "The development and problems of the theory of the instincts." *Int. J. Psychoanal.*, XXI, 1941.
3. DESPERT, L., "Psychotherapy in childhood schizophrenia." *Am. J. Psychiat.*, CIV, No. 1, 36–43, 1948.

4. DEUTSCH, H., "Some forms of emotional disturbance and their relationship to schizophrenia." *Psychoanal. Quart.*, XI, No. 2, 301–321, 1942.

5. EISSLER, K. R., "Limitations to the psychotherapy of schizophrenia." *Psychiat.*, VI, 381–391, 1943.

6. FREUD, A., *The Psycho-Analytical Treatment of Children.* London, Imago Publ. Co., 1946.

7. FRIES, M. E., "The child's ego development and the training of adults in his environment." *Psychoanalytic Study of the Child*, Vol. II. New York, Intern. Univ. Press, 1947.

8. ———, "Mental hygiene in pregnancy, delivery and the puerperium." *Ment. Hyg.*, XXV, 1941.

9. FROMM-REICHMANN, F., "Psychoanalytic psychotherapy with psychotics." *Psychiat.*, VI, No. 3, 277–279, 1943.

10. GREENACRE, P., "The predisposition to anxiety." *Psychoanal. Quart.*, X, 66–94, 1941.

11. HARTMANN, H., "Comments on the psychoanalytic theory of instinctual drives." *Psychoanal. Quart.*, XVII, 1948.

12. ———, KRIS, E. AND LOWENSTEIN, R. M., "Comments on the formation of psychic structure." *Psychoanalytic Study of the Child*, Vol. II. New York, Intern. Univ. Press, 1947.

13. ———, *Ibid*, p. 22.

14. HENDRICK, I., "Instinct and the ego during infancy." *Psychoanal. Quart.*, XI, 1, 33–58, 1942.

15. KLEIN, M., *The Psycho-Analysis of Children.* New York, W. W. Norton, 1932.

16. RANK, B., "Case study of an atypical two-and-a-half-year-old." Round Table, 1947. *Am. J. Orthopsychiat.*, XVIII, No. 1, 1–30, 1948.

17. RIBBLE, M., *The Rights of Infants.* New York, Columbia Univ. Press, 1943.

18. SPITZ, R. A., "Hospitalism." *Psychoanalytic Study of the Child.* Vol. I. New York, Intern. Univ. Press, 1945.

19. ———, "Hospitalism: A follow-up report." *Ibid.*, Vol. II, 1947.

20. SYLVESTER, E., "Pathogenic influence of maternal attitudes in the neonatal period." *Problems of Early Infancy.* New York, Josiah Macy, Jr. Foundation, 1947.

► TREATMENT IN CHILD SCHIZOPHRENIA: PRESENTATION OF A CASE

By J. Louise Despert, M.D.*

INTRODUCTION

Recent Recognition of the Disease Entity

It cannot be overemphasized that the recognition of child schizophrenia as a disease entity is very recent,** and in many countries, and even in certain sections of the United States, the disease is not fully accepted as a clinical entity. For example, in the literature references to "schizophrenic-like" diseases in children are not uncommonly found. The earliest specific mention of schizophrenia in children in the American literature goes back less than twenty years to the article by Howard W. Potter, "Schizophrenia in Children," which appeared in the *American Journal of Psychiatry* in 1933 (5).

Need for Differentiation

It is important to differentiate between "schizophrenic-like" illness in childhood and the true schizophrenic illness. In the former, there may be some isolated behavior, thinking, or feeling manifestations which are of a psychotic character, but the total personality is not involved in the disease process, as it is in childhood schizophrenia. The latter, that is, true schizophrenic illness is to be defined in terms of pathognomic changes taking place in the personality, as related to the loss of affective contact with reality.

---

* Associate Attending Psychiatrist, New York Hospital; Associate Professor of Clinical Psychiatry, Cornell University Medical College, New York City.
** For an historical survey of the subject the reader is referred to my article on "Psychotherapy in Child Schizophrenia." *American Journal of Psychiatry*, CIV, No. 1, July, 1947.

Central Core of the Disease Process

At the first international congress concerned with child psychiatry in 1937, a survey of twenty-nine children admitted to the New York State Psychiatric Institute from 1930–1937 and diagnosed as schizophrenics, was presented (1). An attempt to define schizophrenia in childhood was made. The definition may be inadequate in that it lacks reference to psychogenetic factors, yet it is sufficiently descriptive of the process, and it offers possibilities as a working definition. It has proved helpful in the course of several years of experimentation with psychotherapy.

Schizophrenia in childhood was thus defined: " . . . a disease process in which the loss of affective contact with reality is coincident with or determined by the appearance of autistic thinking and accompanied by specific phenomena of regression and dissociation." With the advance of Kanner's concept of early infantile autism (3), (4), the definition could be modified to include both the failure to develop affective contact with reality, and the loss of affective contact.

To the author it appears then that the first task in child schizophrenia is by any and all means to establish affective contact with the patient, to break into the child's autistic world with a keen alertness for possible associations which might offer insight into the unconscious as it is revealed, yet not legible, in external manifestations. This means also a breaking-down of apparently unintelligible neologisms, the interpretation of which can subsequently be given to the patient. On the whole, this is a very active process but once the contact has been established its activity can be relaxed; interpretations and other techniques as carried out in severe neurotic illnesses can be used.

Types of Therapeutic Approach

In looking over a fairly large series of schizophrenic children since their treatment and/or diagnostic evaluation, it is immediately apparent that from the point of view of therapeutic approaches a differentiation must be made between two distinct categories: the children in whom mutism and negativistic features are foremost; and those in whom the opposite manifestations are found, that is, excessive and distorted verbal behavior.

In the first category which offers additional difficulties since language is such a potent means of communication and contact, the approach is through the observation of subtle changes of facial expression, involuntary gestures, changes in motor reactions to interpretations offered by the therapist.

In the second category, difficulties of an altogether different nature are encountered. The child usually presents motor restlessness in addition to the verbal behavior. It is difficult to approach him even physically long enough to communicate with him. His compulsive outbursts are apparently meaningless verbal content. The irrelevancy of his speech which expresses his extreme ambivalence makes it difficult to offer an interpretation. Furthermore, when interpretation is available and can be offered, one may find it impossible to place a word edgewise into the flow of speech in order to introject the interpretation. From the point of view of treatment, these two categories of children present distinct differences in the order of approach and difficulties.

The extreme ambivalence of the schizophrenic who is torn between emotionally opposite drives will present a similarity between the two categories.

PRESENTATION OF THE THERAPY
IN ONE ILLUSTRATIVE CASE

The patient discussed here was briefly referred to in a previous communication (2). Peter K. was at the time of admission, and still is, an only child. He was three years ten months when first seen. He was referred by the pediatrician who had been attending him since birth, and who was now administering barbiturates for reasons shortly to be given.

Complaint

Three weeks prior to admission the child suddenly manifested excited behavior, acute anxiety, and stupor-like states, alternating with excitement. He seemed to hear but did not answer. He had always been an anxious and excitable child. Furthermore, because of a congenital dislocation of the hip, he had been from age four months to ten months in a cast which extended from midthigh to neck. He had had several illnesses. There was great tension in the home mainly because of clashes in personality between the mother and her own mother, (the latter had practically brought up the boy). In this background of tension and poor emotional adjustment the child developed the acute symptoms which led to admission, as follows: for about a week (at Christmastime) he had been a little more excited than usual. The whole family (mother, father, maternal grandmother) was "on edge" because on the night after Christmas he had slept very little. The following day he asked his father to take him to the Museum of Natural History. There he saw totem poles in the American Indian section. He came home very excited, referring to crocodiles in an incoherent fashion. The next night he appeared dazed for a long period before finally falling asleep. For approximately one year he had been sleeping in his room together with his grandmother, who was in the habit of telling him stories. The second night after the visit to the museum, he refused the story, then suddenly clutching the bed he shrieked, "Mummy, I can't be myself!" He would not let his mother go out of the room. He spent the whole night lying on his bed, dazed, and staring at the ceiling. During the following day and night the same behavior was shown but with alternating periods of acute anxiety when he mentioned "rhinoceros" and "Indians with sticks." Since that time he had continued in a dazed, stuporous condition with outbursts in which he referred to hostile feelings he had toward his mother, but had never expressed before, such as, "you don't let me shovel enough snow," and "you stay too long in stores," all of which referred to specific past episodes.

Parents

The father (age 41) is a professional man, a mild-mannered individual with quiet speech who practices corporation law and is mildly successful in a job which does not require much contact with people. He appears quite even-tempered but his veiled hostility is very close to the surface and on occasion breaks through, to be controlled quickly again. He has centered his life interests on the patient. He had great drives to achieve success, put himself through college, married at twenty-five; through the nearly seventeen years of marriage, at least up to the time the patient was born, he had great doubts as to whether he had "made the right marriage." This refers to considerable tension because in the past his wife, the patient's mother, has had periods of depression and he has had to "nurse her through" these periods. Sexual relations have become very infrequent and unsatisfying. He drives himself as an escape. He is the second of two boys. He states that he had a happy childhood, admired his own father, a compulsive man "who had to do it all himself" and who died when he, the patient's father, was ten years old. The grandfather's death changed the social and economic position of the family, and after it the patient's father determined to rely upon himself for his college education and other aims. He was very close to his mother who died of a cardiac condition in her 60's, a few years after his marriage. She was affectionate, and both her sons were very attached to her. The patient's father has been "all wrapped up" in the patient and considers that his sole happiness comes from him.

The mother (age 38) is the most important member of the family background. Her own family was highly neurotic. Her father died at 46 when she was twenty-four years old. Following his death she had a severe depression. The maternal grandmother is high-strung, given to violent temper outbursts. The mother had an ambivalent feeling toward her own father: she admired him but feared him because of his unpredictable, violent behavior. The grandmother is close to 60, lives with the family, and has had more to do with the bringing-up of the patient than the mother herself. She indulges the boy, but at the same time frightens him by telling him gruesome, worrisome stories, and is in constant conflict with the boy's parents. The maternal grandmother was always "anxious and worrisome, had hysterics," but has been much worse since, at 40, a trolley-car accident caused a fractured skull which exacerbated her personality difficulties. The accident took place shortly after her husband's death and shortly before her daughter's severe depression.

The patient's mother is the older of two sisters, a woman who would be attractive were it not for her constant depressed expression. She speaks in a whining monotone with occasional outbursts of very aggressive speech. She was the favorite of both parents presumably because she was conspicuously more attractive than her sister. Owing to economic difficulties, she did her college work at night, soon after her marriage at twenty-one-and-a-half years. She has done secretarial and editorial work in various non-profit fields. In the past few years she had been a clerical assistant in the public school system which she joined in the hope of securing paid holidays, a hope which was never realized because approximately at this time, after thirteen years of marriage, she decided to stop working and have a child. She had frequent mild depressions with one severe and long period (about one-and-a-half years following the death of her father and her mother's injury). At the peak of the period she had suicidal impulses which were precipitated by the suicide of a woman, unknown to her, who lived in the same house.

Patient

The patient is an only child, born after thirteen years of marriage (mother 34, father 37). On the conscious level this was a wanted and planned pregnancy; however, there is evidence through associative material that the purpose of the pregnancy was to consolidate a shaky marriage. The mother stopped working in the fourth month. Although she was given to frequent mild depressions, she was physically well during her pregnancy. She describes herself as more emotionally stable at this time than at any period of her life.

One month premature, the baby was born after short labor, middle forceps. He was not breast fed, presumably because of some physical difficulty with the mother's breasts. He slept and fed well but was noted to cry "fiercely" for an hour before feedings. As already mentioned, he was in a cast from 4 to 10 months of age, sat up at 14 months, walked at 16, was precocious in every other respect. At 22 months he could recite many rhymes, but also at approximately this time had severe stuttering. Because of the additional difficulty created by the congenital dislocation of the hip, the maternal grandmother was called in to take over. ("It was wrong to have her come.") There has been a continuous conflict over the patient, mostly between the mother and the maternal grandmother. The elimination training was initiated late because of the cast and was met with "terrific resistance."

On admission the child was still enuretic at night. Vigorous thumb-sucking started at the time the night bottle was taken off, and was forcibly interrupted. Masturbation, which has been varying in frequency and severity, has been a major problem to the parents, and in particular, to the maternal grandmother. Repeatedly the patient was told that he would "hurt his penis." Shortly after he was put in the cast he began to sleep poorly, and in recent years this has been accentuated. He also has had frequent nightmares, following a herniotomy at two years, four months. His grandmother sleeps in his room; she responds when he screams, never his parents. The mother has been overanxious, overprotective. She reports, for example, that with the appearance of any minor symptom she frequently "imagines he is going to die." Death wishes toward the patient are thus very close to the surface.

The child has always been very active and has gradually become very destructive, throwing books around, and breaking toys apart, stuffing a variety of objects into the toilet bowl and wash basin. Regressive behavior (tempers, rocking, speaking incoherently) seems to have appeared a few days before the acute onset mentioned above, although the parents do not agree on this point. The father "never saw anything abnormal" prior to the visit to the museum. The mother saw insidious changes for several months prior to the acute onset. During the reporting of the developmental data it became apparent that the mother was depressed, with intense aggressive impulses, generally under control, and with openly expressed strong guilt feelings ("It's my fault, even if it was the grandmother, it's again my fault."). In addition, there was strong rivalry between the mother and grandmother; and also the mother resented both the affection that her son showed to the grandmother and the grandmother's affection to the boy ("he does not respond to me"). While he does not respond to anyone in the family, when he is acutely frightened he is apt to run to his grandmother.

Therapeutic Approach

In advance of the first interview with the child it was suggested that the mother refer to the child's fears and tell him that she would bring him to a lady who would help him as she helps other children. In spite of these recommendations the mother brought the patient, with the sudden, advance announcement to him that: "It's so windy, let's go up and see a lady."

The mother was asked into the playroom because of the child's clinging to her for protection, and the obvious anxiety of the mother at the thought of separation. It appeared that the mother was clinging to the boy more than the boy to the mother, an observation which was confirmed later.

He was an attractive, large-boned, very alert youngster, with pupils widely dilated. There were sudden rigid attitudes of the body which were revealing of the intense anxiety experienced by the patient. It is difficult indeed to give an adequate picture of the intensity of the anxiety, which a good deal of the time was equivalent to an acute panic. His speech was incoherent; however, amid the jumble of words and disconnected syllables, it was possible to make out distinctly a full sentence: "I am not afraid of anything." The mother was asked to sit in a corner of the playroom and as much as possible not to participate actively in the therapeutic session, yet to respond to the child's demands, if any.

The patient let the physician undress him, holding himself in a characteristic way with brief muscular rigidity and intervals of intermittent screaming.

His uttered answers were incoherent for the most part;

he had an extensive vocabulary, both for his chronological age level and as shown in single words and those sentences which were coming through with some degree of legibility, even when it was not possible to ascertain the meaning. The associative links could not be made out, but out of the jumble of words, references to a variety of experiences, realistic and fantastic, could be reconstructed.

There was evidence of visual and auditory hallucinations, as when, staring at the ceiling with a frightened expression, he was seen to cock his ears to listen, and at such moments did not respond to any stimulus. There was catatonic posturing and drooling.

Some of the verbal content which illustrates the nature of his anxiety could be made out in the following expressions: ". . . different . . . things the same . . . things different . . . the wrong floor . . . go to another room . . . crocodiles . . . animals in the same place . . . I am not afraid of anything . . . Indians . . ." With attention for any utterance, single or grouped words which could be made out, reassurance and protection were repeatedly offered: "The physician would not let the animals hurt Peter. Things were different indeed: the bathroom is different, the room is different, I am a new person, but the room also looks different because Peter feels different." When he said that he was not afraid, the physician offered that "Peter was not afraid, but what was the little boy afraid of?" The answer came in the form of incoherent words with the one clearly articulated word "animals." It was offered to him that the little boy was afraid of animals and that the physician would not let the animals hurt him. The whole while the physician kept as close to the child as would possibly be accepted.

Animals and other toys were put on the floor, but the child at first would pay no attention to them. He began to take note of them (after repeated suggestion) and out of a variety of toys he picked the animals and held on especially to a dog and a snake. While handling these toys he announced several times, "must be the same" and seemed to attempt to disarticulate them, concentrating especially on the eyes. He was told that he wanted to see if the animals were alive, that he was afraid of live animals but these were "pretend" animals and they could not hurt him. The concentration on a toy dog and the associated anxiety aroused the suspicion that although the dog was the object of an anxiety at an unconscious level, possibly it was involved also in a realistic episode. In the course of the second interview with the parents (that in which evaluation of the problem and the suggested treatment were discussed), it was learned that a dog left with the family by a maternal aunt had frightened and bitten the patient several times. The word "Echo" which had been used several times in connection with the toy dog was the name of the actual dog. Incidentally, it was suggested that the dog be removed from the environment.

Diagnosis

The pathological manifestations met the criterion for schizophrenic illness as described above. The first steps in therapy were to establish affective contact with the child. Then to relieve the intense anxiety associated with primitive fantasies, such as the fear of being destroyed or devoured, and the loss of self. In particular to provide therapy aimed at bridging realistic, traumatic, conscious experience with the underlying anxiety arising from unconscious fantasies. It was indicated to the parents that the treatment would be a long process and that it could be ascertained within a few weeks whether the child responded or not. The parents, leaning on the suggestion made by the pediatrician that they send the child to an upstate farm, were briefly resistive to the plans formulated, and throughout the treatment showed some ambivalence to the plans. However, because the child improved rather early, he was kept in treatment.

During the initial period he was seen with the mother present three times a week for the first two months, then twice a week for the next four months. The summer vacation intervened; following this, the child was seen alone once a week for a year. The mother was allowed to remain in the playroom not only because of the child's screaming, but also because he fastened himself so tightly to his mother that the result was a sort of physical symbiosis. Some contingencies could not be controlled: such inordinate screaming might be tolerated on the in-patient service of a hospital, but was hardly acceptable in a non-clinical ambulatory set-up.

In one of the initial interviews with the mother she made a statement that was very revealing of the relationship between the mother, the child, and the therapist. She said specifically, "After I saw you with Peter—you were so beautiful, such a beautiful job—I thought, 'she loves children, she hates parents.'" This was presented to her as reestablishment of her own family relationship, in which the physician was the mother and she saw the physician in rivalry with the patient, as if the physician were her own mother (her awareness of her conflict with her mother helped her to accept this interpretation).

It was suggested that the barbiturates which had proved ineffectual be discontinued.

The various relationships in the family were discussed, generally in their superficial aspects; the conflict between the mother and father, mother and maternal grandmother, was pointed up. It was suggested that the maternal grandmother might gradually become less indispensable. The parents were considerably relieved that the child was not to be sent to an institution, which they had feared.

The father, though compulsive, did not seem to have too disturbed a personality and since it was impossible to consider treatment of the whole family, owing to economic limitations, it was decided to deal mostly with the mother. She was the one most in need of therapy. However, intensive therapy was ruled out because of the possibility of a psychotic explosion and even suicide. It was therefore planned that the work with the mother would be on the basis of supportive therapy, with the mother-son relationship as a foremost consideration. It was thought that after the child's improved condition brought some release of the family tension and particularly of maternal anxiety, more intensive therapy for the mother might be considered.

The mother, who had been a secretary, was made to feel useful in the therapeutic situation when she was asked to make notes as she wished; and it was explained to the child that the mother would be helping the physician by taking down some of the things that were being said. This was explained to the boy as "mother helping us." Indeed, in a relatively large series of child schizophrenics treated, this is the only case in which the presence of the mother during such a long period of treatment was deemed necessary. While this was unusual and presented certain liabilities it was also an asset in some respects; for example, it was of the greatest interest to the physician to compare the type of information that the mother would select as significant, with what had actually taken place, in that it revealed areas of emotional blocking which could be used for analysis and interpretation.

The immediate and most important job was to begin with Peter. From the beginning, it was possible to get the child to respond even though this was the briefest sort of response. Owing to his passive attitudes, it was possible to cuddle him and demonstrate affection to him even at such times as he was completely out of contact. This was a considerable asset if one compares such passivity with the negativism and muscle rigidity frequently encountered in child schizophrenics. This asset was exploited to its full possibilities.

The mother, who had been asked to turn to the physician for every minor problem or question that might come up day by day, had reported to the physician one morning that the child had remained awake the major portion of the previous night and that he frequently referred to a dog when he was in a stuporous state. The physician therefore deliberately opened the interview with a toy dog and the child immediately identified with the dog, growling, snarling, in a complex facial pattern which seemed to indicate such complete impersonation as to erase any human facial features. This was dramatized in a situation of acute anxiety which alternated in a mechanistic manner between being the dog and being the victim. He would spell the word "growl," point to the closet door referring to "wild animals in a cage," to "rhinoceros" and "Indians." At intervals he shrieked without verbal content. Again and again it was pointed out to him that he was afraid of being devoured by the animals, especially the dog, not only devoured, but that he feared that other worse things (castration anxiety referred to, but not mentioned) would happen to him and that to stop the dog from devouring him and doing these other things he wanted to be the dog himself. Then again, he was told he was afraid to be the dog because the dog would be doing these bad things. The tenor of the interpretations is merely indicated here; the interpretations had to be repeated again and again, and dramatized. It was evident at once that these interpretations afforded a penetration into the child's fantasies; he would suddenly stop and stare intently at the physician and briefly respond to her in a more positive body contact.

Everything around him was a cause of anxiety because of misinterpretation of objects in the environment. For example, the bathroom fixtures were the "sticks"; "Indians with sticks" which he had frequently referred to. The physician explained to him that the sticks were really something else to him, and, that he was afraid that some bad things would happen to the sticks. He was encouraged to come and touch the pipes, etc.; thus his anxiety was fully recognized, but also evidence of objective reality was offered. This handling of the child's anxiety associated with fantasies and distortions of the reality world, illustrates an approach which was used over and over to the point of monotony and perseveration, namely, the need to establish a distinction between reality objects and fantasies projected into the reality objects. The reaction was always a more positive body attitude and sometimes, though rarely, a verbal acknowledging of the interpretation given. At any rate, the result was clearly a breaking into the autistic world of the child.

It is impossible for lack of space to multiply the illustrations which were all of the order of reality-testing. As an example, when he handled the dolls and seemed intent on pulling them apart and tearing the eyes out, especially in acute anxiety, his confusion about reality and unreality, living and not living, his own concern about himself not being real, not being himself, the people not being live people, was brought up over and over again. This loss of identity of self, extended also to the people around him, as when he referred to his mother as a statue. Once he turned to her in the midst of play and said, "I'll plug you in," (which besides the sexual connotation and in the light of the total context, referred to his feeling that his mother was inanimate).

At the beginning of the treatment the mother was very anxious for the boy to be treated daily. She would "do everything, no matter what it cost," even bring a lunch box for the physician if the latter did not have time to cook, etc. As will be seen from later developments (request for a consultation, insistence on application of shock therapy as suggested by the family physician, etc.) her attitude toward the physician and toward therapy was very ambivalent. Incidentally, the physician was willing to accept the consultation but indicated firmly that it was either shock therapy and severance of all contact with her, or continuation of the current therapy. Following this, the family dropped all further suggestions.

The boy continued hallucinating, laughing irrelevantly, staring into space, shrieking in anxiety, all in rapid succession. Every coherent statement which was made was immediately seized upon for an interpretation of his anxieties. When, for example, he was heard to say, "I am everybody's boy, all people's boy," the physician pointed out to him that he was afraid he was not his mommy's boy, but that he was also afraid to be that.

Pictures of a dog and a rhinoceros were drawn for him again and again, and the drama of a dog and rhinoceros trying to bite or eat a little boy was enacted, always with the reassurance that the rhinoceros (or the dog) was not real but that the little boy was afraid it was real. Through this period (approximately three weeks) it was reported that at night the stuporous periods were considerably shorter; the content was indicated by the following words which were distinctly heard: ". . . dog . . . bone . . . growl . . . it's dangerous . . ."

The mother was especially disturbed by the fact that the patient addressed her almost as though she were a thing.

He would suddenly ask her to stop in the midst of some activity with such comments as, "You can be a statue . . . don't move, I can't use you now . . . I'll plug you in . . ." (the latter as he played with electric fixtures). Considerable time was spent with the mother in an elucidation of the "inanimate" delusion, and it was pointed out that this was a safety mechanism which enabled him to save himself pain, but that it was also the result of his own loss of self.

During this period, while he was not completely sleepless at night, he stayed awake a good deal of the night. Then, in the morning he would be "worn out" and would make such statements as, "Nothing lets me sleep and I want to sleep so hard." These comments were all utilized in the therapeutic situation.

The mother alternated between two opposite attitudes: one of extreme anxiety about the severity and hopelessness of the child's illness, and belief that a short period of contact with the physician would be sufficient to bring him back to normal. "I am sure if you could look after him he would be OK in one week."

During this initial period (the second or third week), the physician initiated the session by taking a boy doll out and asking what the little boy thought about when he was going to sleep. A then cryptic statement came forth: "Elissa with the pokers." Since the pokers had previously been associated with the sticks of the American Indians, this was again brought up in connection with anxiety about the sticks and what the sticks stood for. It was formulated that he feared that the sticks would be used to hurt him and that bad things would happen to the sticks. The meaning of Elissa was not immediately ascertained but was later recognized as standing for an old woman about whom additional reference is forthcoming. At one moment, he pointed to the bathroom door and insisted it must be closed because "Echo (the family dog) might come in and bite you." Actually, the physician pointed out, he said this because he himself was afraid that the dog might come in and bite him. His response to this was immediately to turn into a dog and a wolf, growling, snarling, in space as well as at the physician. This activity was interpreted to him as having to be the dog or the wolf in order to do some of the things he was afraid he might do. It can be said that each interpretation of the kind illustrated here brought responses different in degree, but generally at least some reaction.

The general pattern was one of absence of contact and verbal incoherence; for example, there often was a reference to "an animal a long time after the war" which could never be elucidated and interpreted. Since the anxiety relating to animals was dealt with in a general way, it did not seem imperative to pursue the specific meaning of many references to animals which were at times unintelligible.

The notes taken by the mother during the sessions provide an interesting opportunity for insight into the mother's personality. She was emotionally involved in the dramatization of fantasies, etc., and was singularly blocked in her reporting of them. Of significance is the following: "Peter was glad to see you and advised you on questioning that the wind had given him his red cheeks." The child's dramatization of fantasies related to the wind had been completely omitted. The child on that day showed great anxiety and most of his speech was incoherent. The following is selected from otherwise unintelligible material: "The wind and the sun came to say 'Happy New Year' and the little old lady tapped on the door . . . I was asleep in the bathroom in the toilet . . . I saw the dog eating and then he lifted his leg . . ." At that point the child had acted so realistically and lifted his leg, and the physician pointed out that Peter wanted to know about the dog's penis, wanted to make sure it was there, and he was afraid his own penis might not be there. The castration anxiety which had repeatedly come up in various symbolic ways was thus for the first time pointed out.

At this time the associations with "little old lady" were not intelligible. However, later, when he stated, "I am not going to be afraid of the little old lady," the physician pointed out that the "little old lady" might be a woman whom she (physician) did not know, but she was also like his mother, grandmother, and the physician herself. At a later session it was learned that the "little old lady" was a rather dilapidated woman whom he had seen in the country a year or so before. This particular association was brought in reference to a pump (there actually had been such a connection with the dilapidated old lady). Whenever he expressed anything relevant, the physician was quick to pick it up and hold on to it, to talk about it over and over, dramatizing both sides—the frightening and the frightened. In relation to the little-old-lady fantasy and through bits of associative material it was acknowledged that someone gets into his bed, specifically the little old lady (as he was mentioning) but also it was indicated that the little old lady was not real. In regard to this double dramatization he stated, "Another little old lady comes in the middle of the night. I won't get scared of her; she'll get scared of me." He was encouraged to feel that he could now deal with the little old lady.

He frequently expressed his anxieties by projecting them. Once he said, "You must not talk because something bad will come to you and bite you." This was quickly seized upon to point out to him that it was he himself who was afraid and not the physician, and also that he thought that by asking her not to talk the danger would be removed from himself (magic thought). About this time he frequently expressed an intense anxiety about the physician putting "pennies" into him. He would shriek in a tone of terror, "Don't put pennies into me." Although at the time the delusion was totally unintelligible, it was possible to assume, in view of the total content, that he was referring both to "pennies" and "penises," especially as often the "s" was pronounced to point to the latter interpretation. At first he was told of the double meaning and of the associated anxiety, but the complete analysis of this delusion was made only after additional information was secured. As has been previously reported, this delusion was the end-result of a condensation-phenomenon commonly encountered in schizophrenia. The child, as indicated above had hallucinated a "little old lady" identified both with his grandmother and with an actual dilapidated old woman. The grandmother had brought a dog, and there was anxiety associated with this dog. The grandmother had often overdramatized the story of the Three Little Pigs and the child had, even prior to his illness, identified with the little pig eaten by the wolf; and lastly, he owned a penny bank, in which pennies were frequently dropped. Each fragment was brought up for analysis and abreactive release with the "pennies" content at first only mentioned, and the "penis" content held in abeyance for evidence, later secured, regarding the castration anxiety. This was in a short while brought in by the child in the form of a neologism which will be later described.

Illustrations too numerous to be related here (at first unintelligible, incoherent statements) were analyzed, dissected, as it were, and wherever possible, replaced in their relationship to reality, fantasies, unconscious expressions, etc. One more illustration is given: he kept repeating "lock happening . . . happen . . . it happened . . ." During one of these expressions (always associated with severe anxiety) he glanced toward the closet door and was told that he was afraid to be locked, that if he were locked he would not be able to come with his mother nor his mother to come with him, that he would be alone, strange, and not himself, and that he was also afraid that he might be locked, perhaps alone, perhaps not alone. His reaction to this was some incoherent garbled language with two distinct words which gave it a specific meaning: "cage . . . cage with wild animals . . ." Again this was an expression of his anxiety about being devoured, but, as was learned later, it also referred to an actual event which had taken place several months before the onset of his illness when he locked himself in a closet and had been released almost immediately. At the moment he had appeared very frightened but no after-effects had been noted.

To illustrate the technique in the utilization of apparently unitelligible statements, the analysis of a neologism which was of the greatest importance in the understanding of this child's problem is here offered: Toward the end of the second month, he began to use a neologism, the phonetic rendering of which would be "benishghellaman." It was noted that "Benjamin," the name of his father, came up from time to time in the flow of unintelligible language, and seemed to belong with this neologism. It would be impossible except with mechanical recording to give a faithful reproduction of these phonetics, but some of what seemed significant or intelligible at the moment was taken down by the physician in the course of several sessions, and it became clear that the neologism expressed the fear of castration at the hands of his father. Incidentally, at no time did he refer to his father as "father" or "my father," but rather as schizophrenic children will often do, brought him in descriptively, via a reference to a gesture or special function more or less characteristic of him, in this case, the fact that his father brought in the mail at night. It was only after constant interpolation from the physician, regarding the association, that he finally referred to his father specifically, and to what his father might do to him. When he finally connected his father with the neologism, within a mass of unintelligible material, the castration anxiety emerged, could be, and was, interpreted: "There is benishghellaman . . . the kind that bites off your penis . . . the kind that spoiled your benishghellaman . . . last year . . . don't touch my benishghellaman . . . then Benjamin comes home . . . the night-carrier . . . my daddy's name . . ."

Conspicuous, following the interpretation, were the draining of the anxiety, the improved contact, and the amelioration of intelligibility. This was the end of the second month and the beginning of the third. His contact was much improved and he had become spontaneously affectionate, at intervals.

Throughout the initial period, as condensed above, he appeared at times to have amnestic aphasia. For example, he would place a number of animals on the radiator, look at them with a very anxious expression, seemingly to identify each one, and obviously laboring to find the proper name. Then with a helpless expression, he would wail, "I don't know all the words."

As the contact improved, negativism, which at first had been mild, increased and there was a great deal of perseverance in activity as well as in verbal expression. Throughout, drawings had been used by the physician, in preference to those of the child, whose productions were at first of the scribbling type. The drawings made revolved mostly around a boy, his mother, his father, and animals suggested by the patient's current verbal comments. He sometimes took the pencils, adding protuberances at any part of the body, which were clearly the penises he had mentioned and were so interpreted to him in later sessions. He began to refer to "the other boy inside" and this was again and again used to point to the split in himself between the other boy who used to have bad thoughts, etc., and the boy who now was beginning to be more comfortable with himself.

Through this period (two months to two-and-a-half months) he went through regressive and aggressive behavior, biting, mostly his mother. This was interpreted to the mother as identification with the dog and other animals in order to control his anxiety about being bitten and castrated. It was a difficult period for the mother, as the scenes, temper tantrums, and biting activities worried her considerably. When he was told he was playing "doggy" because he was afraid of a dog and what the dog would do to him, he seemed at first startled, then smiled in acquiescence and his play lost the "vicious" character (a note that the mother herself entered in her "report").

Toward the end of the third month he began to play constructively with the toys and to dramatize play scenes in which his hostility toward his mother, his anxiety relating to his father and to his grandmother were more clearly coming through, with the primitive fantasies associated with totem poles, Indians, etc., appearing infrequently. Whenever the latter were manifested, the mother's own anxiety was of such severity as to constitute a problem in the therapy situation. She was particularly disturbed by the fact that his facial expressions were so realistic. She was also watchful of such identifications outside the playroom and reported, for example, on one occasion that "he makes a face like a totem pole and shouts, 'I don't want anybody in the street.'" At this time, he made frequent references to his mother at home regarding: ". . . going up . . . don't send me up . . ." which were associated with the "totem poles," "rhinoceros," etc. His father had bought him earlier a small bronze rhinoceros, and the physician asked the mother to bring it. This was used for dramatic abreaction for several sessions, during which Peter would reassure himself with, "It's not a rhinoceros from the museum." Then he made it go up and down a thin block which he called a "stick." When it was suggested he might want to go again to the museum, he said he would, "if you take me with you because it's dangerous." Actually, the plan was not carried out, owing to unavoidable circumstances.

In the course of treatment, about the middle of the third month, a light was thrown on an interesting condensation-phenomenon which involved the mother figure, a woodpecker instrumental in the castration fantasy, and, coincidentally, the gradual growth of his hold on reality. He had made frequent references, mostly unintelligible, to a "little lady—and the little old lady who looked like a woodpecker ... the woodpecker and the benishghellaman." He asked the physician to draw pictures of these very subjective experiences and she proceeded to render the requested scenes as best she could, during which the child dramatized more and more comprehensibly this half-realistic and half-fantastic experience. In this connection he made it evident that the lady-woodpecker represented a current hallucination which seemed to be on the wane. He said that the little old lady still "climbed in my bathroom window," then she "melts away." Many abreacting activities at this time (drawing, play, and dialogue) involved the little old lady as woodpecker, or the big wolf and the little boy. He had, for instance, taken the physician's hand to go to her bathroom, which he identified, on the occasion, with his own. "I will have to take you there—now the little old lady is gone—she used to talk 'lad' talk." Incidentally, while it could be assumed that the 'lad talk' referred to threats addressed to a little boy, and was so interpreted, the use of the word in this context was never clarified.

He would also play for a short period with chairs in a "cage arrangement" and was at first in a panic when the physician "opened the door" by removing a chair. His anxiety was interpreted in the light of his ambivalence in wanting to retain the safe closing-in around himself with the mother figure, the fear that he could be closed in with the animals that could devour and injure him, and the fear that he could himself be let loose, abandoned, on his own. This was substantiated again and again by acts such as the drawing (requested by him) of a woodpecker next to a little boy, when he suddenly interrupted the activity, to draw a heavy black line around the woodpecker in order to protect the little boy.

By the end of the fourth month (he was then being seen only twice a week) there was no evidence of hallucinations, but reality-testing continued in a manner somewhat akin to that of the normal 2–3 year-old child who experiments on the "real" and "pretend" objects of his world. An interesting episode which took place at this time illustrates the point: the mother came in on that day with a heavy bandage on her finger. She had reported that she had seen the child holding a broomstick toward the ceiling light in a play which she did not understand, but which had made her anxious. In the sudden movement she made to remove the stick from his hand she had broken the bulb. The child was anxious and guilty over the mother's minor injury and was asked at the beginning of the session to explain the mother's bandage, etc. This enabled him to re-enact the scene and to ventilate the tensions attached. A very illuminating comment regarding his relationship to the therapist was, "You should have hurry up."

With the summer breaking into the therapy, he was not seen for two months, and the mother was prepared to let him come to the playroom alone. (Sessions once a week were started at this point.) The separation, difficult for the mother, was relatively easy for the child because of the positive transference and also because he had in the meantime become relatively independent of his mother. The reality-testing continued for approximately another two months; for example, he would from time to time in the course of dramatization of the family relationships take a large doll and say that she was to cry, then that "she can't really cry—her eyes are wood—my eyes are not wood because I am real, but the doll is not real." The improvement was considered sufficient to warrant his attending school. After initial apprehension in the new setup he adjusted well, made friends, but displayed a tendency to flare up in excited play. This tendency the teachers were able to control readily.

Vacation time arrived (he was then five years, four months), and the whole family moved to the country for a two-month period which was very happy for all. In the fall it was impossible to get the parents to continue with treatment, the reason given by the mother being that since he was so well, further contact with psychiatry would be harmful. Against advice she had insisted that the school be uninformed about any of the youngster's problems. She did not maintain contact with the physician, not even for information; a contact which was actively sought by the physician for a whole year, then given up.

The determination to remain incommunicado continued for four years, when a frantic call came from the mother. The child was then nine-and-a-half years old. The mother explained that he had rather suddenly developed obsessive-compulsive neurotic symptoms. The mother cried on the telephone, making a significant statement: "Don't punish me . . . please see him again . . . etc." Seen several times on this occasion the boy manifested none of the psychotic behavior reported in this communication. Since it was impossible for the physician to take him on for continued treatment at this time, he was referred to an outside therapist working under her supervision. The child is still under treatment; after several months he is considerably improved, and is now seen once a week. He has made a very good adjustment in his family; and for the first time went to a summer camp, where he was happy and free of symptoms.

CONCLUSION

This case was selected because it represents a typical case of child schizophrenia with acute onset in a background of insidious changes.

The therapy, as illustrated, is also typical, with the exception of the unusually long time that the mother was permitted to stay in the therapeutic situation, for reasons previously given. (This is a unique exception.)

The abrupt severing of the therapeutic process was accomplished by the parents, based on their assumption that the child's improvement was sufficient. Such severing is an occasional feature of parental attitudes; it represents an additional obstacle to total therapeutic success.

It has been shown through a number of representative illustrations that the breaking-into the child's autistic world, into his primitive fantasies, and into the initially impenetrable defenses of his neologisms could be and was accomplished. This is considered by the author to be the core of the therapeutic approach in child schizophrenia. The transference relation was built up on this basis of the establishment of contact; otherwise such a relationship could not be realized.

The patient was thus able gradually to achieve subjective delineation between reality and unreality, and ego-boundaries re-emerged. It was also feasible to drain the excessive anxiety attached to the primitive fantasies, which thus made possible the realization of self. When the above was accomplished, therapy could proceed along the more familiar lines, not here elaborated upon, of the therapy of severe neurotic illness.

BIBLIOGRAPHY

1. DESPERT, J. L., "Schizophrenia in children." *Psychiat. Quart.*, XII, 366–371, 1938.
2. ———, "Psychotherapy in child schizophrenia." *Am. J. Psychiat.*, CIV, No. 1, 36–43, 1947.
3. KANNER, L., "Autistic disturbance of affective contact." *Nerv. Child.*, II, No. 3, 217–250, 1942–1943.
4. ———, "Problems of nosology and psychodynamics of early infantile autism." *Am. J. Orthopsychiat.*, XIX, No. 3, 416–426, 1949.
5. POTTER, H. W., "Schizophrenia in children." *Am. J. Psychiat.*, LXXXIX, 1253–1270, May, 1933.

► NOTES ON THE DEVELOPMENT OF TREATMENT OF SCHIZOPHRENICS BY PSYCHOANALYTIC PSYCHOTHERAPY*

*By Frieda Fromm-Reichmann, M.D.***

INTRODUCTION

In the preanalytic phases of psychiatric development, psychotherapists considered schizophrenic states non-treatable. There seemed to be no medium in which the disturbed schizophrenic and the psychiatrist could communicate with one another. The thought processes, feelings, communications, and other manifestations of the disturbed schizophrenic seemed nonsensical and without meaning as to origin, dynamics, and actual contents.

Psychoanalysts know that all manifestations of the human mind are potentially meaningful. This refers equally to the psychotic manifestations of the disturbed schizophrenic while awake, and to the transitory psychotic productions of the mentally healthy dreamer while asleep. Schizophrenic thought processes and means of expression have been successfully studied by Betz (2), Bleuler (3), Cameron (4), Goldstein (25), (26), (27), Hanfmann (29), Kasanin (37), Storch (48), Sullivan (49), (50),

* Reprinted with permission from *Psychiatry*, II, 263–273, 1948.
** Supervisor of Psychotherapy, Chestnut Lodge Sanitarium, Rockville, Maryland; Chairman, Council of Fellows, Washington School of Psychiatry.

Vigotsky (57), and others. Their parallelism with dream processes has been constructively emphasized by Freud, Jung (36), Sullivan (51), (52), Federn (11), and the writer (18), (19). It is now generally recognized that the communications of the schizophrenic are practically always meaningful to him; they are potentially intelligible, and not infrequently actually understandable to the trained psychoanalyst. Thus it was not the nature of the schizophrenic communication that constituted an obstacle to psychoanalytic psychotherapy with schizophrenics.

The reluctance to apply psychoanalytic knowledge and technique to the psychoses stems from Freud's paper on narcissism (14). According to Freud, this concept of the narcissistic origin and the regressive character of schizophrenic disorders excluded the possibility of establishing a workable relationship between the schizophrenic and the psychoanalyst.

Subsequent revisions have led to changes in Freud's concept. It is true that the schizophrenic is hit by initial traumatic warp and thwarting experiences at a very early period of life when he has not yet developed a marked and stable degree of relatedness to other people. It is also true that the final outbreak of schizophrenic disorder will be characterized by regressive tendencies in the direction of this original, early period of schizophrenogenic traumatization. One of the means of defense against warp from the outside, and of hostile reaction against it from within, in the preschizophrenic as well as in the schizophrenic personality, is the withdrawal of interest from the outside world and from other people.

As was pointed out early in psychoanalytic research by Fenichel and Abraham, the withdrawal is not a complete one, nor is the early developmental phase to which the schizophrenic regresses one in which he was "narcissistic" at the exclusion of his relatedness to other people (12), (1).

Sullivan teaches that there is no developmental period when the human exists outside of the realm of interpersonal relatedness (51). From the very early postnatal stage, at which time the infant first learns to sense by empathy approval and disapproval of the mothering person, some degree of interpersonal relatedness is maintained throughout life by everyone, regardless of his state of mental health; its disruption in the schizophrenic is therefore only partial.

Fairbairn (8) has offered another significant revision of Freud's concept. Psychoanalytic theory attributes a two-sided significance to the early phases of psychosexual development. The oral and anal preoccupations of the child or of an adult in a regressive state are first understood in terms of the feelings of lust obtainable from these bodily zones and from their functions; second, in terms of their use for the expression of one's relatedness to significant people. According to Fairbairn, the latter is what counts for the developmental understanding of schizophrenic psychopathology. In his investigation of schizophrenic oral preoccupation from the viewpoint of its interpersonal significance rather than as a source of autoerotic gratification, Fairbairn also made it evident that schizophrenics do not ever totally relinquish their ability to relate themselves to others, even in the most regressive withdrawal states with marked oral preoccupation.

Moreover, the schizophrenic patient has lived and developed personal relationships in his premorbid days—that is, prior to being actually disturbed and given to marked withdrawal and regression. Here is an additional reason why the psychoanalyst is always able to find traces of previous interpersonal developments in the schizophrenic. No matter how tenuous these traces may be, they are sufficient for the establishment of a new relationship, such as the doctor-patient relationship. This experience has been verified by all those who have done psychoanalytic psychotherapy with schizophrenics. In addition to the above-mentioned authors, it has received verification by Federn, Knight (39), (39a), and recently by Rosen (43), (44).

Several authors—for instance, Hinsie—found, as this writer did, that the schizophrenic's expectancy and tendency toward resuming interpersonal contacts were sometimes equally as strong as his original motivation for withdrawal (32), (20). This seemingly paradoxical attitude can be easily understood since the schizophrenic has not resigned from interpersonal dealings freely or of his own design, but is motivated by dire, defensive necessity. Because of this, the schizophrenic is frequently very willing to break through his self-imposed withdrawal if the analyst has been successful in overcoming his well-founded suspicions, not only of the significant people, because of whose malevolence he originally withdrew, but also later of members of the human race at large, including himself and the psychoanalyst.

It appeared then that it was possible to deal with schizophrenic communication as meaningful and potentially understandable and to establish workable relationships between the psychoanalyst and the schizophrenic. So the road was open to follow the hope and suggestion expressed by Freud in his paper "On Psychotherapy" (16) that analytic technique might be modified for application to the psychotic. This has been done since the 1930's by authors quoted elsewhere in this paper and by Bak, Eissler (6), Ernst (7), Hollos (33), LaForgue (40), MacBrunswick, Silverberg (46),* and by other psychoanalysts connected with psychoanalytically oriented mental hospitals.**

I had the privilege of reporting upon work with schizophrenics at two previous meetings of the American Psychoanalytic Association. In this paper I wish to describe the changes in technique as they have been developed in the Washington-Baltimore area since my last presentation in 1945. Also I wish to elaborate on the personal problems arising for the psychiatrist who undertakes to do psychoanalytic psychotherapy with disturbed schizophrenics.

CHANGES IN PSYCHOANALYTIC TECHNIQUE

Before proceeding, I wish to sum up briefly some of those schizophrenic dynamics which have guided the psychoanalysts

---

* After the first publication of this paper, important new contributions in the field have been made by Bychowski, Pious, Sechehaye, Wexler, among others.
** Chestnut Lodge, Forest Sanitarium, The Haven, The Menninger Clinic, High Point Hospital, Dr. Boss' Psychoanalytic Hospital, Zurich, Switzerland.

in developing and changing the psychotherapeutic approach to schizophrenia.

The schizophrenic is painfully distrustful and resentful of other people. This is due to the severe early warp and rejection he encountered in important people of his infancy and childhood, as a rule, mainly in a schizophrenogenic mother. During his early fight for emotional survival, he begins to develop the great interpersonal sensitivity which remains his for the rest of his life. His initial pathogenic experiences are actually, or by virtue of his interpretation, the pattern for a never-ending succession of subsequent, similar experiences. Finally he transgresses the threshold of endurance. Because of his sensitivity and his never-satisfied lonely need for benevolent contacts, this threshold is all too easily reached. The schizophrenic's partial emotional regression and his withdrawal from the outside world into an autistic private world with its specific thought processes and modes of feeling and expression, is motivated by his fear of repetitional rejection, by his distrust of others, and equally by his own retaliative hostility (which he abhors), as well as by the deep anxiety promoted by this hatred.

Changes in the technique of psychoanalytic treatment during recent years are in regard both to the establishment of the doctor-patient relationship and to the approach to the contents of psychotic communication.

History of Doctor-Patient Relationship

Psychoanalysts used to approach the schizophrenic with the utmost sensitive care and caution. We assumed this to be the only way of making it possible for him to overcome his deep-rooted, suspicious reluctance against reassuming and accepting any personal contacts, including those with the psychoanalyst. This was especially true for the initial establishment of the relationship. I have described the work during these years of apprenticeship in my paper, "Transference Problems in Schizophrenics" (20).

I still believe that it was ultimately helpful to start out that way. Retrospectively it seems to have been the only way for the psychoanalyst to overcome, first, his own anxiety in coping with the schizophrenic's aloofness and, later, his amazement at the possibility of breaking through the schizophrenic's state of withdrawal. It paved the way toward enabling us to convince the patient as well as ourselves and our colleagues, of the schizophrenic's and the psychoanalyst's ability to establish workable contacts with one another.

Once a relationship with the patient was established, treatment was continued with as much acceptance, permissiveness, and as little rejection as could possibly be administered without damage to the institution, to personnel, and to other patients. Nothing short of actually destructive or suicidal action was prohibited.

Previously, Sullivan had begun to do most successful and instructive research work along similar lines on his schizophrenic ward at the Sheppard and Enoch Pratt Hospital, Towson, Md. Kempf and Hadley did similar work at St. Elizabeths, Washington, D. C.

Non-professional closeness, pretense of personal friendship, and violation of the schizophrenic's fear of closeness with its concomitant fear of his own hostility were, of course, avoided. Also omitted were those signs of acceptance and permissive gestures which, to sustain or repeat over a prolonged period of time, would go beyond the psychiatrist's endurance. This had to be seriously considered lest what appeared to be therapeutic acceptance would ultimately be reversed into a new case of rejection.

In spite of this background of basic permissiveness, treatment was not just effective by virtue of the "love" offered, as Kurt Eissler has intimated (6). What has been described here is the interpersonal background, not the contents of the treatment.

The psychoanalysts of this area have subsequently learned that this was not the only nor the best way of establishing an effective interpersonal treatment background. One reason is because this type of doctor-patient relationship addresses itself too much to the rejected child in the schizophrenic and too little to the grown-up person he was before regressing. Something in every non-deteriorated adult schizophrenic senses at least dimly that his disaster cannot be solved by one person's offering him a type of acceptance otherwise not mutually obtainable in adult society. Therefore the psychoanalyst should address himself to the patient also on the level of the patient's present chronological age. There is the danger that unmitigated acceptance may be experienced by the sensitive adult schizophrenic as condescension or at least as lack of respect on the part of the psychoanalyst. There is the further danger that oversolicitousness in playing up to the patient's sensitivities will be interpreted by the patient as, and may actually be, a sign of anxiety on the part of the therapist. Such anxiety, as well as other countertransference phenomena and the role of the therapist's personality in general, need serious consideration in the psychoanalytic work with schizophrenics; they will be discussed in the second part of this paper.

Doctor-Patient Relationship at Present

As for the approach to the patient, it holds true for the psychotic as well as for the neurotic that the damage done to him in early life cannot be undone by therapeutically manufactured unlimited acceptance in later life, but only by understanding of and insight into the nature of the early trauma.

For all these reasons, the psychoanalyst learned to change his generalized attitude of permissiveness and acceptance into one of acceptance of and permissiveness toward the regressive infant as part of the patient's personality. This is blended, however, with an attitude of respect and understanding according to the patient's chronological age. This holds true both for the initial period of establishing contact and throughout the treatment period.

For example, initial contact with a patient who previously had to be induced to treatment-acceptance by three months of

waiting outside his door, might now be tried by seeing that patient while he is in a pack or continuous bath until he has
overcome the period of violent opposition (20). The reasons
for this procedure should be frankly discussed with him.

After the initial contacts with the patient have led to the
establishment of a workable doctor-patient relationship, the attempt is made, in the case of the articulate schizophrenic,
to establish a consensus about the need for treatment and its
reasons. With the psychoanalyst as participant observer, the
patient will then be guided into collaborative efforts at understanding, working-through, and gaining insight into the genesis
and dynamics of his mental disturbance until constructive, lasting, and therapeutically valid insight becomes his. In other
words, the goal of treatment is the same as it is with neurotics.
The method is different until manifest psychotic symptomatology
has disappeared.

The investigation of the doctor-patient relationship and its
distortions will be included in the therapeutic process. I do
not agree with Abraham and Federn (10) who suggest the
animation of positive transference phenomena with the schizophrenic, and that one should refrain from analyzing them. Those
elements of the schizophrenic's relationship with the psychoanalyst, the transference character of which is obvious, should
be used for analytic clarification. Only those elements which
are an expression of the real, positive interrelatedness between
patient and analyst need not be touched by the psychoanalyst.
Sooner or later the articulate schizophrenic will take care of
their discussion by himself.

Interpretation of Content of Patient's Communications

The psychoanalytic knowledge of the potential meaningfulness of most schizophrenic productions plays an important
role as presupposition for a therapeutically valid interpersonal
exchange between patient and analyst. However, in recent
years the actual role of the therapeutic use of the contents of
the schizophrenic's manifestations has undergone considerable
change. Formerly the greatest possible attention was paid to the

contents per se of all the psychotic's utterances, be they ever so bizarre, cryptic, and, at times, seemingly unintelligible.

If the analyst understood the content of the patient's communications, he, the analyst, evidenced his understanding by his responses and further questions. Such mutual agreement on the understanding of content was designed to help break through the self-imposed isolation of the patient in his private world. It was also considered an aid in creating a desirable background for collaborative therapeutic endeavor. However, the analyst would not try to "interpret" content (18), (19), (20). "Interpretation" in psychoanalytic terminology means to translate the manifestations of that which is barred from awareness into the language of consciousness. That is what the psychoanalyst has to do for the neurotic in order to help him to become aware of and to understand repressed thought and feeling.

The schizophrenic's problem is not so much that thought or feeling is barred from awareness, but that he is swamped by, from the observer's viewpoint, unconscious material which breaks through the barriers of dissociation. The neurotic and the healthy person have succeeded in keeping such material dissociated. In the schizophrenic most of the time this material is within his awareness. He knows the meaning of his psychotic productions as far as their contents are concerned. It was the psychoanalyst's knowledge of the schizophrenic's awareness of the meaning of his communications which made it seem inadvisable, if not most of the time redundant, to interpret the contents of his productions. My refraining from doing so was not "for the purpose of promoting a type of introjection of the analyst as a good object, which avoided a splitting of the ego," as Sylvia Payne suggested in her paper on "Theory and Practice of Psychoanalytic Technique" (42).

This does not mean that I would advocate exclusion of formulations of vague, indirect schizophrenic communications. These frequently become therapeutically more meaningful to the patient as he hears them clearly and directly re-formulated in the rational language of the therapist.

As far as actual interpretive help goes, it is needed by the schizophrenic when it promotes understanding of and insight into both the genetics and the dynamics of his disturbance. Grotjahn has stressed the same point (28). The analyst has, of course, continued to pay attention to the contents of the schizophrenic's communications so that he, the analyst, may know, if possible, what the patient wishes to convey. However its therapeutic importance is no longer overestimated. The importance of the psychoanalyst's misunderstanding and misinterpretation of the schizophrenic's production has also been overestimated. The patient's therapeutic contact with the analyst, and the patient's progress, by and large, will not be interfered with by a miscarriage in understanding on the part of the psychoanalyst, if it happens in the spirit of therapeutic humility and not in the spirit of any type of overbearing, personal therapeutic ambition. Lack of spontaneity or overcaution may be more detrimental than faulty directness as long as the latter is serious and sincere in purpose. Clear directness is a necessary device in dealing with disturbed schizophrenics. Their one-track thought processes, lack of reality testing and of foresight make it greatly desirable for the psychoanalyst to offer his therapeutic suggestions in terms of one-sided, meaningful, concrete, concise questions and statements. Questioning in terms of "either/or" tends to be confusing, and therefore anxiety-producing to the insecure, indecisive schizophrenic.

John Rosen has re-established the therapeutic use of interpretation of the content of schizophrenic manifestations in a new setting (43), (44). I hope that the evaluation of Rosen's material will clarify the reasons for the therapeutic moves in opposite directions.

Response to Patient's Irrational Productions

Some analysts have wrongly evaluated the significance of the meaningfulness of schizophrenic communications, by operating on the faulty conclusion that they can argue on a rational level with the patient about the rationality of his communications and that they can, for example, try to "talk" the patient "out" of a delusional system.

While this obviously does not work, another similar approach has proved to be therapeutically valid. That method is to respond, for example, to hallucinatory or delusional manifestations in terms of registering disagreement, without, however, arguing about them—for instance, by stating, "I do not hear or see what you hear or see. Let us investigate the reasons for the difference in our experience." The analyst may react similarly to psychotic behavior by remarking: "Your hair-pulling, spitting, and so on, does not convey any meaning to me. Maybe you can verbalize what you want to convey rather than act it out."

Incidentally, discouraging irrational behavior by professing lack of understanding of its meaning is not tantamount to advising in principle to "cut it out" the way the analyst does in his dealings with a neurotic. At times "acting-out" is the only way of communicating that is available to the inarticulate schizophrenic (18), (19). The essential irrationality of his "acts" should then be approached therapeutically. The acting-out, per se, has to be accepted until it yields to therapeutic efforts and is replaced by the patient's re-gained ability to use verbalized communication.

Only in cases where sustained efforts to reach the patient on a verbalized, rational level have consistently proved to be unsuccessful over a period of time, has it seemed necessary to enter temporarily into the schizophrenic's psychotic world. In such cases the analyst participates for the time being in the patient's delusional experiences until the patient gets ready to investigate their dynamics with the psychoanalyst.

Here again our present method in this area differs from Rosen's, and we hope to get an answer to the validity of both approaches through future investigation.

Genetic and Dynamic Scrutiny of Productions

Now, as to the changes tried in this area after the therapeutic approach in terms of overemphasis of contents was discarded. Mainly through the efforts of Sullivan, it was replaced in recent years by developing a technique of focusing therapeutic attention upon the genesis and dynamics which determine the contents of the schizophrenic production (50), (53), (54), (55). As a way of accomplishing this, close attention is paid to, and careful investigation done about certain factors. These include: present timing and circumstances, the original setting, precipitating factors, and bodily and emotional symptoms preceding or concomitant to a psychotic manifestation. The patient is trained, if he is in contact, to join the psychoanalyst in his endeavor to find those connections. We have been gratified by the disappearance of psychotic manifestations subsequent to their consistent, repetitive, genetic, and dynamic scrutiny. Once accepted by the introspectively gifted schizophrenic, this procedure leads automatically toward the investigation and understanding of neighboring symptomatology which has been linked up with the manifestations which were originally under scrutiny. Staveren has given an illustrative example of this technique in his paper on "Suggested Specificity of Certain Dynamisms in a Case of Schizophrenia" (47).*

In cases where the patient is too disturbed to participate actively in this genetic and dynamic scrutiny, it yet has proved ultimately helpful if the analyst directs his therapeutic attention in this direction and tries to communicate this effort to the patient until such time as the patient emerges sufficiently from his psychotic state to follow suit.

Timing of Therapeutic Intervention

There has been much discussion concerning the timing of the analyst's active therapeutic endeavor with the schizophrenic. In my opinion, much valuable time has been lost by waiting too cautiously until the patient was "ready" to accept one or another active therapeutic intervention. Once a workable doctor-patient relationship has been established, the patient is "ready" to be approached with active therapeutic moves. The fact that he may not be able to accept them immediately is not necessarily a sign of the approach being counterindicated.

---

* For other illustrative examples of the above-described method see Tower (56) and Cohen (5).

It may have to be repeated and "worked-through" innumerable times but that is no reason not to get started.

There are only two reasons for being cautious in one's timing of active therapeutic moves. One reason is the sloweddown and narrowed concrete thought-processes of many schizophrenics. These make it necessary to offer only one therapeutic suggestion at a time and not to offer a second one before there is evidence that the first one has been heard, even though not yet necessarily worked-through and integrated.

The second reason is the schizophrenic's anxiety and tendency to go into panic. Therapeutic moves which are liable to produce manifest anxiety have to be offered in such dosage that anxiety does not turn into panic. Also they should be offered at a time when the psychoanalyst will be available if needed to help the patient cope with his anxiety.

The Role of Anxiety

In recent years, Sullivan has succeeded in giving more specific direction and content to the therapeutic scrutiny of the schizophrenic's communications and symptomatology. According to him, the psychodynamics of mental illness, including the schizophrenic manifestations, can be understood as a result and an expression of unbearable anxiety and, at the same time, as an attempt at warding off this anxiety and keeping it from awareness. Full-fledged anxiety is to be considered the most discomforting and disconcerting experience to which a person can be subjected. Remembering this, the analyst will not be surprised to find that the most bizarre and, as to contents per se, unintelligible, irrational, time- thought- and energy-consuming communications and symptoms may be used as security-operations in the presence of threatening anxiety (50), (53), (54), (55).

Anxiety, in Sullivan's definition, is the discomfort which the child learns to feel in the presence of the disapproval of the significant adult who first uses the arousal of this discomfort as a tool while training the child to abide by the basic requirements of acculturation. With great variations as to the ultimate threshold of endurance, anxiety remains effective throughout people's lives in response to disapproval from important people which interferes with a person's security and prestige (50).

In Freud's later formulation, as given in *The Problem of Anxiety,* anxiety is the fear of the dangers which threaten people from within, that is, regarding their culturally unacceptable inner strivings (17).

Without entering into a discussion of the variations in concepts of anxiety offered by other authors such as Goldstein (24) and Horney (34), (35), let me refer to it in terms of the above definitions.

The therapeutic validity of a consistent dynamic approach to schizophrenic symptomatology as a manifestation of the patient's underlying anxiety and his operational efforts to evade its rise and awareness has proved to be most useful and effective with many schizophrenics.

SETUP AND TECHNIQUE

Other suggestions as to setup and technique in psychoanalytic work with schizophrenics are still valid as previously given (18), (19), (20), (21), (22).

Physical Setup

The classical setup of the psychoanalyst sitting behind the patient who lies on the couch is counterindicated. This arrangement interferes with the re-establishment of the patient's ability of reality-testing. It also interferes with the psychoanalyst's use of visual observations which are especially helpful in the case of inarticulate schizophrenics.

Schedules

Equally counterindicated are rigidly scheduled one-hour interviews. Flexible schedules which allow for either cancellation of sessions, sessions of several hours, or non-scheduled extra interviews are indispensable in psychoanalytic work with disturbed psychotics.

Contact during Disturbed Periods

Unlike Schilder (45) and Glover (23), I recommend with Sullivan (49), (50), (51), (52), Weininger (58), and Rosen (43), (44) that the schizophrenic be seen by the analyst through all prolonged states of psychotic disturbance regardless of the visible and immediate gain of insight from interviews during such periods. Later on one usually sees that there has been some gain in insight, even though it could not be acknowledged or verbalized at the time. Also, the maintenance of therapeutic contact through periods of disturbance is useful for the sake of later therapeutic reference. Incidentally, my experience with reviewing these disturbed periods with the patient, following his recovery, has also been a gratifying one— in contrast to some other therapists who warn against it (18), (19), (20), (21), (22).

Free Association

The use of the technique of free association constitutes a definite mistake in psychoanalytic therapy with disturbed schizophrenics. The thinking and expression of the schizophrenic is frequently disorganized or in danger of disorganization. The psychoanalyst certainly does not wish to increase the loosening up and disorganization of psychotic thought and expression by the artifact of free associations for alleged therapeutic purposes. The only time when the analyst may ask the psychotic to express himself in terms of associative thinking will be in regard to a specific problem, its origin and timing, and so on, if direct questioning does not lead to the desired results.

Dream Interpretation

In this connection the problem of dream interpretation with schizophrenics should be discussed. Because of the above-mentioned similarity between the dynamics of thought-processes in dreams and schizophrenic thought-processes in awakened states, psychoanalysts used to consider it contraindicated to work on dreams with schizophrenics; we discouraged the recital of dreams. In recent times, however, three treatment-histories of paranoid schizophrenics were brought to my knowl-edge (Drs. M. Spottswood, J. Hartz, and T. Lidz in Baltimore) which encouraged reconsideration of our viewpoint. Each of the patients in a significant dream anticipated marked improve-ment which he subsequently accomplished upon recital and col-laborative interpretation of the dream with the psychoanalyst.

Direction of Productions

While the analyst does not wish to induce associative thinking but prefers to direct the patient's productions, he must keep in mind that there are many schizophrenics whose verbal-ized productions are so scarce that he cannot direct their com-munications. Then he must use what productions he can obtain for meaningful therapeutic work regardless of the seeming remoteness of such communications from the immediate thera-peutic aim he plans to pursue. If the analyst is sufficiently flex-ible, he will be able to use in his therapeutic plan, sooner or later, any manifestation which he elicits from an inarticulate patient.

This approach is somewhat similar to play technique with children. It will be well in this context to keep Federn's remark in mind: "When we treat a schizophrenic, we treat several children of different ages" (10). Yet the truth of the matter is, as mentioned before, that the psychoanalyst, as he works with a disturbed schizophrenic, is not only treating a child at differ-ent ages but also, and at the same time, an adult person of the chronological age at which he comes into treatment. This is one of the main reasons for the difficulties in psychoanalytic work with schizophrenics. All analysts, in their dealings with schizo-phrenics, seem to struggle with it as they try to develop the technique of treatment most suitable to their own and to the patients' personalities. Psychiatrists who are not sufficiently flexible may find it difficult to address themselves simultane-ously to both sides of the schizophrenic personality. They may behave like rigid parents who refuse to realize that their chil-dren have grown up. The undesirable results of the psychiatrist's reluctance to communicate with the adult part in the patient's personality and his addressing himself only to the regressive parts in the patient have been discussed elsewhere.

On the other hand, if the psychotherapist, out of an erroneous identification with the patient, addresses himself to the adult patient only, he renounces comprehension of, and alertness to, crucial parts of the schizophrenic psychopathology.

The intricacies in the handling of this situation point toward a discussion of the role that the personality of the therapist plays in the treatment of schizophrenics.

PERSONAL PROBLEMS OF THE PSYCHOTHERAPIST

The results of the psychotherapeutic endeavors with disturbed schizophrenics, so far, are not too discouraging. However, cures have not been to the psychoanalysts' satisfaction as to number or durability. Some of the failures are not because of the therapeutic technique used, but because of personal problems of the psychotherapist in his dealings with schizophrenics and because of the personality of the therapist.

Therapist's Role

Every psychotherapist, and especially one who works with schizophrenics, should be clear about his role in the psychotherapeutic process. He should know that he is not called upon to fulfill any noble, magic mission. The schizophrenic, more skeptical of all types of would-be and as-if attitudes than the rest of us, will definitely react unfavorably to a therapist with alleged missionary and similarly God-like attitudes. Such attitudes are usually designed to make the therapist feel good as a self-inflationary measure; but they fail to make him alert to the patient's needs and they certainly fail to impress the schizophrenic.

The task of the psychotherapist is to be the participating observer in the interpersonal process between himself and the psychiatric patient. He must know how to listen and how to elicit the data from the patient. By these means he can guide the patient toward the therapeutically valid genetic and dynamic understanding of his illness and the insight into it which is the goal of psychoanalytic psychotherapy.

In the course of this process, and without himself becoming involved, the psychotherapist must be able to allow the patient to repeat and, by doing so, to resolve old pathogenic interpersonal patterns with him, the therapist, both as a person and as a distorted shadow of other important people of the patient's previous life.

Patient's Aloofness

One more reason for the specific difficulty in doing psychotherapy with the schizophrenic springs from the schizophrenic's aloofness. The active, eager psychotherapist is liable to interpret this general aloofness which long antedates the patient's contact with the psychiatrist as a sign of personal resistance directed against him. He may be liable then to allow himself to be hurt or paralyzed by the patient's state of withdrawal.

Non-Intelligibility of Productions

Another feature of schizophrenic psychopathology which seems to be taxing to many psychiatrists is that many schizophrenic communications, while meaningful to the patient, will not be intelligible to the therapist. Many psychiatrists find it difficult to accept the fact that they, supposedly being of sound mind, cannot make out what the disturbed schizophrenic, who is allegedly "out of his mind," understands and communicates. This experience threatens the security of some psychiatrists and it arouses the resentment of others against the patient by whom they feel humiliated. Either outcome will interfere with the doctor's therapeutic usefulness.

Patient's Resentment and Rage

A fourth personal difficulty for the psychiatrist springs from the resentment and at times rage or fury which are harbored by the schizophrenic in response to his early traumatic experiences and of which the patient himself is afraid. Without any artificial encouragement every schizophrenic will, at times, give vent to this hostility in front of the therapist, thus learning to face and to integrate it, or to overcome part of it. I do not believe, as many classical psychoanalysts do, that man is born to be hostile. However, the personal hostility which is engendered by the early pathogenic warp, rejection, and malevolence he has encountered is among the serious psychopathological problems of the schizophrenic. Nevertheless encouragement of hostile expression in the schizophrenic for alleged therapeutic purposes is not to be advocated. Nor should the psychiatrist expose himself to hostile action or violence on the part of the patient. Schizophrenic violence is seldom malevolent but it should not be endured by the psychiatrist with the erroneous rationalization of therapeutic heroism. Avoidance, if possible, is not only recommended for reasons of the doctor's self-protection but also to protect the patient's self-respect. In retrospect, recall of violence constitutes a serious blow to the self-respect of many schizophrenics.

Therapist's Anxiety

Each time the psychiatrist undertakes one of the therapeutically important frontal attacks against the schizophrenic's defenses in his (the schizophrenic's) avoidance of the rise and awareness of anxiety, he (the psychiatrist) ought to make sure that his own state of mind is one of stability and serenity. Otherwise his own counter-hostility, fear, or anxiety may blind him in the therapeutic evaluation of the patient's experience. Also, they will, in turn, make the patient more hostile and anxious. The psychiatrist's anxiety is a threat to the insecure schizophrenic and it causes an empathic increase in his own anxiety. It is a measuring rod for the degree of disapproval and rejection which the patient expects from his fellowmen because of the anxiety-provoking negative impulses which he suffers and which he, himself, abhors (18), (19), (20), (21), (22).

Another possible unfortunate outcome of the therapist's anxiety is his need to give uncalled-for reassurance to the anxious schizophrenic, thus killing the patient's attempts at bringing his anxiety into the open and in verbalizing it. Constructive reassurance encourages the patient to express and face adequate amounts of hostility and anxiety and their causes. Attempts at mitigation by patting the patient on the back, as it were, are discouraging. The patient senses the therapist's own anxiety or lack of understanding which underlies such a nontherapeutic performance. For all of these reasons it should be evident that it will constitute a serious handicap to ultimately successful therapy if the schizophrenic succeeds in evoking the psychiatrist's anxiety.

Patient's Empathic Ability

The schizophrenic's ability to eavesdrop, as it were, on the doctor, creates another special personal problem for some psychiatrists. The schizophrenic, since his childhood days, has been suspiciously aware of the fact that words are used not only to convey but also to veil actual communications. Consequently, he has learned to gather information about people in general, therefore also about the psychiatrist, from his inadvertent communications through changes in gesture, attitude and posture, inflections of voice, or expressive movements. Observation of all these intangibles is one way of survival for the anxious schizophrenic in the presence of threatening malevolent interpersonal performances which he is always expecting. Therefore the schizophrenic may sense and comment upon some of the psychotherapist's assets and, what is more frightening, his liabilities, which had been beyond the limit of the psychiatrist's own realization, prior to his contact with the schizophrenic patient. An insecure psychiatrist will be made anxious by being exposed to the schizophrenic's empathic ability for this type of eavesdropping and so become preoccupied with his own defenses.

Therapist's Attitude toward Patient's Social Adjustment

Perhaps the greatest threat directly attributable to the therapist to a favorable outcome of psychotherapy with schizophrenics, is the conventional attitude of many psychotherapists toward the question of the so-called social adjustment of their schizo-phrenic patients. The recovery of many schizophrenics depends upon the psychotherapist's freedom from conventional attitudes and prejudices. These patients cannot and should not be asked to accept guidance toward a conventional adjustment to the cus-tomary requirements of our culture, much less to what the in-dividual therapist personally considers these requirements. The therapist should feel that his role in treating schizophrenics is accomplished if these patients are able to find for themselves, without injury to their neighbors, their own sources of satisfac-tion and security, irrespective of the approval of their neighbors, of their families, and of public opinion. This attitude is required because, as a rule, a schizophrenic's recovery will not include the change of his premorbid schizoid personality to another personality type. Schizophrenia, in this sense, is not an illness but a specific state of personality with its own ways of living (18), (19).

I am convinced that many schizophrenics who remain ill could recover if the goal of treatment were seen in the light of the needs of a schizoid personality, not according to the needs of the non-schizophrenic, conforming, good-citizen-psychiatrist.

CONCLUSION

In conclusion, I wish to recommend that the therapist be trained in recognizing and controlling his own dissociated feel-ings and motivations and in overcoming his own insecurity, previous to working with schizophrenic patients. Many failures in the treatment of schizophrenics, due to the therapist's failure in handling his and the patient's mutual interpersonal problems adequately, could then be avoided.

BIBLIOGRAPHY*

1. ABRAHAM, K., "Short study of the development of the libido viewed in the light of mental disorders (1924)." *Selected Papers of Karl Abraham*. E. Jones, ed. 418–501. London, Hogarth Press, 1927.

2. BETZ, B. J., "A study of tactics for resolving the autistic barrier in the psychotherapy of the schizophrenic personality." *Am. J. Psychiat.*, CIV, 267–273, 1947.

3. BLEULER, E., "Dementia praecox oder Gruppe der Schizophrenien." *Handbuch d. Psychiatrie*. G. Aschaffenburg, ed. Leipzig und Wien, Franz Deuticke, 1911.

4. CAMERON, N., "Reasoning, Regression and Communication in Schizophrenics." *Psychol. Monographs*, No. 221, 1938.

5. COHEN, R. A., "The management of anxiety in a case of paranoid schizophrenia." *Psychiat.*, X, 143–157, 1947.

6. EISSLER, K. R., "Limitations to the psychotherapy of schizophrenia." *Psychiat.*, VI, 381–391, 1943.

7. ERNST, M. G., "A psychotherapeutic approach in schizophrenia." *J. Ment. Sci.*, LXXXVI, 668–674, 1940.

8. FAIRBAIRN, W. R. D., "Endopsychic structure considered in terms of object-relationships." *Intern. J. Psychoanal.*, XXV, 70–93, 1944.

9. ———, "Object-relationships and dynamic structure." *Internat. J. Psychoanal.*, XXVII, 30–37, 1946.

10. FEDERN, P. "Principles of psychotherapy in latent schizophrenia." *Am. J. Psychother.*, I, 129–144, 1947.

11. ———, "Psychoanalysis of psychoses." *Psychiat. Quart.*, XVII, 3–19, 246–257, 470–487, 1943.

12. FENICHEL, O., *Outline of Clinical Psychoanalysis*. New York, W. W. Norton, 1934.

13. FRENCH, T. M. AND KASANIN, J. S., "A psychodynamic study

---

* This bibliography includes only literature pertinent to the contents of this paper, which was published before 1948. For literature pertaining to the subject since then, see the author's *Principles of Intensive Psychotherapy* (Chicago, University of Chicago Press, 1950) and *Psychotherapy with Schizophrenics: A Symposium* (New York, Internat. Univ. Press. 1952).

of the recovery of two schizophrenic cases." *Psychoanal. Quart.*, X, 1–22, 1941.

14. FREUD, S., "On Narcissism: an Introduction." (1914) *Collected Papers*, IV, 30–59. London, Hogarth Press, 1925.
15. ———, "The interpretation of dreams." *The Basic Writings of Sigmund Freud*. New York, Modern Library, 1938.
16. ———, "On psychotherapy." *Collected Papers*, I, 249–263. London, Hogarth Press, 1904.
17. ———, *The Problem of Anxiety*. New York, W. W. Norton, 1936.
18. FROMM-REICHMANN, F., "Psychoanalytic psychotherapy with psychotics." *Psychiat.* VI, 277–279, 1943.
19. ———, "Remarks on the philosophy of mental disorder." *Psychiat.*, IX, 293–308, 1946.
20. ———, "Transference problems in schizophrenia." *Psychoanal. Quart.*, VIII, 412–426, 1939.
21. ———, "A preliminary note on the emotional significance of stereotypies in schizophrenics." *Bull. Forest Sanitarium*, I, 17–21, 1942.
22. ———, "Problems of therapeutic management in a psychoanalytic hospital." *Psychoanal. Quart.*, XVI, 325-356, 1947.
23. GLOVER, E. AND BRIERLY, M., *An Investigation of the Technique of Psychoanalysis*. London, Balliere, Tindall & Cox, 1940.
24. GOLDSTEIN, K., *Human Nature in the Light of Psychopathology*. Cambridge, Harvard Univ. Press, 1940.
25. ———, "Methodological approach to the study of schizophrenic Thought Disorder." *Language and Thought in Schizophrenia. Collected Papers*. J. S. Kasanin, ed. 17–40. Berkeley, Univ. of Calif. Press, 1944.
26. ———, "The significance of special mental tests for diagnosis and prognosis in schizophrenia." *Am. J. Psychiat.*, XCVI, 575–588, 1939.
27. ———, "The significance of psychological research in schizophrenia." *J. Nerv. & Ment. Dis.*, XCVII, 261–279, 1943.

28. GROTJAHN, M., "Emotional reeducation in supportive therapy." *Psychoanalytic Therapy*. F. Alexander and T. M. French, eds. 165–172. New York, Ronald Press, 1946.

29. HANFMANN, E., "Analysis of thinking disorder in a case of schizophrenia." *Arch. Neurol. & Psychiat.*, XLI, 568–579, 1939.

30. ――――, AND KASANIN, J. S., "An experimental study of concept formation in schizophrenia." *Am. J. Psychiat.*, XCV, 35–52, 1938.

31. ――――, *"Conceptual Thinking in Schizophrenia."* Monograph No. 67. New York, Nerv. & Ment. Dis. Publ. Co., 1942.

32. HINSIE, L. E., "Schizophrenics." *Psychoanalysis Today*. S. Lorand, ed. 274–286. New York, Intern. Univ. Press, 1944.

33. HOLLÓS, J., *Hinter der gelben Mauer* (Buecher des Werdenden). Stuttgart, Hippokrates Verlag, 1928.

34. HORNEY, K., *The Neurotic Personality of Our Time*. New York, W. W. Norton, 1937.

35. ――――, *New Ways in Psychoanalysis*. New York, W. W. Norton, 1939.

36. JUNG, C. J., *"The Psychology of Dementia Praecox."* Monograph No. 3. New York, Nerv. & Ment. Dis. Publ. Co., 1936.

37. KASANIN, J. S., "The disturbance of conceptual thinking in schizophrenia." *Language and Thought in Schizophrenia. Collected Papers*. J. S. Kasinin, ed. 41–49. Berkeley, Univ. of Calif. Press, 1944.

38. KEMPF, E. J., *Psychopathology*. St. Louis, C. V. Mosby Co., 1920.

39. KNIGHT, R. P., "Psychotherapy of an adolescent catatonic schizophrenia with mutism." *Psychiat.*, IX, 323–339, 1946.

39a. ――――, "Psychotherapy in acute schizophrenia with successful outcome." *Bull. Menninger Clinic*, III, 97, 1939.

40. LaFORGUE, R., "A contribution to the study of schizo-

phrenia." *Intern. J. Psychoanal.*, XVIII, Part 2, 147–162, 1936.

41. LEWIS, N. D. C., *Research in Dementia Praecox*. New York, Nat. Comm. for Ment. Hyg., 1936.

42. PAYNE, S. M., "Notes on developments in the theory and practice of psychoanalytical technique." *Intern. J. Psychoanal.*, XXVII, 12–19, 1946.

43. ROSEN, J. N., "A method of resolving acute catatonic excitement." *Psychiat. Quart.*, XX, 183–198, 1946.

44. ———, "The treatment of schizophrenic psychosis by direct analytic therapy." *Psychiat. Quart.*, XXI, 3–37, 117–119, 1947.

45. SCHILDER, P., *Psychotherapy*. New York, W. W. Norton, 1938.

46. SILVERBERG, W. V., "The schizoid maneuver." *Psychiat.*, X, 383–393, 1947.

47. STAVEREN, H., "Suggested specificity of certain dynamisms in a case of schizophrenia." *Psychiat.*, X, 127–135, 1947.

48. STORCH, A., "The Primitive Archaic Forms of Inner Experiences and Thought in Schizophrenia." Monograph No. 36. New York, *J. Nerv & Ment. Dis.*, 1924.

49. SULLIVAN, H. S., "The language of schizophrenia." *Language and Thought in Schizophrenia. Collected Papers.* J. S. Kasinin, ed. 4–16. Berkeley, Univ. of Calif. Press, 1944.

50. ———, *Conceptions of Modern Psychiatry*. Washington, D. C., The William A. White Psychiatric Foundation, 1947.

51. ———, "Affective experience in early schizophrenia." *Am. J. Psychiat.*, VI, 467–483, 1927.

52. ———, "Environmental factors in etiology and course under treatment of schizophrenia." *Med. J. and Rec.*, CXXXI, 19–22, 1931.

53. ———, "Therapeutic investigations in schizophrenia." *Psychiat.*, X, 121–125, 1947.

54. ———, "Notes on investigations, therapy, and education in psychiatry and their relations to schizophrenia." *Psychiat.*, X, 271–280, 1947.

55. ——, "The meaning of anxiety in psychiatry and in life." *Psychiat.*, XI, 1–13, 1948.

56. Tower, S., "Management of paranoid trends in treatment of a post-psychotic obsessional condition." *Psychiat.*, X, 137–141, 1947.

57. Vigotsky, L. S., "Thought in schizophrenia." *Arch. Neurol. & Psychiat.*, XXXI, 1063–1077, 1934.

58. Weininger, B. I., "Psychotherapy during convalescence from psychosis." *Psychiat.*, I, 257–264, 1938.

59. Zilboorg, G., "Ambulatory schizophrenics." *Psychiat.*, IV, 149–155, 1941.

▶ PSYCHOTHERAPY WITH THE CRIPPLED AND DISABLED

By Gustav Bychowski, M.D.[*]

INTRODUCTION

The following presentation is based on the experience gained by the writer during his work with the physically disabled over the past five years. In this he had the good fortune of being a member of a well-coordinated team of workers. The spirit of cooperation prevailing at the Institute for Crippled and Disabled made possible the joint efforts of workers of such diverse interests as the psychiatric social worker, the physical and the occupational therapist, the vocational instructor, the psychologist, the orthopedic surgeon—and the psychiatrist.

The necessity for cooperation on a wide scale will become manifest in the course of the presentation. However, let us outline at the very outset the theoretical and practical principles underlying this necessity.

PROBLEMS OF THE PHYSICALLY DISABLED

The specific problems facing a physically disabled individual concern his acceptance of himself and his acceptance by the environment. It is imperative also that in the course of his adaptation he should improve his mental and physical equipment. This is necessary in order to strengthen his ego which may have become weakened as a result of various traumatizations. These may have centered around his disability and his subsequently changed position in the family and the social environment.

---

[*] Assistant Clinical Professor of Psychiatry, New York University; formerly Director, Department of Mental and Social Adjustment, Institute for Crippled and Disabled, New York City.

Since it is our general experience that the immature ego continues to be influenced and molded by the environment, work with the family of our disabled patients is of prime significance. This then becomes one of the most important areas of activity of the psychiatric social worker (S. W.). Let me stress a few aspects of this work with the family as an essential part of mental rehabilitation, one of the components of comprehensive psychotherapy with the physically disabled.

Role of the Social Worker

The S. W. helps to clarify the program for the patient and for his relatives. In so doing he (or she) endeavors to smooth or eliminate some of the rough edges and to alleviate if not resolve some of the conflicts centered around the specific position of the disabled individual. If this isn't done, these conflicts and the resulting emotional attitudes of the patient and of his relatives might constitute serious stumbling blocks on the way to rehabilitation. What is worse, such reactions might even become exacerbated during the process of rehabilitation.

There are a number of areas in which the acitivity of the S. W. is vital: He (or she) serves as an intermediary to clarify for the patient his relationship with the psychiatrist; he (or she) enters into the various areas of adaptation and readjustment in which the disabled patient needs help in so many different ways. He (or she) helps to support the patient's ego in the difficult process of rehabilitation.

The ultimate goal of full social adaptation cannot be achieved without vocational training and rehabilitation. This process which, under most favorable circumstances, results in employment and economic independence, is naturally fraught with many difficulties. The disabled patient here too needs constant help and advice in the various steps he has to take. Specifically, his ego requires support in order to overcome all the natural reactions of distrust and anxiety which would weaken his hold on the new reality in the process of rebuilding.*

---

* The psychiatric case work with patients, to be described later, was carried out in a most competent way by Mary W. Douville.

Role of Physical and Occupational Therapist

The work of the physical and occupational therapist hardly needs elaboration. From our specific point of view, however, it is to be emphasized that the relationship between these two on the one hand and the psychiatric personnel on the other is one of mutual help and interdependence.

The psychiatric team learns from the other workers—in addition to the physical and occupational therapists, we should mention various teachers and vocational instructors—of the various difficulties and inhibitions displayed by the patient in the course of activities directed by them. Reciprocally, we interpret these difficulties for the other workers on the basis of our deeper knowledge of the dynamics of our patients, and offer to these workers some cues as to the most successful handling of the patient.

Role of the Psychologist

The role of the psychologist in our team requires comment. Originally, psychological testing was his only function. This has now become no more than an initial, although important, step in the process of rehabilitation. The initial limitation of testing only the functioning of intelligence is aided now by a more detailed assessment of specific cerebral functions, for example visual-motor coordination. Various projective techniques have also been added to offer valuable indications for the evaluation of personality trends and potentialities. We found the Rorschach and the Figure Drawing Test particularly useful. They have been most helpful in a rapid evaluation of the ways in which the ego deals with anxiety and aggression and with its need for dependence and protection.

Conclusions derived from these data offer important cues for psychotherapy, a complex process in which the psychologist is called upon to play his part. In our team the psychologist took over responsibility for what we called "psychological re-training." Psychotherapy proper was reserved for the psychiatrist and the psychiatric social worker. However, such division of competence is obviously a matter of opinion and based largely on the personal preference and special qualifications of the clinical psychologist.

PSYCHOLOGICAL RETRAINING.   The psychological retraining as practiced at the Institute* was handled in the following manner: The psychologist would see the patient for periods ranging from one-half to three-quarters of an hour at regular intervals two or three times a week. In his work he would concentrate on the retraining of such cerebral functions as had been found defective on the basis of both the psychological and psychiatric examinations. Appropriate exercises were devised to be practiced at first by the patient with the psychologist supervising, later on by the patient alone as a kind of home work. We found it particularly useful to concentrate on perception and reproduction of configurational patterns, improvement of attention span, visual-motor coordination, training of memory, and improvement of various speech difficulties, in particular sequelae of aphasia.

Needless to say, this work by no means remained limited to the retraining of the defective functions. The relationship which inevitably developed between the patient and the psychologist had important emotional implications, and helped the patient to express and eventually work-out some of his anxieties. These anxieties were related not only to his functioning in connection with special activities such as reading, writing, and arithmetic, working in the workshop or at various trades (vocational department), but were also aroused in reference to some relevant situations of the personal interrelationship. Thus some overlapping of the role of the psychologist with that of the S. W. was unavoidable. However, the difference in emphasis and the good cooperation between these workers helped us to steer clear of most difficulties.

We found that the contribution of psychological retraining to the general rehabilitation of our patients was very valuable.

---

* At this point I wish to mention the psychologists, Barbara H. Holodnak and Madeline G. Marcus, who were most helpful in carrying out this program.

The functional improvement could be ascertained by the every-day observation of various members of our team, as well as by psychological retesting. The latter indicated, objectively and fairly accurately, the measure of the progress achieved.

Role of the Psychiatrist

We come next to the psychiatrist's role. Ideally, he should see every prospective candidate for rehabilitation. For technical reasons this was difficult to accomplish, but I did succeed in seeing every patient with organic brain defect or with obvious emotional difficulties. On the basis of my own examination, and of all the other data, I would then establish a detailed program of psychological rehabilitation in which the various members of our team had their particular parts to play.

As regards my own function, I was throughout the leader of our team. I supervised each member's work, seeing them at regular intervals and whenever else it seemed necessary. Naturally, I would also see at any time the particular patient whom they wished me to see.

In addition, my responsibility was twofold: first, I treated those selected patients with definite psychopathology who required systematic psychotherapy. Second, I took over patients for a brief period of time, whenever the situation seemed to require an approach more incisive and dynamic than could be offered by other workers. When on the other hand in treating a patient I came to the conclusion that the other methods were sufficient or more expedient, I shifted that patient to the S. W.

CASE HISTORY

In the interest of greater clarity I shall emphasize in the following case histories the various factors responsible for the weakness of the ego:

> Let us begin with the relatively simple history of an eighteen-year old, John B. He was stricken by congenital cerebral palsy with posturing, especially of the left upper extremity, spastic gait, and slight athetoid movements of the arms and facial musculature. His speech was typically de-

fective but intelligible, though marred by his poor command of English (Italian was the language spoken at home).

John was small in stature and looked somewhat childish and immature. This corresponded to his mental status as revealed by psychological testing and psychiatric examination. In his schooling he had been considered as of low intelligence and had had to attend special classes at a public school. Despite his having graduated at the age of seventeen, he was practically unable to read and write.

The psychiatric evaluation read as follows: "This young man's inferiority, originating in congenital cerebral inadequacy, has also caused emotional immaturity and persistence of personality development on a rather childish level. In view of his emotional security his ego will be able to participate actively in the process of rehabilitation. It is to be expected that his cerebral functions will improve and his whole personality will mature in the course of rehabilitation."

The report of the psychologist confirmed this impression of John's infantile personality features and of his emotional immaturity. As to his intellectual functioning, the I.Q. of 89, obtained on the Wechsler-Bellevue Intelligence Scale, classified him as falling toward the upper end of the dull-normal range of intelligence. However, a more detailed analysis led to the conclusion that the low score was a result of his limited educational and cultural opportunities and of his emotional insecurity. His anxiety interfered with attention and concentration. His slight manual disability contributed to his embarrassment and led to poor performance in every social situation. Therefore it was suggested that "the boy has at least average intellectual capacity and good visual-motor organizational ability. Although his marked anxiety might impede his initial progress, he should ultimately succeed in Optical Mechanics in which he is interested and in which he would like to receive training at the Institute."

A more detailed analysis of John's psychodynamics and of his family situation permitted both a clear formulation of the factors weakening his ego organization, and a survey of his assets, to be used as forces of reconstruction.

John was an only son occupying a middle position between two sisters. His parents with their cultural limitations and their emotional immaturity were never able to reconcile themselves to his disability and to accept it. While their individual reactions were different, they combined to provide a fairly common, perhaps typical, pattern.

The mother's disappointment was covered up by an excess of sympathy with John over his personal welfare, leading to exaggerated solicitude and overprotection. This attitude in turn was bound to reinforce the boy's anxiety and his own need for prolonged and complete dependence.

As the boy grew up, maternal solicitude took the form, almost logically, of the desire to see him successful and on the way to economic security quickly and out of proportion to his real abilities. The mother showed manifest disappointment when such wishes proved unrealistic. These attitudes on the mother's part met with and fostered the boy's understandable tendency toward imaginary overcompensation of his inadequacy. Hence, John entered the Institute with the idea that he would get quick training in a good trade and would be able to reach complete economic independence in the near future. This would enable him to marry, have a car, a house in the country, and to raise a family. He explained that he wanted to have his sons as soon as possible so that they could support him. (Such a wish-fantasy, found in a great number of our immature disabled patients, may be described as an unrealistic, reactive [compensatory] ego-ideal. Later we shall discuss its impact on rehabilitation.)

As to the attitude of John's father, his disappointment assumed the typical form of rejection. His masculine pride was deeply wounded by this misfit of a son, and his constant feeling of frustration resulted in a release of primitive hostility, as is customary on this cultural level. The boy was blamed for his poor achievements, yet the father, a manual worker himself, would avoid instructing him in any mechanical skill and introducing him to his friends. When irritated, the father even became physically violent.

Obviously this attitude constituted a grave obstacle in the development of John's masculine identification. In this area, too, he was driven to fantasy since real achievements seemed so far beyond his reach. Feeling rejected by his father, he could hardly conceive of himself as being accepted by other men and hence was pushed further toward seclusion and isolation.

Reflecting such parental attitudes, John developed rejection of himself as a disabled person. His ego thus evolved two opposite sets of reactions: on the one hand, he avoided situations which made him aware of his deficiency; on the other, he kept denying his deficiency in his fantasy and derived solace from his unrealistic ego-ideal.

As was natural, this basic pattern was a source of serious resistance against the various phases of rehabilitation. It started with John's reaction to psychological testing when he displayed "marked reticence in responding unless he felt the answer to be correct, a situation which was accompanied by his characteristic comment, 'I think I know, but I don't want to say it—I don't want to make a fool of myself,' and by his self-disgust as evidenced by his lament, 'I'm disgraced!' when unable to respond."

Next, John was subjected to various vocational tests; the results were poor. This was not only because of his motor deficiency and his lack of skill but also because of the blocking defense mechanisms, the effects of which were most noticeable in the following stages of rehabilitation. Fortunately, however, the therapeutic results of our combined endeavors came to the fore concurrently.

Like all of our trainees, John was started with tests in the Guidance Test Class. The result was discouraging: "Results of Guidance Tests would seem to indicate that there is little possibility of successfully undertaking training in any of the Institute trades. He follows instructions poorly, both written and oral. He does not appear to be able to distinguish between good work and poor work. He does not handle tools well. Sheltered workshop* tasks were not done neatly and he is very slow."

Yet despite such poor performance of relatively simple as-

---

* A "sheltered workshop" is a charitable or philanthropic organization or institution, conducted not for profit, but for the purpose of carrying out a recognized program of rehabilitation for physically, mentally, and socially handicapped individuals, and to provide such individuals with remunerative employment, or other rehabilitation activity of an educational or therapeutic nature.

signments, John considered such activity as beneath his dig-
nity, and demanded immediate training in a complex and
lucrative trade. Our first problem therefore was to make him
accept his limitations and comprehend the time element involved in learning and in attaining his goals. After an initial
period of depression and bitter rebellion, he became able to
accept without resentment the necessity of spending a considerable period of time (nine months) in the workshop occupied with such simple tasks as folding papers, and making
baskets. He also came to realize the necessity of passing
through successive stages of simple work under constant
supervision before any strictly vocational training could be
considered. The concept of accomplishment as a function of
effort had to be conveyed to him as a new and revealing insight.

In anticipation of the end-result I may here recount that
after two years of combined vocational training and rehabilitation John was rewarded by the fulfillment of his great
desire: he was able to be trained and employed as an optical
mechanic. One may say that an improved ego-organization
permitted him to achieve in reality a goal which formerly
his fantasy had only conjured up.

How was this accomplished? While the executive functions
of the ego were being strengthened and developed by work
in the sheltered workshop, and in the academic class, by
psychological retraining and, at a later stage, by speech therapy, the S. W. dealt with the various tasks and situations
which were confronting the ego, which caused anxiety and
which evoked unrealistic and blocking defense mechanisms.
Once proper transference relationship had been established,
it became possible also to work-through reactions of suspicion
and hostility which originated in the family situation and
were transferred from there to the wider environment.

A decisive step forward was accomplished when John was
made to accept himself as a disabled individual with limited
yet sufficient potentialities. In this way his ego learned to
accept the possible reactions of non-handicapped persons to
his deficiencies. Thus his development was no longer hampered by constant comparisons between himself and normal
individuals or, in terms of mental anatomy, by the confronta-

tion of his actual performance with the demands of an unrealistic, fantastic ego-ideal.

This important process of what may be called "the shading
of the ego-ideal" is well illustrated by an excerpt of a S. W. report centered around finger painting—another adjuvant method
used in our work with this patient:

"We looked at all three of the finger paintings. The third
picture, the one he did today, he criticized by saying that the
barn was crooked. It belonged to a man, maybe to John. He
then quickly said that if the barn were his it would be straight
and strong. He told me that he does not like his pictures, but
that I do. I wondered why this was so and he said that maybe
I knew more about the shame of others having been in this
business longer than John. Maybe in relation to other people
his pictures are not so bad. He then immediately added that
he was not trying to be better than anyone else and kept
repeating over and over again that his pictures were bad but
maybe not as bad as they seemed to him."

Three months after the start of finger painting, a note in
the record reads:

"It was interesting that his finger painting improved this
week and that for the last few sessions he has given up painting his fantasy house in the country, and now draws scenes
of recreational activities available to city dwellers such
as Miniature Golf Course, Beach at Coney Island, Picnic
Grounds, and finally the George Washington Bridge."

In a similar fashion, every step of the way to rehabilitation
was discussed with John with attention focussed on its emotional impact.

As the treatment progressed, parental figures, that is, the
parents themselves, his sister, a former school teacher, and
others were drawn into the picture, with a discussion of
John's reactions toward them and vice versa. Conferences
with the parents, especially with the mother, helped them,
too, to gain a more realistic outlook and to develop reactions
more conducive to John's progress. The pressure of their disappointment was relieved, and full acceptance of John with
his limitations was firmly established.

Day by day we could watch the influence of this change on the boy's ego. We were especially impressed by the effect of the acceptance by the father. It was indeed a decisive step forward when father and son began to do things together and to meet the former's friends.

Psychological retraining helped to overcome John's anxiety accompanying all intellectual assignments, to develop better concentration and attention, to improve memory as well as perception, and reproduction of various configurational patterns.

Feelings of humiliation connected with his various handicaps were an object of frequent discussions which helped John to discharge an emotional burden which had weighed heavily on the ego and blocked every step toward reality.

An important element in John's self-evaluation was disposed of when he was enlightened about the etiology of his disability. It had been his belief that the doctor who delivered him had not taken proper care of his mother and had "ruined" him at birth. He was full of hatred for this man and felt that no punishment could be severe enough; he had fantasies of how he would kill him. All this happened to him, he felt, because his family was poor and had been treated accordingly by this "butcher of a doctor."

Thus he interpreted his disability as caused by poverty and social injustice. Such masochistic interpretation of disability is a frequent element in the self-evaluation of our patients and is a serious factor interfering with self-acceptance and emotional adaptation. The substitution of a realistic insight into the natural causes and mechanics of disability proved very helpful in this case as in many others. It gave John, among other things, a proper understanding of psychological retraining as help offered him in order to retrain his brain which indeed had been injured, though through nobody's fault.

The growing strength of his ego was best demonstrated by John's ability to stand frustration when he had to be discharged from his first try-out placement in optical mechanics because his speed was found insufficient.

He was returned to the Optical Mechanics Class, and two

months later was rewarded by another, this time successful, placement.

Psychiatric evaluation at that time showed a considerable change in John's total personality and greatly improved functioning in various areas. Though he still displayed naivete and immaturity, he was able to control it in a much better way. We felt that now at last he was able to evaluate and internalize experiences in a more constructive way.

I have called this case simple because of the relatively simple and undifferentiated structure of John's personality. In the course of our rehabilitation work at the Institute we had to deal with cases where, despite a similar basic etiology of brain damage at birth, the personality structure was much more complex, and the neurotic involvement more elaborate.* In such cases, in addition to all the other methods of treatment and rehabilitation, we applied systematic psychotherapy.

How to balance psychotherapy in relation to other methods of rehabilitation, in particular to psychiatric case work, offers problems of a special kind.

CASE HISTORY

Let me illustrate this by salient points from the case history of Jim Q.:

Jim Q. is a young man of twenty-three suffering from congenital cerebral palsy affecting to a moderate degree both legs, the right hand, and speech.

His intelligence and personality structure were on a much higher level than John's case (see above). There was, however, a definite indication of organic brain damage though without impairment of conceptual thinking. There was significant disturbance in intellectual functioning most marked in the areas of visual-motor organization, in shifting to form new associations or to learn new tasks, and in arithmetical reasoning. There was also a suggestion of a disturbance in concentration due to neurotic anxiety.

While this type of cerebral deficiency poses definite tasks

---

* See my paper on "The Ego of the Brain Wounded." *The Psychoanalytic Review,* XXXVI, No. 4, 1949.

to psychological retraining, the emotional difficulties required close cooperation between the psychiatrist and the S. W. Manifest anxiety was blocking the functioning of this patient on all levels. Above all, it was seriously interfering with his speech. He would stammer and stutter, would gasp and fall into a whisper only suddenly to regain full tone; all of this while uttering a single sentence.

Psychiatric interviews and social work revealed a deep gap between the surface picture of the family situation and reality. It was natural that Jim's ego had to develop a great many defenses in order to remain seemingly unaffected by the family drama. The mother, although living at home, had been psychotic for many years. This peculiar situation led to the typical neurotic split in Jim's sexual attitude, with division of women, on the one hand into objects of sexual gratification, and on the other, into unattainable idols. Any approach to the latter group was a source of anguish setting in motion a series of inhibitory reactions.

Ambivalence toward the mother was also a result of her inconsistent attitude; in early childhood she had "spoiled" him and in later years she held against him the sacrifices she had made for him. She also accused him of ingratitude when he did not side with her wholeheartedly in her permanent strife with his father.

The father was a typical self-made man, efficient and energetic, yet tense, irritable, and lacking in any psychological understanding. The necessity to repress the considerable amount of hostility which Jim felt against him was a powerful source of blocking and anxiety. The unreasonable demands of the father were largely responsible for the development of an irrationally demanding superego which prevented Jim from ever being satisfied with any achievement, and instead made him feel ashamed and humiliated by his inadequacy. The oedipal conflict resulted in serious castration anxiety. The boy's allegiance was divided between the parents, at constant odds with each other. Actually neither showed any real understanding of Jim's problems and difficulties and each rejected him in his own way.

One consequence of this situation was that Jim found it extremely difficult to accept any help from a woman, a matter which proved of great importance in the transference situation, in his initial work with the S. W.

His ambivalence toward those engaged in helping him was a direct outcome of his deep wish for dependency on the one hand, and his fear of dependency, on the other. In repetition of his infantile patterns he felt both utterly helpless before the entire therapeutic personnel, and hostile against them. Help is experienced as a painful humiliation when an individual feels the need to be not only strong but stronger than others, and really powerful.

From this attitude there was only a single step to the same kind of masochistic distortion that has been described in the discussion of John's case (see above). Indeed Jim had experienced various situations in the past, when he was given physical treatment "without being consulted," as a dictatorial enforcement on the part of ruthless and overpowering adults. On the other hand, lending a willing ear to praise and encouragement meant to him the fulfillment of his unconscious infantile wish to accept the narcissistic version of parental love, an indulgence which in turn was immediately opposed by the punitive superego.

In Jim's case after an initial period of case-work with constant psychiatric supervision and consultation, it became desirable to introduce a period of deeper psychotherapy. While, for instance, some of the hostility aroused by the father could be ventilated in the discussions with the S. W., psychiatric or rather analytic technique seemed indicated to help the patient realize the full impact of this hostility and the intricate ways of its internalization. Similarly, Jim was able to describe some of his sexual problems, but he needed deeper insight into the dynamics of his erotic "split" which could be given him only in deep psychotherapy. Meanwhile the S. W. continued to mediate between Jim and the significant figures of his environment, and to help him with his difficulties related to various stages of rehabilitation.

In a discussion of psychological retraining Jim offered an excellent definition of what case-work was accomplishing for him: "It is like emotional retraining," he said. At a certain point, in a sort of rehearsal, the S. W. helped him to face his father in a more assertive way. She also had a talk with the father and did her best to open the father's eyes to his son's problems.

After he had been prepared for the sessions by the S. W., I began seeing Jim twice a week. Despite this preparation, there was at first a good deal of resistance, due mainly to Jim's identification of the psychiatrist with his father. Under these circumstances, positive maternal transference to the S. W. increased, and made her appear as a most desirable contrast to the "harsh" and "cold" psychiatrist. This attitude had to be worked-through so that Jim was able to accept the cooperation between his two main helpers as a natural team-work of two wise parental figures, each working in his own way.

The task of the psychiatrist in direct therapy with Jim centered around clarifying the psychodynamics and conveying deeper insights. Obviously, the working-through of the transference situation had to be divided between the psychiatrist and the S. W., with the final formulations reserved for the psychiatrist. Yet, every progress achieved by the patient in his work with the psychiatrist immediately reflected on his attitude during case-work which, gradually, reached a high degree of true insight and conceptualization. Thus, early situations prevailing between himself and his mother in early childhood became thoroughly understood and tied up with his present inhibitions and learning difficulties.

In this case, delicate situations arose when problems of transference toward one of us became the topic of discussion between the patient and the other worker. However, with proper handling, what might at first sight have seemed a stumbling block became an additional source of insight for the patient. As time went on he was able to see various shades of his transference reactions in relation to both of us; this helped him considerably in working-through his basic libidinal and emotional attitudes.

The process of clarification went so far that at a time when his conscious transference reaction toward the S. W. was most positive he was able to see his anticipation of hostility and derision on her part, as a repetition of his father's attitude at an earlier stage of his life. The following is an illustration of the way in which he was able to formulate his insight at this point:

"Toward the conclusion of our interview he began to discuss the fact that the more important any people were to him, the more he was aware of his expectation of hostility, the more definitely he withdrew, and the more he experienced inability to operate."

At a later date, after an objective discussion of his visual-motor difficulties and the progress he had made in his arithmetic operations, he began to understand the difference which throughout his life he had felt in his reactions toward formal learning situations as opposed to those in which he had felt less anxiety since it was not expected and demanded that he learn. He illustrated this from his school experience, and related his anxiety to the feelings of hostility against the person who "forces" him to learn. "He seemed less upset today while discussing his hostility. He felt that the area of comfortable operation with his father has been extended and that his anxiety has decreased since he has recognized his hostility."

The effectiveness of the S. W. and the excellent transference situation undoubtedly took a good deal of wind out of the sails of direct psychotherapy. Accordingly, after a brief period of psychiatric interviews it was decided to discontinue them, since a point had been reached when nothing short of systematic psychoanalysis would have accomplished a more incisive solution of Jim's personality problems. Accordingly, preparations were made for him to start psychoanalysis with a psychiatrist outside the Institute.

In the meantime his rehabilitation program was continued and yielded remarkable results, largely due to the systematic observation by the S. W. of his reactions to various parts of this program and to those who carried it out.

In reviewing this entire material I concluded that this carefully detailed observation, supported by Jim's understanding of the connections between present helpers and parental figures as they functioned and were active in his early childhood, was the decisive factor in the psychological rehabilitation.

Although both patients discussed above had been afflicted by their disability from birth, they had not been able to adjust to it adequately before coming to the Institute because of unfavorable environmental influence.

CASE HISTORY

The following case history illustrates the problems of an individual who was stricken with disability at a relatively mature age and who failed in adaptation through neurotic conflicts fostered by an inadequate and maladjusted mother. In discussing this case I shall emphasize the effect of case-work and of brief incisive psychotherapy on the process of adaptation of the ego to physical disability.

Marjorie S. came to the Institute at the age of twenty-two. Five years earlier she had been stricken with poliomyelitis which left her with paralysis of the trunk and both lower extremities. She was wearing a long brace on her right leg and was able to walk haltingly on a level surface with Canadian crutches, but she was unable to step up or down on the curb or climb stairs without help.

Prior to entering the Institute she was described as "uncooperative" by various agencies that had been trying to help her, was leading the life of a recluse confined to her quarters with her widowed mother, and was relying on public assistance for her support.

After spending two-and-a-half years at the Institute she showed remarkable improvement in her mental and physical functioning. Her physical progress was described by the orthopedic surgeon as follows:

"She has learned to do the swing-thru gait and is able to walk 48 feet in 14 seconds which is a tremendous improvement over the 90 seconds it took her on her initial test. She is able to ascend and descend all curbs and bus steps, steps with and without handrails."

Marjorie at the completion of her training period at the Institute, obtained employment as an office secretary and was awarded by the Institute the Clifford Beers Memorial Prize, "since it was through the disciplined use of her mind that she was enabled to fit together again the pieces of her life."

A tabulation of the various contributions to this remarkable result by the various members of our team may be of interest. The treatment comprised: seven months of case-work; six months of psychotherapy by the psychiatrist; seven months of case-work guidance; one-and-a-half years of physical therapy; and two-and-a-half years of vocational training in office work.

To be sure, Marjorie's original mental endowment was very good. The report of the psychologist classified her as falling toward the upper end of the Average range of intelligence (an I.Q. of 106 on Form I of the Wechsler-Bellevue). Even this result was not optimal because of marked insecurity and anxiety which interfered with performance.

Over a five-month period, case-work alone helped Marjorie to overcome some of her difficulties and laid bare her precarious emotional and reality situation. Then psychotherapy was started at a rate of one session a week. This was continued for six months. During this period case-work was less intensive and was focussed on actual situations in the areas both of family life and of rehabilitation.

It appeared that Marjorie's early environment had been extremely unfavorable. A great deal of tension had existed between her parents, so that she, as the only child, had been exposed to heavy emotional pressures. She had remained entrenched in a deeply conflictual oedipal situation, having been very close to her father, which aroused her mother's resentment. She had adored her father and idealized his image after his death, which occurred when she was seventeen. This was three months before her illness.

By the father's death, the two women were left destitute. The father had been an extrovert, convivial, and generous person, while the mother, full of grudge and resentment, had always tended toward seclusion, and considered most people as below her social status. This attitude gained momentum after she was left alone with Marjorie. Her neurotic trends expanded rapidly, and she used her poverty and Marjorie's illness as a rationalization for keeping the two of them in complete isolation. Whatever occasional contacts the girl might have, in particular with men, were frowned upon as not worthy of her social status.

Before her rehabilitation, being crippled had made Marjorie completely dependent on her mother. This situation the mother thoroughly enjoyed and exploited, since it gratified at last her possessive love. Accordingly, she would discourage any attempt at independence on Marjorie's part, no matter how timid and inadequate.

The mother's general attitude was evident in her initial reaction to rehabilitation. It unquestionably posed a real problem for the S. W. and required handling with particular tact and diplomacy. On the one hand, Marjorie was caught as a pawn in her mother's power, and made to feel guilty for every ever-so-slight effort at independence. On the other, Marjorie's attachment to the mother involved deep ambivalence: she hated her mother for old oedipal reasons, for her own need of her, and for the power that her mother had over her.

Psychotherapy in this case had three main problems to deal with: first, the mother-daughter relationship as described above; second, the patient's general attitude toward other human beings turned out to be to a large extent a reflection of her mother's supercilious air of superiority. Marjorie displayed a rather typical mixture of feelings of inferiority with both primary and secondary compensatory narcissism, all of which gave her a slightly paranoid touch with superficial ideas of narcissistic injury and reference, ready to emerge at any moment. She was constantly projecting her own hostility on her environment, going around with a chip on her shoulder, always ready to withdraw in order to protect herself against some imaginary insult.

The third problem was offered by the particular kind of defenses Marjorie's ego had built up to ward off her sexual impulses. A slight obsessive-compulsive syndrome with emphasis on repugnance against bodily odors and bodily contacts helped her to protect her ego against oedipal hatred and jealousy. She could not forgive her father, she said, who had been such an "extraordinary" human being, for having engaged in this "dirty, animal behavior" (meaning intercourse) with her mother. By such mechanisms this charming and attractive girl was protecting herself against any possible erotic temptation and finding a doubtful and superficial consolation for her loneliness in her precarious feeling of lordly superiority.

As regards therapy, one problem deserves special discussion. The attitude of the patient toward her disability was deeply embedded in her neurosis and had to be subjected to thorough clarification.

In speaking of the acute onset of her illness she said at first that her recollection of this period was somewhat dim. She thought at the beginning that she was going to be completely paralyzed and then found herself rather better off than she had expected. Having been reared in the Catholic tradition, she felt that the Lord had chosen her to help others or to set an example of right behavior. She also felt that the Lord had taken her father purposely before her sickness, since her father loved her too much and, consequently, would not be able to bear her misfortune.

Her mother accused her of having herself caused her misfortune since it struck her while she was working, in addition to her job with the telephone company, as an usherette in a theatre, a position her mother had violently opposed. An aunt had once told her and had reaffirmed it recently, when asked for financial assistance, that she (Marjorie) had been stricken because the curse of Christ was on her. Marjorie herself felt that people might think that she had been crippled because somebody had put a curse on her in punishment; this had been a common belief in the olden times, and people have not changed, she felt. "They used to look down on the sick as outcasts."

With all these superstitions as a background, Marjorie was firmly convinced that her kind of sickness befalls only poor, uncouth people, belonging to the "lower" social strata. Thus her disability stigmatized and lowered her in her own eyes. In an interview during a premenstrual depression it became clear that in addition she was unconsciously superimposing her disability on her womanhood as another "crippling" handicap.

What then in this case were the reasons for the particularly successful outcome of the relatively brief psychotherapy? An analysis of the main factors may provide us with an answer to another important question, namely that of the limitations of psychotherapy with the disabled.

Certainly good intelligence proved as important an asset in this patient, as it is in any non-disabled patient selected for psychotherapy. The amount of Marjorie's secondary defensive narcissism was not too excessive and yielded to our endeavors. She had intellectual and emotional resources to draw upon and had a genuine and strong wish for independence. Finally, the masochistic distortion and exploitation of her disability by her ego was of only moderate degree. It is my conviction, based on experience with the disabled, that such a masochistic distortion, especially when combined with a serious disability, provides the main obstacle to successful psychotherapy.

TRAUMATIC NEUROSIS

Let me mention briefly the problems confronting us in psychotherapy of individuals disabled as a result of a recent injury, such as war veterans, and amputees and paraplegics who are victims of accidents. In these cases the presence of emotional sequelae of an acute trauma accounts for elements of actual and traumatic neurosis in their clinical picture. Accordingly, in such cases the psychiatric treatment will benefit from emphasis on abreaction either under conditions of fully awakened consciousness or in some hypnotic trance. In cases like these I have used with advantage both narcoanalysis and hypnoanalysis.

SUMMARY

In conclusion, I would like to review the main points of our study. Psychotherapy of the physically disabled is best considered as a part of a general program of rehabilitation. All factors responsible for a neurotic attitude toward disability should be considered and dealt with, if possible by a team of workers. While psychological retraining helps to restore cerebral functions which have been impaired and thus, in its own way, helps to alleviate some of the actual anxiety, case-work and psychotherapy aim at removing external and internal obstacles in adaptation of the ego to impaired physical functioning. Among these obstacles an important role is played by the immediate environment whose attitudes contribute so much to weakening the ego.

Healthy family members can feel frightened by a disabled individual. Parents, in particular, may feel lowered in their self-regard and wounded in their pride and ambition. The result is rejection in its various forms even when it is covered up by an excess of solicitude and protection. In this way the crippled child is prevented from forming the significant identifications, and the process of acceptance of himself and his impaired body-image is interfered with. Thus he is unable to utilize all his resources for the build-up of a modicum of independence.

This then is the rationale for making the enlightening and influencing of the environment a significant part of therapy, a part usually incumbent upon the social worker. Other aspects of the therapy are delicately balanced between the social worker and the psychiatrist. Various elements of actual adjustment are taken up in coordination and cooperation with other therapists and educators. At the same time the emotional reactions with their significant unconscious background and undertones are subject to working-through and readjustment on the basis of accepted psychotherapeutic techniques.

▶ DYNAMIC THERAPY FOR THE STUTTERER

By I. Peter Glauber, M.D.*

INTRODUCTION

This paper presents a formulation of a concept of stuttering in terms of the total personality, especially of one of its components, the ego. It attempts to bring our concept of stuttering in line with current psychoanalytic theory and practice. A special aim here is to highlight among the various clinical data and working hypotheses those that are significant to the point of being specific for the stutterer and that therefore have a decisive bearing on therapy.

STUTTERING—AN "EGO-DEFECT" NEUROSIS

Stuttering is generally classified as a pregenital conversion neurosis, as a borderline disorder, or as a narcissistic neurosis. Perhaps the term "ego-defect" neurosis, after Hendrick (23), gives us the best description and insight. Two distinguishing features characterize stuttering: First, unlike the transference psychoneurosis, the symptoms of which precipitate during adolescence, stuttering emerges either shortly after the onset of speech or at the beginning of school. That is, stuttering starts during the incubation stage of neurotic development. Thereafter the stutter continues indefinitely; there is no latency period of freedom from the symptom, just as there is not in some other disorders characterized by ego-dysfunction (25). Second, espe-

* Director, Private Treatment Service for functional speech disorders; Chief of Speech Clinic, University Hospital, New York University-Bellevue Medical Center; Member of Faculty, Department of Psychiatry, Post Graduate Medical School of New York University-Bellevue Medical Center; Attending Psychiatrist, Hillside Hospital; Consultant, Jewish Child Care Association.

cially among some of the older patients, it is frequently and insistently presented as a monosymptomatic disorder (28), indicative of the fact that many and early personality difficulties find expression through one and the same speech disturbance.

It should hardly be necessary to add that the disorder is not organic. As regards constitutional predisposition, there is no agreement among the various writers on the subject (7), (30). This factor seems to be no different in the case of stuttering than in neurosis in general. Likewise there is no convincing evidence* in the contention of some (4), (33) that the neurotic manifestations are secondary to a neurologic constitutional disturbance, such as confusion of cerebral dominance. The very early onset of the pathogenic influences and of the symptom, and the relative intractability of the symptom suggest a resemblance to the organic. The suggestion is understandable, but a resemblance is not an identity.

The core of the stuttering syndrome can be understood best through a description and elucidation of its etiology. "Etiology" has been defined (31) as "the science of efficient, as distinguished from final causes." In medicine both types are studied and especially the precipitating. In psychiatry and in psychoanalysis the efficient, that is, proximate or specific causes are the autoplastically maintained conditionings, complexes, defenses, and conflict "solutions." They derive from the genetic history, especially from the earliest relationship with the parents, which may be regarded as the final cause. In all neuroses this relationship is fundamental; in stuttering it has special features relating to the character of the mother, and her peculiar hold upon the child. The genetic history of every stutterer uniquely reflects the mother's basic conflicts as they emerge in the mother-child relationship. For this reason in treating stutterers, it did not seem sufficient merely to understand the mother through reconstruction, as is sufficient in other disorders. It became essential to involve her in treatment for her own sake, which in turn was indispensable in the treat-

---

* Cf. Abram Blau, *The Master Hand.* New York, American Orthopsychiatric Association, 1946.

ment of the child.* This approach to treatment was a departure from the work of other investigators on the concept and treatment of stuttering.

THE PERSONALITY OF THE MOTHER

The following characterologic description of the stutterer's mother is necessarily a composite one. It stresses pathology and does not touch upon modifying and compensatory factors. The description includes elements common to narcissistic mothers in general, in addition to elements that are particularly characteristic for the mothers of stutterers. Especially with regard to the mother-child relation both in the antecedents and in the descendants, the mother's character structure was repeatedly found to be similar in a number of respects. Usually the mother was an infantile person unconsciously burdened by separation fears, guilt, and aggression. All too frequently she suffered from masochistic dependence on her own mother who, though she too might have been infantile in some ways, appeared to be a much stronger character than her daughter. Both mother and grandmother idealized active and aggressive people, usually personified in some male relative of theirs, a nephew, grandfather, etc. Later, idealization referred primarily to an image of their ego-ideal. Thus the children, the stutterer and his mother (as a child), in the lives of their own mothers witnessed oscillation between extremes of weakness and strength. The strength, really pseudo-strength, took the form either of futile strivings toward an ego-ideal, or of impotent rage at failure to attain it. Generally it was impressed upon the child as genuine strength. The image of the mother as a powerful figure was maintained for a very long time. Her weaknesses, on the other hand, were recognized only at a much later age.

Psychosexually, the mother had a poorly differentiated sense of self: part child, part tom-boy, part wife-husband. Penis envy and competitiveness with males were very frequent, as

---

* This paper is based upon long-range psychiatric studies of more than 75 family units of stutterers, upon the analyses of a number of stutterers—adolescents and adults—and upon the analyses of several mothers of stutterers.

was a history of being in love with a masculine, oedipal type of man, and marrying another, weaker type. The marriage could usually be characterized as sado-masochistic, propelled by a need to control or by a sense of duty, but very little by conscious pursuit of pleasure. The husband stood for her passive self or for her own mother, a type incapable of adequate or consistent love; or else, he represented her own phallic ideal self. In the latter case she envied him when he was successful or mocked him when he was not. In a word, the mother's marital relationship was one of identification and projection.

Pregnancy meant her own transformation into the ideal phallic mother, complete and powerful, and a denial of separation from this mother figure. It also denied femininity which was despised as synonymous with passivity, exposing her to hurts and humiliation. Labor of childbirth was often dramatically described as a painful experience of being dismembered, etc. Giving birth led to a redistribution of self-images by a projection upon the child of these introjects of her passive, inadequate, hated self-image and also of her idealized, narcissistic, phallic self-image. Which of these images was accented, in many cases depended upon the sex of the child or its physical resemblance to real or idealized individuals significant in the mother's life.

THE MOTHER-CHILD RELATIONSHIP

Invariably traceable to a hesitant or uniquely ambivalent attitude on the part of the mother, there were almost always feeding difficulties during the first year of the child's life. Closer scrutiny revealed the special characteristics of the ambivalence: alternations of aggressive feeding gestures with sudden withholding, both accompanied by anxiety. One might call this mother a stuttering feeder, stamping the pattern of hesitation upon the oral musculature, and secondarily upon the respiratory musculature of the child. This pattern was to reappear in the child when the same organ systems were later to be adapted for the function of speech. Here we see the first instance of characteristic maternal behavior following the mother's projection upon the child of her own antithetical self-images. In other words, the mother fluctuated between a wish to feed the child and make it independent, and a wish to reincorporate the child and thus to regain the image of her perfect or ideal self which she had in pregnancy. One mother stated that her nursing difficulties stemmed from a fear that the child would eat her up— a projection of her own wishes and an identification with the child's oral fantasies. What was striking was the sense of realness with which this fear existed in the maternal mind. Nursing was acted-out as a repetition of aggressive feeding and sudden weaning acts, reaching their climax in the final weaning from breast or bottle. Work with children showed that they mimicked the maternal fears. Thus in many stutterers mother and child were found to simulate and stimulate each other's fantasies.

Various happenings in the child's life such as the experiences of birth, nursing, and onset of speech were felt by the mother as anxious experiences for her of separation of a special quality, compounded of both separation and clutching. Also, the child's taking control of his own locomotion, elimination, the development of his will in its negative and positive aspects, and of his intellect—all these landmarks of his ego-development —were felt by the mother to be provocative acts of moving away from her, or aggressive acts of biting into and out of the idealized mother-child unity. What was the effect upon the growing child of such a series of spoken and unspoken signs of anxiety on the part of the mother in response to the onset of each successive stage in his own ego-development? It was apt to be the emergence, at each stage, of parallel fearful and hesitant attitudes, later augmented by feelings of guilt and pent-up aggression. It follows logically, as could be observed clinically time after time, that stripped of the ramifications of defenses, the psychopathology of the stutterer was based either upon the inadequate development of certain of his own executant functions (8), or upon the inadequate libidinization of certain of his effective reality-oriented ego functions. Paradoxically, it sometimes seemed that the young stutterer like the compulsion neurotic had a precocious ego-development, but this ego-development generally referred to certain perceptive intellectual abilities, unmatched by similar development in reality-testing and in the capacity to bear frustrations.

THE MOTHER'S ARCHAIC ATTITUDE TOWARD SPEECH

It is obvious that speech makes use of the organs of the oral apparatus—the lips, mouth, pharynx, etc.—which are the first organs of contact of the infant with the mother. It has been pointed out that from this first contact, anxiety and ambivalence characterized the mother's feelings and behavior. She behaved as if she were anxious about what she and the extension of herself, her child, might do with their oral apparatus. At the onset of speech the anxiety, though not its meaning, became more overt. When a child begins to speak, toward the end of the second year, it is quite normal for him to repeat the first syllable. These normal iterations were envisaged by his mother as stuttering, and its "dire" consequences on the child's personality were soon established in her mind. This fear represented an apprehension that self-expression on the part of the child was an oral aggression upon her, the mother, with the aim of separation. Paradoxically, the possibility that the child might express passive or nursing wishes was also feared. During this early stage of the child's learning to speak, the mother often compared the child with her husband or her brother who frequently actually was a stutterer. Consequently the child, whose oral apparatus had already been impressed with hesitations from his nursing experience, sensed that to his mother speech was overdetermined with forbidden content, that it was in fact itself something of a forbidden act. As speech is an object (29) created by the magic act of speaking, it became for the child both a magic and a forbidden object. The mother was unusually speech conscious; speech for her had retained its archaic quality of possessing special motor and hallucinatory meaning (16), (12). Good speech was highly overvalued by the mother and feared for this irrational reason. Speech became the tool of her own oral dependent needs and of her two-fold identifications with passive and with aggressive images. By appersonation, the stuttering child became the instrument of expression for her own aims which were at once passive and aggressive. Speech, a symbolic expression of self-revealing thinking and feeling, that is ordinarily experienced as a substitute for action, was felt by the mother more nearly as an action than as a symbol. The stutter, then, represents an attempt to inhibit an act symbolizing exhibitionistic wishes which are ultimately aggressive and masochistic.

The mother's general relationship to the stuttering child may best be characterized as a "sticky" involvement of mutual need and mutual exploitation. A statement made frequently by the mother was that the stuttering child occupied her more than all the rest of her children combined. An example of this tenacious tie of the mother to the child was the history of the mother's frequent discontinuation of treatment of the child after it had gotten well under way, unless in the original treatment-plan proper attention was given the mother, simultaneously with or prior to the child's treatment. The maternal affect was most commonly shown in great anxiety centered around the child's speech, his general behavior, his masturbation, his school or social life. Below the surface, envy, disappointment, and hostility were also found. But it must likewise be noted as a characteristic fact that much maternal affection and patient care were bestowed on almost all of these stuttering children, together with the imparting of social anxiety. This anxiety had a special capacity for disturbing speech, the instrument of social contact. In a related manner, this type of mother showed still another form of ambivalence: seduction of the child into helplessness, along with more or less subtle proddings toward active, perfectionistic goals.

THE ROLE OF THE FATHER

In this family constellation, the father contributed both to the development and to the maintenance of the stuttering disorder. His contribution to its development was significant to the degree that he was in flight from his proper relationship to his wife. His contribution to the maintenance of the disorder depended upon the degree of his involvement as a father figure with the stuttering child. Thus the father might be lacking in a two-fold way. Realistically, he was generally in flight from playing a consistent and meaningful role. It can readily be recognized that this flight from the child resembled his withdrawal from his proper marital role. In our experience, when the father did take a consistent and active interest in the stuttering child the prognosis was invariably more favorable. Furthermore, the home situation frequently appeared paradoxical. Articulated strife and contention between the parents often produced relatively less disturbance in the children, and a better prognosis, than when the atmosphere was all quiet. Often this was the quiet of fear and resignation on the part of one parent to the domination of the other. Here the child incessantly had to witness the same unmitigated control under which he himself suffered. On the other hand, the quiet of mutual parental acceptance was often based on mutual acceptance of each other's neurotic ties. This usually meant an exchange of normal roles between parents, and led to confusion of identity in the child. Also, a protesting mother or father was therapeutically more reachable than a frightened, resigned, or guilt-imbued parent. A neurotic parental combination which led to a united front often excluded the child from real closeness to either one. While there was no doubt that the primary pathogenic relationship was that between mother and child, the father had the possibility of mitigating the mother's infantile traits and assisting in the emotional development of his wife. In the same way he could also help the child. Thus, the pathogenesis of stuttering like its therapy was shown to be a total family problem.

The clinico-pathological picture of highlights in the family background here described doubtless resembles that encountered in other types of disorder. However, the various levels of ambivalence on the part of the mother, especially involving the functions of nursing, eating, and speech, the burdening of speech with archaic cannibalistic concepts and primitive motor elements, the confusion by the mother of her own oral acts with those of the child because of appersonation, and finally the confusion of diverse mental activities and behavioral patterns with oral acts—the particular combination of all of these factors we have not encountered in the analyses of any other type of mother. Therefore we regard this combination of factors in the case of mothers of stutterers as significant to the point of approaching specificity. In our reading of the literature describing mothers of patients suffering from related oral-narcissistic borderline states such as asthma, tics, addictions, etc. —admittedly a rather meagre literature—we have not gained the impression of quite the same pattern on their part of oscillation of ambivalences, multiple identifications, or speech consciousness. Further study, however, direct as well as comparative, will be necessary to attain a sharper focus.

THE PSYCHOPATHOLOGY
OF THE STUTTERER*

This somewhat detailed description of the mother-child relationship and the general family background of stutterers has been given to render easier discernment of the psychopathology of the stutterer, some anlagen of which have already been sketched. In what follows, special clinical and theoretical features of the stutterer's character will be described as observed during the treatment process. It will be shown how the special features of the stutterer's character make necessary the specialized techniques in his treatment.

We look upon the stutterer's disorder as an "ego-defect" neurosis. The ego is "a substructure of personality defined primarily by its functions" (21), also by total feelings (8) which are characteristic for the various developmental stages, that is, the ego-states. Some of the important functions to be considered in this paper are perception and memory, motor activity,

---

* In anticipation of the objections of readers who may contend that they have not encountered stutterers whose psychopathology is as serious as here described, it may be pointed out that pathology only is being stressed; the mitigating conflict-free ego-elements and the moot question of quantitative factors are not discussed.

reality-testing, synthetic or creative activity. There are elements in the ego-organization which determine the stutterer's character and it is to these that therapy must be directed. They consist of a number of unconscious physical images which, together with their mental attributes, act like multiple personalities. They are the result of inadequate differentiation of the child from the mother because of her own symbiotic needs and separation anxieties, which have led to identical needs and anxieties on the part of the stuttering child. Fear of losing the mother's breast results in the child's identifying itself with that organ. At a later stage the idea of losing the phallus is felt as another manifestation of the fear of losing the mother or her breast. This in turn results in a similar identification with the phallus, and fear or loss of one may heighten the value of the other. Thus phallus and breast become interchangeable. This incredible phenomenon of an individual's total ego-organization being patterned after the structure and function of one part of the body was first discussed by Abraham (1) who named it "identification with a part-object."

Identification with a Part-Object

In the unconscious of the stutterer we recognize three such part-objects: breast and phallus in a state of ablation from the body and the resultant complement—the castrated body.* From direct statements and reconstructions, we learned that the subjective state in the part-objects consisted of feelings of incompleteness, separation, helplessness, even death. These subjective states were charged with aggressive energy rather than self-love and filled with what Federn (9) called "unsatisfied

---

* These pathological ego-states may be elaborations of normal early and transient phases of ego-development which have been called pleasure-ego (16) and mouth-ego (24). Obviously these multiple personalities are quite different from those to which Wittels (34) referred as "phantoms" representing identifications among transference neurotics with individuals as total objects. Fuller discussion of this problem was contained in two papers read by the author before the New York Psychoanalytic Society, abstracts of which have appeared in the *Psychoanalytic Quarterly* (17), (18).

narcissism." The fourth of the multiple personalities, operating at the opposite pole from the other three, is that of a total-object, libidinized and idealized to the point of omnipotence and self-sufficiency. The deepest fantasy wish of the part-object is to become or attain the attributes of this narcissistic ego-ideal. Realistic fulfillment, however, as will be shown, is fraught with dangers, among which is the fear of being eaten; hence this fantasy-wish is blocked by defenses. Stuttering results when these strongly cathected archaic images, seeking expression of their libidinal and aggressive aims, tend to give mere symbols the frightening appearance of powerfully realistic acts.

Inhibitions and Passivity

From the first, the monosymptomatic nature of the complaint of stuttering appeared significant. We saw in it an acceptance by the ego of inhibitions which the extensive personality study revealed to be many-sided. Of these inhibitions the patient was unconscious; he had to be made aware of them at the outset. For example, a telephone call might be postponed, ostensibly because the patient disliked to stutter over the telephone. Actually, his stutter represented a wish to block that call which in turn would mean pursuing an active curiosity and then planning a course of action, both of which were inhibited. The stutter thus was an attempt to fortify the inhibition. In another example, a desired vocational goal was not obtained by a patient, and the employer was blamed. At the same time the patient behaved as if he had already obtained the new position, as if in fact he were the employer. Here the stutter represented mainly an attempt to block the articulation of the wish for and act of becoming the other person through passive incorporation. In the two cases the defenses and rationalizations were varied, but the underlying facts in both revealed fears of being active, and defense against these fears through being inhibited. In addition to the reactive passivity, other observations suggested a deep-seated fixation in passivity which might be regarded as primary. Perhaps these were the results, in turn, of the mother's active defense of her appersonating her child and of her behavior based on this tacit assumption of an incontrovertible fact.

Inevitably related to this passivity, was waiting before beginning to act. In reality, this was waiting for the other person, the object, to initiate, so that subject and object could act together and be as one. The phenomena of oscillation and exhibitionism were pressed into the service of the same aim. Oscillation represented a swinging from the behavior of one ego-image to that of the other, that is, from part-object to ideal image. The part-object was unable to act in separation from the ideal image; the ideal image did not have to act as he experienced himself in any case as part of an active ideal union. The exhibitionism might be expressed through quiet posturing or through frantic activity. The aim, however, was the same—loss of self (as part-object) by passive incorporation into the ideal image.

For example, a young man of thirty, returning to treatment after an interruption prior to which his passivity had been discussed at length, began the hour by saying, "What I need is an earthquake." Associations referred to being pushed out and being born. He added, "I expect to be given energy for activity that I ought to have from within." After working-through his dissatisfactions with his job he said, "Where do *we* go from here? Where do *we* start?" This was followed by periods when this problem would not be mentioned at all, as if it were solved by the mere act of discussing it with the therapist. Another patient, dramatizing his hardship in traveling to the therapeutic hour, added that on arrival he felt like an RAF pilot returning from a bombing mission and about to be dined and wined. He complained that the interpretations given him by the therapist were like weak wine and when he was asked a few questions by way of elaboration he fell fast asleep. The sequence of the oral act, talking with the analyst, followed by a period of quiescence in the one case and sleep in the other, indicated the method and the aim of changing from the image of a part-object to that of the narcissistic ego-ideal. However, quiescence

and sleep were also used as a defense against the desired closeness.

Further Defects of Ego-Function

Most of these stuttering patients, feeling discontent with
their state of adjustment to reality, made many efforts at self-
improvement. Analysis of their activity, and of their failure to
attain the desired goal, revealed some of the fundamental defects
of their ego-functions. For example, it is self-evident that to
solve a problem it is essential to have a feeling that one has a
right to solve it. But when the stutterer's ego-image was that
of a dependent part of another person, his feeling in the face
of such a task was that he was being dangerously presumptive
and provocative or that he was usurping the authority of "head-
quarters," felt to be outside of his ego-boundaries, and thus was
being out of bounds. By the same token, such a patient felt that
he had not the "wherewithal," a term frequently used to denote
independent action, mind, and voice, and on a deeper level—
phallus, or libidinized total self. The end result was: being
blocked. The same held true for the functions of imagination,
volition, and synthesis. However, as stated above, within the
scope of doing an assignment in which the individual functioned as a faithful part of a larger entity, considerably greater
plasticity of thinking and action was available to the stutterer.

Apart from having a right or its equivalent (having an
organ), for independent functioning it is also essential that one
have a clear perception of a problem requiring solution. Such
clarity was obscured, in different degrees of intensity, by the
startling fact that many of these stuttering patients acted in
reality and in treatment as if they were walking in their sleep,
or acting-out a dream. The dream-content began with a wish
for complete passivity and was merged with an anxious escape
from the destructive consequences of such extreme passivity.
This was analogous to the merging of their expectant, "waiting"
silence with anxious, tense silence—a defense against expressing
mounting hostility. In real life one often noted their wishful
thinking and daydreaming, accompanied by inhibition and gen-

eral ineffectuality. It was as if they were acting-out their wish to "sleep away" their lives, a combination of nursing and running away. In treatment, it was common to note amnesia for the content of their therapeutic hours, frequent actual drowsiness, and occasional falling asleep. One patient after a lengthy working-through of his drowsiness and falling asleep during his analytic sessions, remarked that ne thought of his treatment prior to this period as sleeping in an expensive hotel. This was understood to mean his deepest wish for change through the archaic method of passively fusing with the ideal, phallic mother in sleep (that is, being eaten and becoming her breast or phallus), and thereafter living-out a dream-state, the feeling of which was one of narcissistic omnipotence and self-sufficiency. At the same time sleep also served as defense against the fear of being incorporated.

Following this patient's attainment of the ability to stay more fully awake, in reality and in transference—a milestone in the treatment—further difficulties emerged, revealing some of his other deep fixations. To fully perceive a problem he had to "grasp" it, "get" it, "bite into" it, "see" it from all angles. In his impatient desire to "drink" it in all at once, with the aid of an encouraging and energetic "feeder," one could recognize the inevitable regression to nursing and drinking, as a defense against his profound fear of oral aggression. However, the regression itself was also feared and defended against. A manifestation of repetitive shifts from attempts to "bite into" to "drinking in" was his jumping from one facet of the problem to the next—his "flightiness" and psychomotor hyperactivity,* culminating in complete failure of understanding.

In these patients the same difficulties pertained to problems of volition, imagination, or action. Inhibition at the beginning of words and sentences, the essence of the stutter, tended to recur at every new step in making use of the various ego-functions. It seemed as if all activity, mental and motor, had come to bear the imprint of the struggle with oral aggression

---

* This may be one explanation of the constancy of these two symptoms in the manic reaction.

which first emerged during nursing. This struggle in the stutterer appeared to antedate the usually stated period of emergence of oral sadism, at the time of eruption of the teeth (2). It seemed to have begun with the vigorous action of the orbicularis oris and masseter muscles used in sucking and biting before the onset of teething. It was rather a fear of aggression emanating toward and from the breast. The mother feared being devoured by the child's vigorous sucking, and the child feared the forceful maternal feedings (3). Later on it also feared biting with its own teeth. A vicious cycle was established in which interference with sucking stimulated and accelerated biting, and inhibition of biting increased the need for sucking.

Difficulties in Identification

Repeatedly the patient's fundamental conflicts oscillated between efforts to adjust to inner and outer pressures with an ego-image of an organ, and efforts to function with an ego-image of an organism. In terms of emotional investment, the stuttering patient tried to establish feelings about mental and motor activity as different and distinct from oral destructiveness or passive annihilation. With regard to aims, he had to shift from archaic fantasies of passivity to realistic plans of activity. In this way the foundation was laid for growth. Sooner or later the patient encountered the need to identify with his therapist. This is a fundamental mechanism of growth. Once more a significant struggle with his fixation took place. The only technique he "knew" was through becoming one with the therapist by passive submission. Because this wish (26) was felt as nursing or yielding or being consumed and overpowered, even annihilated, he often fell prey to shame or conscience qualms, or even to fears of physical attack, the last representing the well-known homosexual panic.

In our experience, it was in this context that anal obscenity was most often elicited in the stutterer. This stutter was the result of an attempt to block its expression. Intrapsychically, obscenity represented reprimands and threats of punishment by the primitive conscience. The early ego-state which functioned with the wish to be incorporated orally and anally, was derisively equated with abdominal contents or feces, and finally threatened with expulsion. This was in line with Nunberg's (32) contention that the sense of guilt followed activity on the oral level, while the need for punishment was mediated by the anal level of instinctual organization. Externally, obscenity stood for a pseudo-aggressive defense against the same passivity. The term "pseudo" here indicates the use of the aggressive instinct for defense.

In addition, the active taking of a new role was also fraught with dangers. In healthy identification, the individual masters the fear of his own aggression toward objects by actively taking the role of another person. Thereby the other person is eliminated, but only symbolically. In reality one cannot literally be another person but can only emulate the role of another. This was difficult for the stutterer because for him symbolic activity was felt as real activity, as illustrated in his speech. However, to make this change from the impossible to the feasible, constituted separation from the person of the therapist. Again, this separation was difficult for the stutterer because it flew in the face of one of his earliest and severest traumatic experiences—the separation anxiety, which lay at the very root of his abortive or multiple identifications. The same drama of identification would be repeated in the last hurdle, the termination of treatment. Here again much stubborn resistance stemming from the fixation in passivity was encountered, requiring repeated working-through.

Summary

The foregoing has been a description of the genesis and nature of stuttering, in the form of decreasing concentric circles, beginning with the infantile and ambivalent character of the anxious mother, the mother-child relationship, the family backgrounds, ego-elements in the character of the stutterer, and their effect on the functioning of the total personality. Then followed more detailed description of defects of ego-functioning, including the stutterer's identification with part-objects, his inhibitions and passivity, his sense of inadequacy, his flight into sleep, his difficulties in identification.

We turn now to a presentation of the special treatment of the disorder, arising out of its genesis and nature.

THERAPEUTIC FEATURES

General

Before elaborating on the recommended therapy for stuttering, a word should be said about types of treatment that are lacking in psychological rationale and therefore are not regarded as therapies of choice. There are numerous types including hypnosis, vocal and rhythmic exercises, and various devices of distraction. In speech therapy which focuses its attention exclusively on the symptom, speech is overemphasized; the patient lives, as it were, to speak. Further, the symptom which is already isolated due to character disturbance is singled out additionally. This only strengthens the resistance to its treatment. When an improvement or cure of the stutter does occur, it is a transference phenomenon and not the result of this or the other exercise or regimen. In line with these therapies, which in the past have often been conducted in groups, a more rational and promising therapy is beginning to evolve, namely group therapy. This is a form of psychotherapy that presupposes identical insights and standards of adequacy substantially similar to those of individual psychotherapy.

This brings us to the therapies of choice for the stutterer. They are: analysis or analytically oriented psychiatric and casework therapy conducted by individual therapists and by a therapeutic team. The basic principles of psychoanalytic therapy serve as the foundation for the treatment of the character distortions. Upon it are engrafted special approaches and emphases which we found useful and appropriate to the specific needs of the stutterer. Needless to say, these special therapeutic features cannot be regarded in isolation, apart from the underlying psychoanalytic foundation or in place of it.

From Organ to Organism

Succinctly stated, treatment of the stutterer is aimed at a transformation of his ego-organization, so that the image and the functioning which were modeled after an organ may become the image and the functioning of a total organism. The stutterer's inhibitions, symptoms, and character traits have flowed from traumatic experiences; of these the first and most fateful was the nursing and early feeding situation. For him significant mental and physical activity had acquired the archaic attributes of eating and speaking. However, the infantile amnesia for these early traumatic events was seldom broken through. Almost all of them had to be reconstructed from later recallable links of the same chain. In the cases of many stutterers, the mother supplied details of the nursing and feeding history.

First and foremost, the passivity-activity equilibrium had to be repeatedly exposed. For a number of reasons, this was difficult. In accordance with his character, the patient preferred to swallow interpretations whole rather than to break up what he was told into usable tools for further observation and validation. Therefore for a long time what he was told was not very usable to him. This contributed to the defense of isolating related phenomena. His passivity also interfered with comprehension and the application of insight, and blocked that expression of affect which is crucial for acquisition of insight. Furthermore, expressions of passivity seldom appeared directly. They had to be worked-out through their defenses, maintained by deep pleasure premiums. Successful defenses of passivity served indirectly as defenses for inhibition of activity.

Defense Reactions to Orality

In the stutterer a number of defenses against oral regression were noted. The most important were the schizoid and masochistic reactions; less important, the depressive, manic, and schizophrenic ones. The schizoid defense (20a) was the most stable and comparatively the least painful; it was observed very frequently. It provided a defensive distance against fears in interpersonal relations. Objects were serenely enjoyed through their representations in the unconscious, though in actual relationships there was a minimum of conscious pleasure.

More baffling was the masochistic defense, which could best be understood in terms of its dynamic content. The wish to become one with the idealized phallic mother was countered by two fears: the fear of complete regression into passivity as a kind of inertia or death; and its opposite—the fear of getting enough satisfaction to be stimulated or maneuvered sooner or later into activity and separation. Against these fears a patient would defend himself by unconsciously maintaining a passive attachment to a "traumatizing" mother-figure, a distorted version of his actual mother. It was she who, as has been indicated, first induced separation anxiety in him through her active feeding and sudden withdrawals, but who also actively dominated him by her control. He became one with her—treated himself aggressively and harshly as he thought she would treat him—and projected this image onto others. An arrangement such as this offered several gratifications: The real mother, even as she was distorted in the child's mind, was authentic. His wished-for ideal mother-figure was not authentic, as she was part of a dangerous outside world and thus could not be trusted. Besides, the relationship offered a vent for much pent-up aggression through complaints and accusations expressed or unexpressed. It was impossible to feel or express one's self in that way toward a non-frustrating parental figure, at least not without much guilt. Since this defense protected the patient chiefly from separation anxiety, gave him the illusion of activity, and served other needs as mentioned above, it offered him much unconscious satisfaction which overbalanced the consciously felt galling dominations, frustrations, and failures. In the main this is the masochistic content as seen in the stutterer.

The complete flight from reality of the schizophrenic, and the pendulum-like contacts of the depressive and manic—defenses that are comparatively much more sweeping than stuttering, rendering it unnecessary—were therefore seen much less often than the schizoid and the masochistic described above, and will not be discussed here.

The following traits of the stutterer had features of masochistic and compulsive reactions: pseudo-activity, a kind of busy work to avoid anxiety associated with waiting or with real activity; or, being busy "to sign the adoption papers", following which it was hoped endless passivity might be enjoyed under more ideal circumstances; or pseudo-aggression, behavior actually provocative or deemed so, aiming among other goals at caricaturing genuine productive activity in extreme terms and thus avoiding it or laughing it out of court. Related to pseudo-aggression was phallic exhibitionism, the character trait of acting as if one's body were a phallus (27). These patients liked to strut or to appear to be doing something for others. Their real aim, however, was passivity—to be incorporated by the onlookers.

Critical Moments: Speaking, Drowsing, Identifying, Weaning

The stutterer's fixation in passivity and his abhorrence of activity, affecting the use of the oral functions and their derivatives—speech and intellectual activity—has an immediate bearing on the therapy of stuttering. Its chief tool was found to be oral expression, affective and intellectual; this was at the same time the patient's battleground. Speech had to come from the therapist and to the patient it meant life and love (13). These he wanted to imbibe, as long as what the therapist had to say did not convey the idea of separation. To the patient, the therapist's silence meant rejection and hostility. Therefore, at the beginning of the treatment, the therapist had no choice but to speak to the stutterer. He might find that he had to initiate conversation, to speak volubly on many subjects. The particular subject matter was of relatively little importance to the patient, compared to the assurance that the therapist would not be sparing of words. He had to pass this important initial test. At this stage even the Socratic method of questions and answers was no substitute for the therapist's speech, as the patient resented being pumped, in what was to him the wrong way.

This early treatment phase resembled early life experiences described by Freud (13) as "the parent's giving words to the child", and described by Ferenczi as the stage of magical omnipotence of words (11). This latter contained elements of omnipotence and magic through gestures and thoughts in addition to the words. These experiences bore a special significance for the stutterer whose conflict, starting with the oral period of development, pivoted so much around activity versus passivity. The first phases of treatment reflected the aim of passing from passive to active oral activity in the complementary roles played by therapist and patient. Beginning actively, the therapist gradually changed to longer periods of silence, interspersed with the activity of offering confrontations and interpretations. The patient experienced this first period as a libidinal feeding. The next period appeared to the patient increasingly tinged with a kind of aggression suggestive of weaning and having a similar aim. His need to shift to complementary roles produced great difficulties for him. When these difficulties were kept in the forefront by the therapist, they had informative and therapeutic value.

On his side, the patient began by imbibing silently and passively. Fairly secure in this he proceeded to speak; often long stretches of speech followed. Before long he was silent again, and needed encouragement for his activity. When such encouragement was not forthcoming he again waited patiently, then became angry and aggressive. Since he feared above all to express his aggression orally, the formerly relaxed, quiet silence was now followed by tense, controlled, fearful silence. This latter silence might be subsequent to the therapist's silence or to some interpretations to which the patient was resistive. The characteristic reaction of the stutterer to silence or to interpretations dealing especially with his passivity was a clouding of consciousness, or drowsiness, often to the point of momentarily falling asleep. This was an overdetermined reaction, the successful working-through of which was most important for the success of the treatment. For one thing, it was a condensed example, in treatment, of his type of relatedness in life —"sleeping away" his days in passive identification with an ideal figure, yet at the same time fearfully withdrawing from it as if he were acting-out a dream. It was a gesture of selectively imbibing libido from those components of the therapist's speech, such as the sound and resonance, that suggested caressing qualities, leading to drowsiness and sleep. Further, it was a "jamming" or braking gesture which meant that the stutterer did not wish to hear, recognize, accept, or apply the logic of the ideational content of interpretation, to wit: that he needed to awake and cease striving to live in a state of psychological symbiosis and escape from external reality; that he needed to become separated, and to have distinct ego-boundaries.

The successful working-through of this reaction often marked a turning point in treatment, leading to more realistic attitudes and behavior, in the transference and in life. However, the pervasive passivity had to be ferreted out from all hiding places in all levels of treatment. To do this meant to confront the stutterer with his character traits, his varied inhibitions and their defenses, and to interpret their meaning and purpose. One example is the character trait of unemotional or "dead-pan" speech. Incidentally, the stutter represents a partially successful attempt at such speech. When there is no aim to block speech at all, as in psychosis, or when discriminate blocking is successful, as in health, there is no stutter.

Another trait in the stutterer is endless doubt about behavior which aims to maintain the inactivity of the status quo. A third characteristic consists of such sexual symptoms as excessive masturbation, premature ejaculation, fellatio, "aspermia," and the use of obscenities. For a time, the passive drives are even strengthened by the open discussion. Their rationalizations seem more compelling as the necessity grows to finally relinquish them, a necessity implicit in the logic of the treatment, and also made explicit by the therapist. Finally, there is the accentuation of the underlying trauma of separation and its resulting anxiety.

The simultaneous struggle to attain pleasure from genuinely active goals has to be experienced by the patient, both in and out of the treatment process while it is still in progress, in order to break the sense of identity between oral destructiveness on the one hand, and mental and motor activity in general on the other. Such identification is felt to be destructive to both patient and therapist. A most fruitful area for this important experience lies in the patient's many futile attempts to identify passively with the therapist. For when the stutterer finally reaches the point where he can actively select and embody elements of the role of another without himself feeling destroyed, he has attained perhaps the most that analytic therapy has to offer—the freeing of the capacity for growth (23).

Toward the end of the treatment the following was often encountered: Because of the long-standing mother identification, sibling and oedipal rivalries had been obscured. The patient had been above the battle. It had been less a matter of competition with sibling or father as a case of hurt feelings of an unrecognized crown prince or matriarch. Often real sibling and oedipal envy and rivalry-feelings first attained their height of awareness late in the treatment process. "Crown prince" and "matriarch" were derivative images of "his majesty, the baby" and his nuclear traumatic separation from the mother. Since such separation was invariably felt as some form of castration, the mother remained as the only meaningful castrator. Therefore such a patient would attempt to heal his castration anxiety even at oedipal levels, that is, in problems of sexual and general potency, through gaining success with women only, while avoiding important contacts with men and the chance to master his difficulties with them.

The tendency to regression was ever-present in treatment. Understandably, termination of treatment activated the characteristic weaning trauma of the stutterer. One such patient, in the last hour before a vacation trip, referred to his proposed driving alone as a fear of losing himself in himself. He well illustrated the decathexis of the ego-boundaries and the resultant introversion. To set a date fairly long in advance proved helpful in mobilizing this anxiety. Empirically we have found that after one or several interruptions and resumptions there was a somewhat greater sense of reality as to the harmlessness of separation. The stuttering type of patient may have a greater need to master his earliest anxiety through such a repetitious acting-out. However this is not advocated as a shorter method. There seems to be no substitute for repetitious working-through of the stutterer's passivity and its defenses.

The secondary gain through illness—that satisfaction derived from a symptom after it is formed, apart from the deeper satisfaction that caused it to form—was rarely observed in patients who were already in treatment. A surgeon once remarked to a colleague that his patients, especially the women who admired him very much, referred to his stutter as cute. He, it might be noted, was not in treatment. The large majority of patients, however, were eager to be rid of their disturbing symptom; this same desire can also be attested to by the existence of so many speech clinics.

In rare instances there was a type of stutter that in its bizarreness definitely attracted a great deal of attention. This was an extreme example of the clonic form of stutter observed among those patients with the most regressed and masochistic characters. There the stutter served masochistic ends comparable to clowning and being the butt of one's own jokes. A few instances of bizarre stuttering were found among the most disturbed and pre-psychotic patients. Incidentally, as mentioned above, with the advent of psychosis based on the giving-up of many of the defenses, the stutter ceased altogether. On the other hand, for the same type of patient, therapy while at times it intensified the stutter, nevertheless robbed it of its bizarre nature.

This is proof of the general fact that the stutter is usually amenable to improvement and to loss of its phobic quality. This latter attainment is especially important, as the speech phobia is a great burden. In turn, disappearance of the phobia loosens the hold of the symptom before it is finally given up entirely, or to all intents and purposes. Indeed, the symptom amelioration takes much less time than the character changes.

TREATMENT ADAPTATION FOR THE STUTTERING CHILD: THE THERAPEUTIC TEAM

In the following we present a few points about the adaptation of these concepts and therapeutic principles for the treatment of the child stutterer on the clinic level (in the optimal sense of that term). So far, however, such adaptation has had a more intensive trial in private practice and an approximate application in only two public clinics. The team consisted of two therapists. These were analysts, psychiatrists, and/or psychiatric case workers. Psychologists were utilized for part of the diagnostic survey. The case workers used had been analyzed and had had advanced experience in case-work. All therapists were regularly supervised.

Based securely upon the logic of the mother's appersonation of her child, one imperative was that from the start separate therapists be assigned to mother and child. One corollary of this logic, amply attested to by experience, was that the mother was able to relinquish her child if she got a substitute for it, in treatment, in the form of her own therapist. Another was that it helped her to see herself as a separate individual. It was found that she usually was able to relinquish her child (a boy in 80 per cent of the cases) if his therapist was a man. From many experiences we learned that treatment of the boy by a female therapist very frequently was interrupted by the mother. Our experience has also been that for the mother herself a woman therapist was preferable, offering as she does a substitute experience and a basis for identification, to counteract her own identification with a narcissistic and masochistic woman, her own mother. The girl stutterer did about equally well with either male or female therapist, but here too the mother's attitude was important. It goes without saying that the therapist of the mother has to have the conviction that the mother is a neurotic individual who has a legitimate and often urgent therapeutic need in her own right. Some therapists who had a splendid capacity for working with children and for identifying with them, were incapable of reaching these mothers precisely because they lacked such conviction.

The program began with a diagnostic survey in which child, mother, and father received separate and joint interviews, extending over at least four or five hours. In addition, projective psychological tests were given by a clinical psychologist to both mother and child. The primary objective of getting anamnestic and observational data was to aid in deciding on the most suitable treatment plan for each case. Severity of the neurosis, degree of flexibility, analyzability of each patient, and practical factors entered into the determination of the specific plan. The following combinations were then decided upon. (For the sake of completeness all possible ones are listed here, though strictly speaking the term "team psychotherapy" referred only to sessions held once a week.) In private practice it was frequently possible to integrate the analysis of one patient with "team psychotherapy" of the other. The combinations were:

Analysis or psychotherapy of the mother as the only therapy. Unexpectedly this method often proved to be efficient for the removal of the stutter as well as for significant characterological improvement in the children. In the younger children the changes were most marked and they were quite real in the adolescents as well.

Analysis or psychotherapy of the mother and concurrent psychotherapy of the child. The age of the children varied from four to sixteen.

Analysis or psychotherapy of the mother and concurrent analysis or psychotherapy of the child. Analysis of the child was limited to the mid- or late-adolescent. The therapy of the mother facilitated and shortened the course of therapy of the child.

It sometimes happened that during the diagnostic survey, the mother for the first time spontaneously verbalized a causal relation between the child's stutter and the family constellation, especially the mother-child relation. This came to her as a shock and a surprise. Then, and later on, she would repeat that it had never occurred to her that she had any pathological relation to, or involvement with, the stuttering child. This was due both to repression and to acting-out of what was in repression, namely that the stutterer was felt to be a part of her. She generally accepted submissively the suggestion that she be treated; up to that point she had masochistically resigned herself to her "destiny."

As soon as the mother entered treatment it became the first task to work-through her acceptance with really mixed feelings of her own need for treatment, a need that became more convincingly apparent in the discussions of her relationship to her own mother. Next it was essential to expose and work-through the pent-up anger and anxiety connected with unresolved deep disappointments and frustrations at the hands of this mother. These affects emerged in discussions of her own fears of separation from her mother and from her stuttering child; they re-emerged when she was helped to become aware of her loss of self. Her masochistic submission was a major defense against fear of separation. To uncover these affects and mental structures, very much time had to be spent; to develop a realistic sense of self, very strong new identifications had to be formed. In all this, it was imperative to go deeply into the influence of her own narcissistic mother. While in principle this is a truism in the most varied disorders, in the treatment of the stutterer's mother, the fear of separation appeared as a unique result of the maternal influence. Two factors seemed to be responsible: the mixture of clutching influences and weaning influences, and the fact that the control exerted was usually quite subtle. The tie to the narcissistic mother and the fear of breaking from her were also related to the patient's rejection of the feminine role, to penis-envy, and to the overinvestment of the unconscious equation: child=penis. In this connection, the treatment also helped to work-out the difference between infantile and feminine dependence. The patient was therefore helped to view her husband not as a disappointing mother-father image, but as a real person to whom she could turn to share in their common problems of raising their child.

Bringing the husband as a real person into the therapeutic picture was a recurrent theme, but became so especially at the time that the mother was ready to work-out her relationship with him. She was generally frigid. As a result of working-out the marital relationship, a psychological shift frequently took place in the relationship when the husband was willing to try to relate to the child and to the wife in a more positive way. The father who at the start of the treatment was in flight as father and husband, had been deliberately excluded from treatment. Now, to aid it, he was deliberately brought in by the boy's therapist for an occasional interview. With the shifts in the mother's and boy's personalities, positive, constructive qualities in the father were freed toward promoting the treatment. He was greatly encouraged, his natural role strengthened, when he was given the feeling that he was the bulwark in the family, and that he was needed by the therapist to stand-by in the treatment of the boy. The several interviews by the boy's therapist exploited the immediate objectives of being informative and explanatory about the boy's behavior that resulted from the treatment and fluctuations in it.

Insofar as the presenting symptom is not attacked directly, as it is not in analytic psychotherapy, the treatment of the stuttering boy or girl is basically no different from the treatment of any neurotic child. Therefore speech therapy per se could not be integrated with it. However, as the stuttering child presents special characterologic features, the treatment has to be modified accordingly. His inordinate separation anxiety, as already mentioned in the treatment of the adult stutterer, makes necessary an informal, completely permissive atmosphere, in which the therapist speaks freely and does not necessarily expect the stuttering child to speak. Such permissiveness is also necessitated by the need to free the child's expressions of anger and aggression through play. Sometimes after only a few weeks the stuttering was lessened when the patient had expressed some of his aggression through the use of toys, through biting, chewing, or smearing activities. Later when he became more involved in the treatment, the stutter tended to reappear, especially in the process of resolving oedipal conflicts. It was noteworthy how in the course of treatment the stuttering child regressed often and deeply, and how this extremely infantile behavior in treatment contrasted with well-contained behavior at home.

After about six months of treatment, there was generally much less concern in the family about the stutter. In quite a number of instances the stutter had disappeared before then. The increase of aggression or recurrence of enuresis during resolution of neurotic behavior naturally irritated the parents for the time being. The smooth progress of the child's treatment was often an indication that the mother's treatment was progressing smoothly. It was noted, interestingly, that her regressive behavior in treatment preceded the child's regression, and further, that by this time the mother was generally aware that she precipitated the regression in the child.

The main reasons for the acting-out of mother and child during treatment were their basic symbiosis, and the characteristic feeling they both had about speech as action. The child was thus induced to "speak" or act-out for the mother, and when he was "taken away" by his therapist, the mother acted-out herself—toward her husband and toward the therapist. In this way her relationships were observed to shift during treatment. The negative transference was constantly kept in the open, along with her related submissive, masochistic trends which together constituted some of the elements for a negative therapeutic reaction. This reaction was frequently encountered, but it was not insurmountable.

SUMMARY

The major dynamic factors in relation to stuttering, which are regarded as significant to the point of being specific, and from which the therapy naturally flows, include the following:

Profound symbiosis exists between mother and child with the result that the ego-images of the child-stutterer are those of part-objects—breast, phallus, castrated body.

Maternal attitudes toward nursing are archaic; toward speech they retain archaic motor and conceptual elements.

Anxiety as to separation from the mother occupies a central position in both the stutterer and his mother.

The paternal role complements and fortifies, less often ameliorates, the maternal role in the pathogenesis of stuttering.

Oral aggression and oral passivity and their defenses serve as prototypes for diverse ego-functions; of these inhibition is the main defense and is structured through schizoidism and masochism.

Because of multiple identifications with part-objects and fixation in passivity, the stutterer is unable to make use of the normal process of identification essential for development.

The chief difficulty in treatment of stutterers is the simulation of active genital, phallic, and anal aims for passive incorporative aims, and the simulation of the quest for realistic objects for the self as object.

The presentation emphasizes critical moments in the treatment which are inseparable from the significant elements in the character structure. A special feature is a pattern cut from deep insight and geared to the needs of treatment of both mother and child on the basis of weekly interviews, a conjoined therapy conducted by a "therapeutic team."

BIBLIOGRAPHY

1. ABRAHAM, K., "A short study of the development of the libido." *Selected Papers,* Chap. XXVI. London, Hogarth Press, 1924.
2. ———, "The process of introjection in melancholia." "Two stages of the oral phase of the libido." *Selected Papers,* London, Hogarth Press, 1924.
3. BERGLER, E., "Three tributaries to the development of ambivalence." *Psychoanal. Quart.,* XVII, 173–182, 1948.
4. COBB, S., *Borderlands of Psychiatry.* Cambridge, Harvard Univ. Press, 1943.

5. CORIAT, I. H., *Stammering, A Psychoanalytic Interpretation.* N. Y. & Wash. D. C., Nerv. & Ment. Dis. Publ. Co., 1928.

6. ———, "The psychoanalytic concept of stammering." *Nerv. Child,* V, No. 2, 167–171, 1943.

7. DESPERT, J. L., "Psychopathology of stuttering." *Am. J. Psychiat.,* No. 99, 881–885, 1926.

8. FEDERN, P., "Some variations in ego-feeling." *Intern. J. Psychoanal.,* VII, 434–444, 1926.

9. ———, Personal communication.

10. FENICHEL, O., *The Psychoanalytic Theory of Neurosis,* Chap. XV. New York, W. W. Norton, 1945.

11. FERENCZI, S., "Stages in the development of the sense of reality." *Sex in Psychoanalysis.* Jones, E. (Tr.) New York, Basic Books, 1950.

12. ———, "On obscene words." Ibid.

13. FREUD, S., *The Interpretation of Dreams.* New York, Macmillan, 1931.

14. ———, Footnote in Victor Tausk—"On the origin of the influencing machine in schizophrenia." *Psychoanal. Quart.,* II, 542, 1933.

15. ———, "Instincts and their vicissitudes." *Collected Papers,* IV. London, Hogarth Press, 1948.

16. ———, "Wit and its relation to the unconscious." *The Basic Writings of Sigmund Freud.* New York, Random House, 1938.

17. GLAUBER, I. P., "Ego development and the character of the stutterer." Paper read before the New York Psychoanalytic Society. May, 1949. In Press. Abstracted in *Psychoanal. Quart.,* XIX, no. 1, 142, 1950.

18. ———, "The mother in the etiology of stuttering." Paper read before the New York Psychoanalytic Society. May, 1950. Abstract in *Psychoanal. Quart.,* XX, No. 1, 160, 1951.

19. ———, "Psychoanalytic concepts of the stutterer." *Nerv. Child,* 172–180, 1943.

20. ———, "A social-psychiatric therapy for the stutterer." *News Letter of Am. Assn. Psychiat. Social Workers.* Autumn, 1944.

20A. ———, "Observations on a primary form of anhedonia." *Psychoanal. Quart.,* XVIII, 67, 1949.

21. HARTMANN, H., "Comments on the psychoanalytic theory of the ego." *Psychoanalytic Study of the Child*, V. New York, Intern. Univ. Press, 1950.

22. ———, "Early development of the ego. Identification in Infancy." *Psychoanal. Quart.*, XX, No. 1, 1951.

23. HENDRICK, I., Remarks in panel discussion on "Psychoanalysis and Character." Mid-Winter Conference, December, 1950.

24. HOFFER, W., "Development of the body ego." *Psychoanalytic Study of the Child*. V. New York, Intern. Univ. Press, 1950.

25. LEWIN, B. D., "Obsessional neuroses." *Psychoanalysis Today*. Lorand, S. (ed.) New York, Intern. Univ. Press, 1944.

26. ———, *The Psychoanalysis of Elation*. New York, W. W. Norton, 1950.

27. ———, "The body as phallus." *Psychoanal. Quart.*, II, 24–47, 1933.

28. LIEBERMANN, H., "On monosymptomatic neuroses." *Int. Ztschr. f. Psychoanal.*, X, 213, 1924.

29. LOWENSTEIN, R. M., "The problem of interpretation." *Psychoanal. Quart.*, XX, No. 1, 1–14, 1951.

30. MEYER, BERNARD C., Oral discussion synopsis. (See reference No. 18) "Psychosomatic aspects of stuttering." *J. Nerv. & Ment. Dis.*, CI, 127, 1945.

31. *New Standard Dictionary*. New York, Funk & Wagnalls, 857, 1925.

32. NUNBERG, H., "The sense of guilt and the need for punishment." *Intern. J. Psychoanal.*, VII, 64–78, 1926.

33. ORTON, S. T., *Reading, Writing and Speech Problems in Children*. New York, W. W. Norton, 1937.

34. WITTELS, F., "Unconscious phantoms in neurotics." *Psychoanal. Quart.*, VIII, 141–163, 1939.

▶ PSYCHOTHERAPEUTICS OF ALCOHOLISM

By Ruth Fox, M.D.

INTRODUCTION

One of the simplest and most practical of all the classifications of alcoholics so far attempted is that of Knight (10), and Haggard and Jellinek (8). They categorize abnormal drinkers as: symptomatic drinkers, primary addicts, and secondary addicts. The symptomatic drinkers are the fewest numerically and they are relatively unimportant as alcoholics except as they pose a problem in diagnosis. They are the persons whose drinking is endogenously determined. Drinking with them is secondary to some well-defined mental illness such as schizophrenia, manic-depressive psychosis, etc. It is usually only one of many symptoms and may actually be quite superficial. Generally, the underlying morbid condition can be diagnosed by a careful life history, by minute scrutiny of drinking behavior (which is often bizarre), by the use of projective tests, and by a study of the individual psychodynamics involved.

The primary addict is one whose drinking is also endogenously determined, but he differs from the symptomatic drinkers in that he has no other demonstrable mental illness except his alcoholism. He seems to have a definite need for alcohol and as soon as he is introduced to it he uses it as an aid to adjust to his environment. It seems that only through the use of intoxicants can he achieve a psychological state of harmony. He craves the effect that alcohol produces, and as he can obtain this with relatively small amounts, he often escapes, or at least postpones, the physical and mental damage of those who require large

---

* Director, Alcoholics Treatment Center of New York City; Chairman, New York Medical Committee on Alcoholism.

amounts of alcohol. Even before he began to drink, he was a sick individual showing many neurotic and sometimes psychopathic features. Bacon (1) describes him "as one whose emotional development was unhealthy from infancy or childhood on. The maladjustment might be seen as an inability to compete with equals or superiors without feeling extreme anxiety or apprehension of undefined, future pain. Or it might be seen as an unusual fear of contact with those of the opposite sex, or as a general conception of the self as unworthy, inefficient, and socially awkward . . . Alcohol allows him relief from whatever his problem may be." Later comes remorse and guilt for his behavior under alcohol, assuaged by more alcohol, until a vicious circle is initiated. Added to his own sense of unworthiness comes apparent confirmation from family, friends, employer, etc., who begin to use punishment, threats, and withdrawal of affection and approval. This unbearable state is then drowned out by further alcohol.

The secondary addicts do not form a clearcut group, "since the origins of their drinking habits are heterogeneous and no single personality type predominates . . . Their drinking is exogenously determined." (5) They are persons who at the onset of drinking do not have any special psychological need for alcohol but who develop this need and become addicted as a result of many years of consistently heavy "social drinking." In their younger years they have a high tolerance for alcohol and can often drink prodigious amounts, so that when they do break down, usually in the 40's or 50's, mental and physical changes are apt to be evident. These may be delirium tremens, Korsakoff's psychosis, polyneuropathy, advanced liver disease, or merely a deterioration of the personality. This is the group which is often termed the "chronic alcoholic." They are differentiated from the primary addicts in that their early psychological adjustment to life was apparently fairly good, many had previously excelled in their work and many have real accomplishments behind them.

Secondary addicts have a much better prognosis in treatment than primary addicts, provided they come for help before the physical and mental changes have become irreversible. As they had once attained a fair degree of adjustment they have something to return to in sobriety. The primary addicts, however, never having learned the techniques of living, have a much harder time of it.

There is pretty general agreement that compulsive drinking may be a symptom of any underlying personality maladjustment, and that the soil in which alcoholism grows is almost always the neurotic character. The personality traits most often present show a profound emotional immaturity which may denote a lack of development in the primary addicts, or a regression in the secondary addicts and symptomatic drinkers. It is also generally agreed that addictive drinking, though "merely" a symptom, can assume the proportions of a disease in itself with a profound alteration of the total personality. An important part of the disease entity is the gradual but eventual withdrawal of the alcoholic from all social participation and responsibility.

THERAPY OF ALCOHOLISM

Since alcoholism has no single cause (or if it has we do not know it as yet) and since it may be symptomatic of many underlying pathological conditions—psychological, physiological, or social, or, most often, all three—therapy can be expected to succeed only if each case is studied individually in its many aspects. Just as the causes are many and various, so are the effects. We know that one cannot become a problem drinker without an involvement of the total personality in the progressive process of addiction. Thus the task of rehabilitation is a long and often complicated one, in which we need all the help we can get. We need the cooperation of psychologists, social workers, nurses, experts in vocational guidance and recreation, hospitals and rest homes, schools, colleges, courts, churches, social and fraternal organizations, Alcoholics Anonymous, etc. Because of the necessity of this team work, I think the individual alcoholic is best treated in special outpatient centers or clinics such as those now operated by a few of the states.

In spite of the public health aspect of the problem, the personal relationship of the alcoholic patient to his therapist is a peculiarly close one. Without a deep and lasting rapport and a mutual respect, I do not believe there will be a successful outcome to treatment. Indeed, psychotherapy starts with the very first interview, whether it is with a receptionist, a social worker, or a doctor—and whether the patient is drunk, in the depths of a hangover, or in a free interval. The therapist takes the cue from the patient, as it were, responding to each of these phases of the illness differently but at all times in a friendly way. The therapy required for each phase is quite distinctive: treatment which might be good in one phase might be bad in another. One has to develop a certain flexibility not usually demanded in the treatment of other illnesses, but as a result, more often than not, one will be rewarded by a cooperative patient.

Many secondary addicts, if given some counseling and help for the immediate disaster which has resulted from their drinking, and if deeply convinced that the bulk of their problems are the result of alcohol, can get their affairs in order and function quite well, by the mere removal of alcohol from their lives. In a great many cases they need only short-term therapy with the opportunity for further interviews if or when the going gets rough. During the first few shaky weeks and months, "Antabuse" may make the difference between success and failure. Alcoholics Anonymous also can often help this patient with his fears, his sense of inferiority, and his isolation. There, perhaps for the first time in his life, he finds friends who do not punish and condemn him—no matter how "bad" he has been—and gradually his preoccupation with himself may shift to an interest in helping other alcoholics to recover. Alcoholics Anonymous is based on sound psychiatric principles and does much that no psychotherapy can do.

For the neurotic drinker and for the primary addict, psychotherapy is imperative. It is my feeling that the psychotherapeutic approach must differ in several respects from the usual procedure with "merely" neurotic cases. Though it is admitted that excessive drinking is a symptom of an underlying personality disturbance, the symptom gets out of hand and may over-shadow all other manifestations. Tiebout (20) likens it to a fever which one treats specifically for itself, regardless of its cause, once it becomes high enough to threaten life. Thus, early in psychotherapy, one must tackle the drinking itself to which the alcoholic has become a victim. Alcohol can be looked on almost as an outside force against which the patient carries on an endless struggle.

One of the most important tasks of psychotherapy is to bring the patient to the point of accepting his inability to drink. This is only a part of his total unwillingness to accept reality and it may take months or years of painstaking analysis before the partipotent (18), in contrast to the omnipotent, attitude of the normal adult becomes fixed in the personality.

There are different degrees of the ability to accept reality which are directly proportional to the ego-strength of the individual. We know the ego-strength is low in an alcoholic who comes for treatment, and we must be prepared to give him much support in the early months of treatment. This can be done through a strong transference relationship, through the ego-building of A.A., or through the protective influence of "Antabuse." Since one cannot analyse an alcoholic while he is drinking, or at least make much progress, these adjuncts to treatment are extremely important.

One of the outstanding characteristics of alcoholics is the low frustration tolerance which is present perhaps in most orally fixated individuals. Also, the patient's great dependency and the unsatisfied longing to be loved and approved of must be partially gratified before a working relationship can be established. Once established, analysis of transference and resistance can proceed as in any other analysis, with special emphasis on the unique function alcohol has played in each individual. Alcohol may have served to overcome a sense of inadequacy by giving a spurious self-esteem, or it may have been the means of rebelling against society or asserting independence against present or past authority figures. There is deep and intense hostility which is often repressed and acted-out during drinking bouts. There is an ever-present guilt in the drinker due to the strong instinctual drives, both aggressive and sexual, which are lived-out under the influence of alcohol—either actually or in fantasy. A strong primitive superego besets the alcoholic when sober, and prohibits all such instinctual gratification. As therapy proceeds, these drives can be recognized and expressed in less destructive behavior.

Techniques of Treating the Acute Phase

The majority of the patients coming to a clinic for alcoholics come during a free interval or during the stage of hangover, but a few come intoxicated. These last are admittedly disruptive of schedules, yet somehow time should be found for them if at all possible. Some may need hospitalization to pull out of their benders, but an astonishing number can be sobered up through office procedure alone. Even in a short informal interview a great deal can be learned about a patient. Observations on the type of behavior under alcohol can give valuable clues for later understanding of the psychodynamics involved. The very acceptance of the patient as ill rather than perverse may be the first step in rehabilitation.

At the Alcoholics Treatment Center in New York City we have worked out a technique which is proving helpful to those who are not too drunk or who are in the hangover state. After a few words of reassurance, we explain in a simple way that much of the craving for alcohol can be abolished by supplying certain things that the body lacks because of drinking rather than eating. We then give the patient 2 gms. of salt, 500 mgs. of vitamin C by mouth, and a quart of milk to drink. Vitamin B complex is given by injection. Unless the patient has specific complaints or shows evidence of injury, we generally omit a physical examination in this state, except for blood pressure reading. If there is restlessness and nervousness we may give one grain of phenobarbital and suggest that the patient lie down on one of the cots kept in a quiet room for this purpose. This suggestion is almost always gratefully accepted, and the patient will sleep for two or three hours. Usually he wakes feeling refreshed. If no doctor is available at this point, some other member of the staff gets a little more information, offers him coffee or coca cola or further milk. Another short interview with the doctor or nurse, more salt and vitamin C, possibly more phenobarbital, occasionally adrenal cortical extract in those patients with low blood pressure, some sedatives for the night, and a little discussion of alcoholism in general, with an outline of various therapies, will almost invariably bring the patient back sober and grateful the next morning. Tolserol,* 1-2 gms., is given with instructions that it be taken on awakening in the morning to control any tremor. In these cases, Social Service may be equally as important as the supportive psychotherapy or the medication, for the patient may be totally without funds or a place to sleep.

It should be noted that alcohol is not given in a tapering-off process. Indeed there are very few doctors treating alcoholics who still advocate this. By the above treatment the phenomenon of craving is so quickly abolished that patients rarely ask for alcohol. Psychologically, it is important to demonstrate that in order to feel better they do not need alcohol.

Treatment of Hangover

Far from being the legitimate butt of humorists, the hangover is a serious, ever-recurring crisis in the lives of problem drinkers. It is so unbearably painful that many of them postpone facing it by taking more and more alcohol until the body finally rebels. The physiological and psychological components of the hangover are inextricably mixed, and both must be treated. As Lolli (12) has pointed out, as the blood level of alcohol falls the organism is unable to cope with the overwhelming excitations suddenly flooding it. He compares the nameless fears of the hangover to those of a traumatic neurosis. As sensibility and awareness of reality return with sobriety, the initial tension which preceded and precipitated the bout is magnified. Self-confidence, always basically low, is

---

* Tolserol is the trade name (Squibb) for Mephensin.

shattered and the hunger for love and approval seems now to remain unsatisfied forever. The patient is in a state of acute emotional decompensation.

If, at this moment of inner hopelessness and helplessness, condemnation comes from the outside also, the alcoholic may turn further in on himself, may react with deep depression or, unable to endure the terrible loneliness, isolation, and loathing for himself, he may try to drink again or to kill himself. Or he may project all the blame outward and become aggressive.

If, on the other hand, in his crisis he finds real understanding and sympathy, actual help for his physical pain, and genuine interest in him and his problems, his resistance and hostility may suddenly melt, and much material of dynamic value may be poured out. In a sober interval it might take many sessions to get the equivalent; and it might never come again with an emotion so deep and so convincing to the patient.

During the hangover state, the patient should be seen daily to cement the early gains. As tension decreases and the patient's control over his impulses strengthens, he will probably want to forget his recent helplessness. He may want to deny it altogether and with it his whole problem of alcoholism. The daily interview (with its implied acceptance of the patient as a worthwhile individual as well as a sick one) will give him courage to face himself, possibly for the first time. The therapist may come to be considered his "alter ego," and his dependence on alcohol may shift to dependence on the therapist. In a later working-through of the transference and resistance, the patient should be able to give up both dependencies and to replace his flight-reaction by a more mature handling of his problem.

Treatment during a Free Interval

Most patients come into a treatment center for alcoholics during a sober period between bouts. If they come voluntarily, this implies that they have at least partially "surrendered," to use Tiebout's phrase (19), but if they are dragged in by an irate wife or sent by the court, it may mean nothing but surly submission to the inevitable. I agree with the oft-repeated statement that unless the patient wants to get well, no power on earth can keep him sober. However, this wanting to get well is a highly complex and variable thing (2). A given patient may want to get well at 11 a.m., but not at 4 p.m.; or he may want to when talking with an ex-alcoholic but decidedly not when talking to his wife; or he may insist with apparent sincerity that he does want to get well, but to him this may mean only that he wishes to be helped to feel better physically so that he can then enjoy alcohol again. He may honestly wish to get well yet not realize that this means total abstinence for as long as he lives. Or he may consciously want very much to change the conduct of his life but unconsciously cling to the old infantile patterns. In short, in each case one must study the motivation for recovery. No alcoholic will ever give up alcohol until he can envisage for himself a life without alcohol as more satisfactory than one with alcohol.

INITIAL INTERVIEW. In the first interview the therapist gauges the patient's assets and liabilities, his beliefs and attitudes, as well as the practical aspects of the case. One must discuss frankly the nature of alcoholism, the concept of it as a treatable illness, answer the questions about the various available types of therapy, and elicit the patient's interest and cooperation. A dispassionate but friendly and non-moralizing attitude may swing the patient over from a rebellious, angry, hurt, and hopeless person, to one who is friendly and hopeful. This is an absolutely necessary first step for the patient. For those who can take this step, the prognosis for ultimate recovery is good.

There are, of course, many excessive drinkers who are not at all ready to stop drinking. The advantages of drinking may still outweigh the disadvantages. As the A.A.'s put it, they have not as yet "hit bottom." They may still have jobs or private incomes, may still have wives or husbands who will take care of them and cover up for them. They are still "getting away with drinking" and see little reason to give it up. Among the wealthy group, this cushioning against the consequences of drinking may delay treatment for a long time. All one can do with such a patient is to point out the facts about alcoholism and its inevitable downhill course, and to determine with him just where he personally is in this descent. One must be friendly but firm about the facts and the inevitability of the outcome if drinking continues. If possible, an inroad should be made on the feeling of invulnerability so characteristic of the alcoholic. One invites the alcoholic to look at facts, but he will see only those facts which he wishes to see. The frank appraisal of the situation by the therapist, however, may plant a seed which will later bear fruit. Such a patient may then return in one month, six months, or even in several years, ready for real therapy.

PHYSICAL AND SOCIAL REHABILITATION. When the patient has finally accepted the fact that he needs help, one must determine which type of therapy or, usually, which combination of therapies is indicated. Though it seems too obvious to mention, physical rehabilitation is an essential beginning.

In evaluating the social situation of each patient, a psychiatric social worker or specially trained counselor is extremely valuable. Some member of the family, preferably the spouse, should be seen at least once or twice, but probably more frequently, for a series of interviews. His (or her) attitude toward treatment may make the difference between success or failure in the outcome. In a study of the wives of alcoholics, Gladys Price (17) found that many of them were basically dependent people who became hostile and aggressive toward their husbands on finding them also dependent. The husband's drinking is often interpreted by the wife as a rejection or lack of love, and so "to get even" she may become more and more demanding, or may assume more and more responsibility. In either case, the husband feels less and less adequate. The wife may even fight treatment for her husband, usually unconsciously, since his alcoholism is continuing proof of her own superiority and his inadequacy. Boggs (4) speaks of this need to treat the "alcoholic marriage." The wife is just as important a person as the husband and should be made to feel so. For example, the maternal type of wife may fear that her husband will no longer need her if he recovers. By the auxiliary help available after getting the various members of the family to modify their attitudes and behavior, the psychotherapeutic progress of the alcoholic can be greatly speeded up.

Psychological Study of the Patient

Before deciding what type of psychotherapy is needed, there should be a clinical evaluation by a trained psychiatrist. Since even a severe alcoholic can put up a very good front when he is not drinking, several interviews may be needed. The patient's own statements should be checked and as objective a picture of him as possible should be obtained from relatives. A description of the patient's behavior when not drinking as well as when intoxicated is indispensable. When alcohol brings out wild, bizarre, chaotic or extremely brutal acts, one should consider an underlying psychosis, psychopathy, or possibly an organic involvement, for in almost all cases the drunken behavior gives the clue to the unresolved conflicts. It is valuable for the psychiatrist to see this himself, but if he cannot, a good description will suffice.

In diagnosis and prognosis projective tests may be of definite help. At the Alcoholics Treatment Center in New York City we use Rorschach, Bellevue-Wechsler, Word Association, and Figure Drawing routinely. Occasionally the Thematic Apperception Test is given. (The figure drawings of alcoholics have been studied by Minear (16) who contrasts them with drawings of normals and psychoneurotics.) Each drawing is scored on a five-point scale, as suggested by Machover (14). We are now paying more attention to this test and find it simple to give, since it requires very little time, is difficult to falsify, and in its application there is no barrier of education or language.

Each patient also fills out an exhaustive questionnaire which covers vital data, childhood influences, personality study of parents, siblings, and patient; psychosexual development; marital, educational and employment history; entanglement, if any, with the law; previous therapy, and a study of the drinking pattern in minute detail. When all the data on the patient has been collected, a staff conference is held and a tentative diagnosis is made on each case as to whether the patient is a symptomatic drinker, a primary addict, or a secondary addict, and a tentative plan of therapy is mapped out.

After eliminating the psychotics and organic cases which are referred elsewhere for appropriate treatment, an estimate is made of the depth of the psychopathology in the primary and secondary addicts. In the primary addict the involvement is more profound. He is an inadequate, immature person with personality maladjustments before his drinking began. Drinking usually started early and was pathological from the start. He has grandiose hopes but has rarely achieved any degree of success in school, work, marriage, or social life. For him psychotherapy can be successful, but it is apt to take a long and stormy course with frequently recurring slips, and the protection of a hospital during treatment may be necessary. However, "Antabuse" may be successful in maintaining sobriety during the period of psychotherapy.

The secondary addict, on the other hand, though he may present an identical picture at the onset of treatment, is a much more hopeful prospect for treatment. His drinking has generally become a problem only after years of excessive social drinking, and he frequently gives a history of former good adjustment in work, in marriage, and in social life. More careful study will reveal that although neurotic conflicts were present before he became alcoholic, his neurotic defenses allowed him to function in an apparently normal manner. As Bacon (2) has pointed out, he once used socially acceptable channels of self-expression and with treatment can be brought to use them again.

It is important to group the patients according to the severity of neurotic involvement. The least sick include the so-called "normal" drinkers and the secondary addicts. These will probably do well on almost any kind of therapy provided they have truly accepted the fact that they are alcoholics, and the further fact that being alcoholic means that they can never again drink socially. If there is deep conviction on these two points, plus an equally deep conviction that recovery is possible, it makes little difference what type of therapy is chosen. Alcoholics Anonymous, "Antabuse," superficial supportive therapy, a period of hospitalization, clinic outpatient therapy, aversion treatment, Salvation Army, a re-entry into church work, etc.— any of these will work singly or in combination. Perhaps the chief function of the therapist in helping this type of patient (representing perhaps 50% of all alcoholics) is to inspire him to believe in the possibility of recovery and then to help him choose which type of treatment is best suited for him.

Alcoholics Anonymous

The remarkable accomplishments of Alcoholics Anonymous attest the value of this social and religious approach to therapy of alcoholics. Often the greatest service to the alcoholic and his family is in getting the patient to accept the fellowship of this group. Though every alcoholic cannot or will not accept A.A., for those who can there are so many immediate and lasting advantages that every effort should be made to see that a suitable contact is made. Except in the completely irreligious and in the deeply neurotic or psychotic alcoholics, A.A. can be the mainstay of treatment, or indeed, the only treatment needed. Psychiatrists, ministers, and sociologists have studied this group approach of A.A. and have tried to interpret its success. The movement has drawn much from both medicine and religion and is a great therapeutic weapon. As one of the founders has said (15), "A.A. is a society where men and women understand each other, where the clamors of self are lost in our great common objective, where we can learn enough of patience, tolerance, honesty, humility and service to subdue our former masters, insecurity, resentment, and unsatisfied dreams of power."

Tiebout (21) believes that through the force of religion in an atmosphere of hope and encouragement, the typically egocentric and narcissistic alcoholic personality, dominated by defiant individuality and drives for omnipotence, undergoes a profound change by the acceptance of the A.A. program. The prevailingly negative characteristics of aggression, hostility, and isolation are replaced by peace and calm and a lessening of inner tension. This change—or conversion—may come suddenly with cataclysmic force: however, in most cases it is effected gradually through the living-out of the program. The defiant individual no longer defies help, but accepts it and allows positive feelings, such as love, friendliness, and contentment, to replace his former feelings of restlessness and irritability. Perhaps those alcoholics who are able to accept the program of A.A. without at the same time undergoing intensive psychotherapy are secondarily addicted.

Aversion Treatment

The purpose of the conditioned reflex (11) type of treatment is to establish an aversion to the sight, smell, taste, and thought of alcoholic beverages. It is done by administering emetine, which produces nausea and vomiting of alcoholic drinks. The technique of the treatment must be carefully learned and meticulous attention to detail is required. During a period of sobriety from four to six treatments are given in a hospital, usually one every other day, and later reinforcing treatments are given throughout the first year. At the Shadel Sanitarium in Seattle, Washington, in addition to the conditioning itself, there is a great deal of informal psychotherapy both with members of the staff and with other patients. The counselors who undertake the rehabilitation work are all former patients who act as living examples of the possibility of recovery. They help in a practical way also with family problems, job placement, recreation, etc.

A recent follow-up of over 5,000 patients treated during the past 14 years at the Shadel Sanitarium gives an over-all abstinence rate of 51 per cent for the period covered by this survey.

"Antabuse" Therapy

About four years ago it was discovered accidentally in Denmark that the organic compound tetraethylthiuram disulfide had the peculiar property of rendering anyone who took it extremely sensitive to alcohol. The possibility of using it to control alcohol addiction was immediately investigated. After three years of intensive research, covering over 12,000 cases in 100 investigating centers, it was released for prescription use in the United States by the Pure Food and Drug Administration in October, 1951. Its mode of action apparently is to block some enzyme system in the liver necessary for the complete metabolism of acetaldehyde. (Acetaldehyde is one of the intermediate products of alcohol breakdown in the body.) The resulting accumulation of acetaldehyde is responsible for the toxic symptoms which occur when an individual who is saturated with "Antabuse" drinks alcohol. These symptoms are flushing, palpitation, difficulty in breathing, pounding headache, sense of apprehension, and frequently nausea and vomiting. There may be an abrupt and alarming fall in systolic blood pressure, so that a picture very like that of surgical shock may occur. The severity of the reaction depends on the previous dose of "Antabuse," upon the amount of alcohol imbibed, and upon the type of patient. Two or three hours after the alcohol has been given the patient falls asleep and wakes refreshed a few hours later. My own experience with "Antabuse" covers two and a half years of work on approximately 300 patients. My study covered three objectives: to determine the safety or non-safety of the drug; to establish the type of alcoholic on whom it might work; and to evaluate the long-term results of its use.

During the first year of work on the first 149 patients, "Antabuse" was not given until after one week of sobriety and only if the results of a complete physical examination, intensive laboratory work, electrocardiogram, chest x-ray, and psychological tests were within normal limits. The patient was given four pills the first day, three the next, then two a day for the next two days. On the fourth day the patient was hospitalized and given an alcohol-"Antabuse" test dose. It consisted of 1-3 ounces of whiskey which invariably brought on the typical symptoms described above. These were truly alarming in many cases, with unconsciousness and collapse in several.

In addition, I found about half the patients had toxic effects from the "Antabuse" itself even before the test dose of alcohol. These symptoms varied from slight malaise, fatigue, headache, and gastro-intestinal disturbance to motor incoordination, difficulty in concentrating, peculiar floating sensations, hypochondriacal preoccupation, anxiety, depression and lethargy. After reassurance to the patient that these effects were due to the withdrawal of alcohol (which I do not now believe) and not to "Antabuse," I sent them home on 1½ tablets a day for the next 2-3 weeks, asking them to call if there continued to be the above symptoms. In a few men impotence developed, and in several the above symptoms became progressively worse. Fifteen cases, or 10 per cent, developed mild psychotic reactions lasting from a few hours to a week or ten days after discontinuance of the "Antabuse." Prodromal signs of psychosis were drowsiness, fatigue, indisposition to work, and mild depression. Next there developed disorientation with amnesia for the preceding few weeks, with a replacement of the lethargy by restlessness, insomnia, and anxiety. In some there were paranoid delusions and hallucinations, and in others a manic-like type of overactivity. A number of other investigators describe similar reactions (13), (6), (7), (3). Gottesfeld and his co-workers (6) at the Blue Hills Clinic in Hartford reported that eight of their 42 patients developed these transitory episodes. The clinical picture resembles the schizophrenic reaction pattern in most cases.

Because of these severe side reactions from "Antabuse" alone and because of the collapse-like symptoms during the "Antabuse"-alcohol reaction, the dosage of "Antabuse" and the quantity of alcohol used in the test dose were drastically reduced in the last 150 of our cases. I now give one pill daily for 2-3 weeks before giving the test dose in the hospital. Three-fourths to one ounce of whiskey will generally elicit a mild but sufficient reaction of flushing, malaise, headache, and palpitation. If such a reaction has not occurred in 20 to 30 minutes, the same amount or less of whiskey may be repeated. After this test, the daily maintenance dose of "Antabuse" is cut to one-half tablet (.25 gm.). In some cases it may be cut to one-fourth tablet. With this new dosage schedule of "Antabuse," we have treated 151 cases without any adverse symptoms to date. The sensitization effect takes place within 3-4 hours after the first dose of "Antabuse" but does not reach its maximum until 12-24 hours later. No tolerance to the drug occurs on prolonged administration, and it seems not to be habit forming. It should *never be used for sobering up and should never be given without the patient's full knowledge and consent. Otherwise death could occur from the rapid drinking of 2-3 ounces of whiskey.*

We have found it unnecessary in most cases to wait for one week of sobriety before starting "Antabuse." It may be given after 24-48 hours, provided the patient is in good physical and mental condition and provided there is some member of the family or a friend to take over the responsibility of administering the pills. The patient signs a waiver of responsibility and is given an identification card which reads as follows:

TO WHOM IT MAY CONCERN:
            The bearer of this card,
is taking the drug *ANTABUSE*. This drug alone is harmless, but when combined with alcohol, symptoms of flushing, perspiration, redness of eyeballs, difficulty in breathing, palpitations, vomiting and low blood pressure will be observed. If such a reaction occurs and is severe, please call Dr. . . . . (Tel. No.) or the emergency ward of the nearest hospital. Treatment should consist of coramine 2 to 4 cc. intramuscularly and Vitamin C 1000 mg. intravenously. Oxygen and saline solution 1000 cc. intravenously may also be necessary for shock.

Until more is known about the drug, I believe it is imperative that the same complete physical, laboratory, and psychological work-up be instituted on each patient, as was required during the period of investigation.

It is my conclusion that indiscriminate use of "Antabuse" by physicians who have not studied it in detail can be not only ineffective but dangerous. "Antabuse" is useful mainly as an adjunct to psychotherapy, and its use should be limited to those physicians who are prepared to give each patient the many hours and painstaking attention he will need to recover from his addiction. Good psychotherapeutic technique means special training, as in any other specialty of medicine. "Antabuse" should not be given to those with suicidal tendencies, nor to vagrants, psychopaths or psychotics. Though there are no proved contraindications to "Antabuse" therapy in modified doses, special caution is required in the following types of cases: arteriosclerotic heart disease, cirrhosis of the liver, diabetes, tuberculosis, convulsive disorder, and Korsakoff's psychosis. However, with the exception of the last mentioned, I have successfully given "Antabuse" in all of the other conditions mentioned.

As in any other method of treating alcoholism, the results of "Antabuse" therapy depend on the general management of the case, the sincerity of the desire on the part of the patient to stop drinking, the degree of premorbid personality adjustment, and the personality and ability of the therapist. In the fairly normal secondary addict, the results can be expected to be very good even with a minimum of psychotherapy. In the primary addicts, however, long and intensive psychotherapy may yield meager results despite "Antabuse" combined with A.A., environmental manipulation, group therapy, etc. Though psychopaths may do well for a very short time, they invariably revert to drinking. The real derelict type is so undersocialized and so unable to cope with life that he rarely if ever wishes to stop drinking and here the problem is largely a sociological one.

A detailed statistical report covering the 300 cases treated with "Antabuse" at the Alcoholics Treatment Center in New York City is being prepared for publication at an early date. There have been no harmful effects as measured by periodic physical examinations or laboratory tests; in fact, the patients have in general improved remarkably in health and sense of well being.

The results of treatment with "Antabuse" are unusually consistent from investigator to investigator. The reports of most value are those which cover the longest time since the institution of treatment. Dr. Ebbe Hoff (9) has made a recent survey of 200 alcoholics who had been treated for periods from 10 months to one year. One hundred received "Antabuse" and one hundred served as a control group. Both groups received equivalent psychotherapy and social rehabilitation. A period of two-and-a-half years has elapsed since the study began, so this evaluation is of particular importance. Table I summarizes Dr. Hoff's findings. When corrected statistically, especially as regards age, it is found that in the 35-49 age group, 64 per cent of those who were given "Antabuse" could be rated as socially recovered, while only 36 per cent of the control group of the same age could be so classified.

TABLE I

	100 cases who Received "Antabuse"	100 cases who did not Receive "Antabuse"
CLASSIFICATION I Patients who have maintained sobriety since beginning treatment	39%⎤	31%⎤
CLASSIFICATION II Patients who have maintained sobriety after one relapse	20%⎦ } 59%	11%⎦ } 42%
CLASSIFICATION III Patients who have shown improvement in family relations, who have lengthened periods of sobriety, whose drinking sprees are materially reduced, and whose employment is on a considerably improved basis	15%	19%
CLASSIFICATION IV No improvement	20%⎤	23%⎤
CLASSIFICATION V Died, unclassified or could not locate	6%⎦ } 26%	16%⎦ } 39%

SUMMARY

In summary, we should stress again that alcohol addiction may be a symptom of any underlying personality maladjustment; that the soil in which alcoholism grows is almost always the neurotic character; that this neurotic pattern was formed in infancy or early childhood because of disturbances in the relationship of the child to the significant persons with whom he came in contact; that the vicissitudes in the early life of an alcoholic are no different from those which underlie neurosis, psychosis, or psychopathy, i.e. the choice of symptom may be influenced by many factors, perhaps both constitutional and environmental; that the egocentricity and immaturity characteristic of the alcoholic may denote a lack of development in the primary addicts or a regression in the secondary addicts; that in addition to the profoundly disorganizing effect of excessive drinking on the psyche, there are accompanying physiological disturbances; and finally, we might point again to the fact that this illness is an extremely complex one with not only medical and psychiatric aspects but social ones as well. To control and prevent it will take the combined efforts of many types of therapies but, most of all, it takes an informed public. We can take courage and comfort in the realization of the excellent beginnings which have been made in the past decade. A short ten years ago we had almost nothing to offer, whereas now we have a great deal.

BIBLIOGRAPHY

1. BACON, S. D., Alcoholism: Its extent, therapy, and prevention. *Federal Probation*, XI, No. 2, 1947.
2. ———, Alcoholism: Nature of the problem. *Federal Probation*, XI, No. 1, 1947.
3. BENNETT, A. E., McKEEVER, L. G. AND TURK, R. E., Psychotic reaction during tetraethylthiuram disulfide ("Antabuse") therapy. *J. Amer. Med. Assn.*, CXXXXV, 483–484, Feb. 17, 1951.
4. BOGGS, M. H., Role of social work in the treatment of ine-

briates. *Q. J. Studies on Alcohol,* IV, 557–567, March, 1944.

5. FLEESON, W. AND GILDEA, E. F., Study of the personalities of 289 Abnormal Drinkers. *Q. J. Studies on Alcohol,* III, 409–432, Dec. 1942.

6. GOTTESFELD, B. H., LASSER, L. M., CONWAY, E. J. AND MANN, N. M., Psychiatric implications in the treatment of alcoholism with tetraethylthiuram disulfide. *Q. J. Studies on Alcohol,* XII, 184–205, June, 1951.

7. GUILD, J. AND EPSTEIN, N., Psychosis during the treatment of alcoholism with TETD. *Q. J. Studies on Alcohol,* XII, 360–365, Sept., 1951.

8. HAGGARD, H. W. AND JELLINEK, E. M., *Alcohol Explored.* New York, Doubleday, Doran and Co., 1942.

9. HOFF, E., From a talk given at the National States Conference on Alcoholism, New Haven, Conn., Aug. 6, 1951. Division of Alcohol Studies and Rehabilitation, Dept. of Health, Commonwealth of Virginia.

10. KNIGHT, R. P., Psychodynamics of chronic alcoholism. *Jour. Nervous and Mental Diseases,* LXXXVI, 538–548, Nov., 1937.

11. LEMERE, F. AND VOEGTLIN, W. L., An evaluation of the aversion treatment of alcoholism. *Q. J. Studies on Alcohol,* XI, 199–204, June, 1950.

12. LOLLI, G., Hangover in relation to the theory and treatment of alcohol addiction. *Q. J. Studies on Alcohol,* VII, 193–213, Sept., 1946.

13. MARTENSEN-LARSEN, O., Psychotic phenomena provoked by tetraethylthiuram disulfide. *Q. J. Studies on Alcohol,* XII, 206–216, June, 1951.

14. MACHOVER, K., *Projective Personality.* Springfield, Ill., C. C. Thomas, 1950.

15. MEDICAL SOCIETY OF THE STATE OF NEW YORK. From a talk by one of the originators of Alcoholics Anonymous presented to the Medical Society, Hotel Pennsylvania, New York, May, 1944.

16. MINEAR, V., From a talk given at the National States Conference on Alcoholism, August, 1951, New Haven, Conn. Washington D. C. Rehabilitation Center for Alcoholics.

17. PRICE, G. M., A Study of the wives of twenty alcoholics. *Q. J. Studies on Alcohol*, V, 620–627, March, 1945.

18. SILVERBERG, W. V., Factor of omnipotence in neurosis. *Psychiatry*, XII, 387–398, Nov., 1949.

19. TIEBOUT, H. M., Act of surrender in the therapeutic process. *Q. J. Studies on Alcohol*, X, 48–58, June, 1949.

20. ———, Psychiatry in the field of alcoholism. *Q. J. Studies on Alcohol*, XII, 52–57, March, 1951.

21. ———, Therapeutic mechanisms of Alcoholics Anonymous. *Amer. J. Psychiat.*, C, 468–473, Jan., 1944.

▶ SOME ASPECTS OF TREATMENT OF SEX OFFENDERS

*By David Abrahamsen, M.D.**

INTRODUCTION

Psychiatric treatment of sex offenders is a new venture in the field of psychiatry. The reasons for this spring first, from society's reaction toward sex offenders, and second, from the fact that psychiatry has only lately taken an interest in this particular type of offender. Heretofore society's reaction toward sex offenders has been to punish the individual for his crime without any effort to see why he committed that particular crime; it is understandable then that society has not been concerned with treatment of sex offenders. In fact, even today any treatment which indicates leniency toward the offender still tends to evoke a strong negative reaction in the public at large. With the advent of the new law which the State of New York introduced in 1950, and which was based upon our research findings of 102 sex offenders at Sing Sing Prison, psychiatric treatment of sex offenders has begun to take its place in the broad field of psychotherapy. It states offenders who forcefully commit crimes of rape, carnal abuse, or sodomy may receive an indeterminate sentence of from one day to life, and that the decision is to be left to the discretion of the judge. Such sentence is to be passed only after a complete psychiatric examination of the offender and report thereof. The law further provides that any man receiving this type of sentence is to be given treatment and re-examined by a psychiatrist at least every two years, and the report is to be submitted to the Parole Board.

---

* Research Associate, Department of Psychiatry, Columbia University; Director of Research Project, Department of Mental Hygiene, State of New York.

The goals of the law are twofold: the protection of the community from dangerous individuals, and the rehabilitation of such individuals. As the law can be effective only if there are psychiatric facilities to implement it, it was with the understanding that sufficient psychiatric facilities would be established that the law was first suggested.

SURVEY AT SING SING

In our research at Sing Sing the first question with which we concerned ourselves was: Is there such a thing as a sex offender, that is, a man who commits only sex crimes? We made a survey of 1800 inmates at Sing Sing, which showed that 25 per cent of them had committed sex offenses. However, according to legal definitions and the convictions, only 10 per cent of them had been sentenced for sex crimes.

Differentiation of Sex Offenders

In our study we found that several of the sex offenders also had committed other types of offenses. One of them had committed seventeen offenses that were not ostensibly of a sexual nature. Possibly the only types of sex crime which reveal overt sexual behavior are exhibitionism and homosexuality. In investigating other types of offenses, such as rape or incest, we found that many of the perpetrators had also committed burglary and robbery. Psychiatrically considered, robbery may be a symbolic expression of rape. Men who take women's pocketbooks frequently reveal in therapy that what they really wanted was to rape the women. One offender in our study held up women with a toy pistol, then tied them, untied them, and tied them again. He always took something from women so that the crime would appear to be burglary, and usually it was so considered by the courts.

Since we were dealing primarily with legal and not psychiatric definitions, for the most part we studied and treated only those men who had committed overt sex crimes.

In our research at Sing Sing, we found that out of 102 overt sex offenders, seventy-eight had committed previously both sex crimes and other crimes. Sixty-four of them had committed crimes other than sex offenses. Thirty-four of the 102 had committed sex crimes previous to the sex offenses for which they had been sentenced. These last numbers indicate that sex offenders repeat their misdeeds. Indeed, there is an element of repetition in their behavior which assumes the character of compulsion.

Diagnoses

Apart from these difficulties in differentiation of sex offenders, they also pose a problem with regard to their particular diagnoses. Even in those of our cases which were closely examined by a team of psychiatrists, psychologists, and psychiatric social workers, we are still in doubt about the diagnosis because several of the patients showed traits of which at the present time it is not possible to make a diagnostic interpretation. This diagnostic uncertainty is due to the fact that the total constellation of traits in criminals is often very different from that of patients in psychiatric institutions, yet the psychiatric classification was originally developed from hospital patients.

Thus the accepted psychiatric diagnostic procedures proved inadequate in work with criminals. For instance, when the term "psychopath" was introduced for diagnosing offenders, it was mainly to designate persons who are capable of committing crimes; later, however, this concept was broadened to include difficult borderline cases. In our diagnostic procedures, however, we found that most of the 40 per cent of the sex offenders who previously had been diagnosed by others as psychopaths, with or without psychoses, in addition were psychotic, or neurotic, or they suffered from a character disorder. During our psychiatric treatment it was possible for us to elicit material which guided us in arriving at a more correct diagnosis.

Despite these various handicaps, psychiatric treatment of sex offenders was started at Sing Sing in the fall of 1948. Many of the sex offenders after being paroled also have been in aftercare treatment at the Psychiatric Institute in New York City.

TREATMENT PROCEDURE

Before treatment was initiated, each offender was examined by a psychiatrist, a psychologist, and a psychological social worker; at a subsequent staff meeting, the patient's entire personality make-up was discussed. For practical purposes we felt we had to divide the prisoners into four categories on the basis of diagnostic and prognostic features: offenders who are violent and untreatable at present; those who are not violent, but are untreatable at present; those who are treatable in a hospital; and those who are treatable in an outpatient clinic.

The forms of therapy used have been a form of psychoanalytic psychotherapy,* supportive psychotherapy, narcosynthesis, and group psychotherapy. There are now four groups,** varying in number from five to nine. One group meets the therapist twice a week, and three groups meet the therapist once a week. One group consists of sex offenders only; another consists of non-sex offenders, and two are made up of sex offenders and non-sex offenders together. The group of offenders is selected on the basis of their identification with each other, their standing and age, rather than on a similarity of diagnosis. Therefore, we have had to explore each individual before we could take him on in group therapy.

Etiology

As a rule, with sex offenders, the etiology does not reveal any one predominant traumatic event. In all our cases we found any number of traumatic events, spread out from early infancy into adolescence.

Case History

Take, for example, Case 88:

He himself has no memory of his earliest years. However,

---

* This psychoanalytic psychotherapy consists of interpretations and follow-up questions. In cases where it seemed indicated, particularly in those cases which we suspected of having a predominantly psychotic core, no interpretations were given in order not to weaken the ego.

** Since this has been written, treatment has been curtailed.

the records of the social service agencies are loaded with details about him. When a social worker first visited his home the mother threatened to use her small baby as a weapon with which to strike the visitor. Both parents were alcoholics, given to violent brawls. When the patient was eleven months old his father was sent to the workhouse for kicking his pregnant wife in the stomach. The children were taken to an orphanage. Soon afterwards the mother died of alcoholism.

Thereafter the baby was turned over to his grandfather, who was a brawling drunkard like the baby's parents. Then he was left to his father who lived with a succession of women. It was recorded that, when he was four, he had witnessed his father's sexual relations with at least two different women. His earliest memories, confirmed by documents, are of the continued beatings his father gave him. Several times he ran away and was beaten soundly when brought home. He remembers that he was always running away and never knew where he was running. From the age of twelve to sixteen he lived in an orphanage and an institution for juvenile delinquents, from both of which he ran away numerous times, to live by petty crime.

At thirteen, he had sexual relations with a girl in the orphanage, but even before this he had begun the practice of sodomy with younger boys. At sixteen, on request of his custodians, he was sent to a State School for delinquents with a maximum term of three years. A year later he was released on parole.

He had been at liberty a month when a policeman picked him up for trying to persuade a little girl to go into a cellar with him. Then he confessed that a few days previously he had taken the five-year-old daughter of an acquaintance into a basement and had abused her sexually. Probably he had also committed offenses against other little girls and boys. He said he saw nothing wrong in this and had no pangs of conscience about this kind of act. He was sentenced to serve from five to ten years in prison.

This man had had so many deeply disturbing experiences in his dealing with authority figures that he had become entirely uncooperative. When treatment started he had been at Sing Sing for five years. He was depressed, felt misunderstood and did not see any particular purpose in continuing to live. He had no understanding of why he had gotten himself into trouble. Because he had suffered such intense deprivations all his life, a relationship therapy, with occasional interpretations, was used with him at first. Gradually, as his trust in the therapist developed, a deeper therapy was found acceptable to him.

As a result of treatment he has broken through his defensive barriers, has acquired a better knowledge of himself as a person, and has even learned to accept certain frustrations. Originally he spent much time venting his wrath on the Parole Board. He is now able to divert this pent-up emotion to more worthwhile efforts. He has a strong positive transference to the therapist, which makes it possible to give him insight into his compulsive reactions. In fact, he has developed a hopeful outlook on life and actually looks forward to being a useful citizen. He has even abandoned homosexual practices and himself feels that alcohol is a minimal problem. By and large his behavior is amazingly well adjusted, in spite of many occasions which are bound to tempt him to rebellion.

Psychology in the Prison Situation

In general, success in psychiatric treatment depends upon the constitutional strength of instinctual drives and on the modifiability of the ego. With a sex offender, however, one is faced with a particular problem since as a rule his instinctual drives are constitutionally so strong as to make it difficult to alter the ego which usually by then has already been distorted or crippled. In fact, certain types of sex offenders are entirely inaccessible and refuse treatment. By and large, as in all cases, including the neurotic or psychotic, it is the struggle between instinctual drives and the ego which decides the outcome of whether or not the person will be able to function.

As we know, psychotherapy cannot simply be "applied," it presupposes the patients' voluntary cooperation. It is obvious from the outset that any psychiatric treatment within a prison is seriously hampered by the fact that the inmate cannot act in freedom and under his own responsibility while he is thus confined. In fact, it is easily seen that the confinement itself may practically counteract the effect of psychotherapy. First, the inmate is afraid to reveal anything about himself that might be used against him, notwithstanding constant reassurance as to the confidential nature of his revelations to the psychiatrist. Second, the attitude of many of the prison personnel often constitutes an obstacle to successful psychotherapy. Some of the guards "disapprove" of psychotherapy, and they often make it difficult for the prisoner to keep his appointment with the psychiatrist. Third, the inmate constantly identifies himself with other inmates, and his identification raises another barrier against treatment. Fourth, a main prerequisite for every psychotherapy is the establishment of a transference situation. In the prison however such a situation is difficult to keep on an even level. Also the fact that the prisoner does not have to pay for his treatment may at times encourage his secondary neurotic gains; this, too, disturbs the transference situation. Finally, the prison instills in criminals feelings of hostility and aggressions to degrees higher than before the incarceration; this tends to make the offender more incommunicable. This is particularly true in the cases where the offender does not accept any blame for his crime, but considers himself innocent. Only in those cases where the offender understands that he has committed a crime and would like to know why he did it, has psychotherapy fewer obstacles to overcome.

On the other hand, in the prison setup there are always, or at least most of the time, "secondary gains" when an offender seeks treatment. Nevertheless, originally there was much objection to our unit at the prison. Not only were we another authority, but we were treating the sex offender, who is considered the lowest type of offender. This meant an additional stigma. As the prisoners became aware, however, that we were there to help them, many came to us voluntarily for help with their own specific problems.

GROUP THERAPY. In the group-therapy session we have tried to encourage the inmates to express their feelings, be they negative or positive. Gradually it has been possible to see changes in their attitudes and their behavior. Some who had previously been withdrawn, became assertive; some who had been aloof started to show interest and to talk particularly about the problems of other offenders. After two or three months it was possible to discern a group identification. We have tried to allay their fears and anxieties by helping them to talk openly about their problems. When the aggressive emotions have been expressed it becomes possible for the psychiatrist to discover the underlying anxiety and hostility and to discuss it.

INDIVIDUAL THERAPY.   In addition to group therapy, many of these offenders have also been given individual therapy. In the individual therapy we have found it possible to go into deeper psychological levels so that the patient may discuss more freely his relationship to the group and interrelationships and interaction between the various group members.

There is no doubt that among our cases there has been definite improvement which is expressed in a reduction of fears, anxieties, and aggressive trends, antisocial or otherwise.* Repressed material also has been brought to consciousness, and to a reasonable extent the resistances have been overcome. In many cases it can be assumed that there will not be any repetition of offenses or of any other pathological actions.

Case History

One illustrative case was that of a twenty-one year old youth who had been sentenced for the rape of a young girl. This was not the first time he had committed crime; he had been arrested for the first time at the age of sixteen and several times thereafter. At that time he used to tie up women, and while doing so would have an erection, though never an ejaculation.

Upon further investigation much was revealed about the offender's home life. His father was aggressive, hostile, and domineering. Although his mother was a frustrated woman who frequently submitted to her husband, nevertheless to

---

* This has been verified by the psychological tests.

some extent she was able to control the situation. Her relationship with her son had always been very close. As a youth, the boy considered himself a woman hater and was too shy even to ask a girl for a date. Psychological tests performed on the boy indicated a grave disturbance in his ability to test reality.

At school he had always been a good student, and was particularly interested in mathematics and science. However, when he started his criminal activities, his school achievements decreased, undoubtedly due to his increasing need to deal with his intensified sexual urges.

The boy's crucial early traumatic experiences stemmed from his punitive father who severely restricted his sexual activities. Not only did he punish the boy brutally for masturbation, but he would tell him that every time he had an ejaculation it meant loss of a pint of blood, and the like. All this left its mark on the patient's personality structure. He developed a distinct rebelliousness against all authority figures, became extremely inhibited in all social and sexual activity, and markedly hostile toward people in general. He felt that his inhibitions were imposed upon him by authority without any justice.

The feeling that his life was interfered with unjustifiably also made him extremely suspicious of others. He constantly feared rejection. When we began to examine deeply into the psychodynamics of this boy we knew only of his hostility against the punitive and threatening father who had prohibited all sexual gratification. Then unresolved oedipal ties emerged. The boy also displayed marked hostility against his mother who he felt should have preferred him to his father. Because of what he experienced as his mother's rejection he had come to feel extremely inadequate and had, therefore, become oversensitive to any defects within himself. Thus he could not believe that he was able to win love by what he had to offer but felt rather that he could gain sexual gratification only by force.

His incestuous sexual drive generated strong guilt feelings and made him less ready to accept his father's teachings that masturbation and other sexual activities lead to seri-

ous injury. He was constantly afraid that his rebelliousness
and sexuality would overrule his conscious control.* The
fear that he would not be able to control his own incestuous impulses seemed to be based upon his inability to identify with his father. Because he had always felt his father's
restrictions to be unfair, he could not allow himself to submit to them. His main concern was to be free from the control of authority. This was one reason why he resented
school which he was forced to attend. After he had finally
graduated from high school, an event which to him symbolized freedom from control of authority, he began to tie
up girls (and occasionally to expose their breasts). This
seemed to be the only way for him to obtain sexual gratification.

It should also be emphasized that when he tied up a girl,
he thereby frustrated not only her but also himself. He castrated the girl, as it were, but simultaneously castrated himself as if he were saying, "Look, Mother, I am tying you up.
I don't want you but you are not going to get me either."

Psychiatric treatment in the form of psychoanalytic psychotherapy was started with him three years ago. In the beginning he was depressed, and kept repeating, "Mother is
the same way." Gradually, he began talking about himself,
his father, the pimples on his face, masturbation, and at
last he mentioned that he had been frequently frightened by
his father's threat that he would go insane if he continued
to masturbate.

In the following sessions, he was again depressed, talked
about suicide, about hanging himself, and then said, "I had
no desire to hurt women. I never thought of the danger before. I couldn't rape a girl even if I had the opportunity." It
then came out that when he was ten or eleven years old he
almost hanged himself. "I had a rope, and I was fooling
around to see what it felt like." Suicidal tendencies appeared again later on, and a possible transfer to a mental
hospital was discussed. In later sessions he spoke about
dreams he had had of tying women with ropes and exposing their breasts.

---

* The weakness of this conscious control was confirmed by the
Rorschach.

At that time, the psychotherapy was taken over by another psychotherapist;* then, when he had to leave, the writer continued the work with this patient. Early in the treatment the patient related that he had entered five apartments, in one of which he found a pistol, and that he had begun using that pistol to hold up women. He would tie them up by the hands or by the hands and feet, and leave them. In the Middle West he had once tied up a woman and walked her to the edge of town, where they spent the night on the side of a hill. He was very tired and fell asleep. In the morning he walked the woman back to town and released her. He had the feeling that the whole thing was "screwy"; in order to provide some rational motive he always took some money from the pocketbooks of women involved.

During the following months in treatment the patient appeared somewhat withdrawn and did not speak much. At one time he wanted to sit up rather than lie on the couch. He said that he mistrusted anyone connected with the state and then spoke very harshly about authority and his intense dislike of it. He liked authority only when he himself was the authority. All of this indicates that this was a case extremely difficult to treat in prison.

The resistances the patient showed in the following hours were centered about his fear of revealing himself to people. He was afraid of being despised. He also said that he was afraid to talk to people because they would find him ridiculous. His next question was how this could be related to his tying up women. The psychotherapist pointed out to him that what he wanted was the attention of women, but that he feared he was unable to win it and hold it. Therefore, he decided that he would compel women to stay with him by using force.

The next two sessions were taken up with his feelings of isolation and his fear of ridicule if he revealed himself. After two or three months he found himself surprised to be able to talk with people and felt that this was due to the treatment. Later on, he began to discuss the idea that if masturbation was harmful, then certainly sexual intercourse would be much more harmful. He discussed at great

---

* Nathan Ross, M.D., who deserves much credit.

length his anxiety about his frequent masturbation. He was then assured that his anxiety about masturbation was an expression of his fear of sexuality. It was explained to him that what he was doing was to put the woman on a pedestal which made him feel inferior and at the same time created such a barrier between himself and the girl that he became unable to approach her.

In the following months the patient dealt at great length with his fear of criticism, his guilty conscience, his hostility against people and in particular with his difficulty in revealing himself to others; also with the fact that he expected people to harbor the same distrust and hostility toward him that he felt toward them.

In the subsequent therapeutic sessions the fact was brought out that he never carried out orders because by doing so he would have to give up a pleasure which, as the patient himself said, was that of masturbation. Thereupon he was made aware that he was experiencing his frustration in prison and the deprivation in his sex life as a rejection. This the patient seemed to understand and accept. He started to get some insight into his feeling that he would prefer to be mistreated and insulted so as to have a reason to complain; all this revealed to what extent the patient himself engineered all his own difficulties.

He also recognized that while he believed that masturbation had impaired his mental functioning he had at the same time an unconscious wish to behave in such a manner as to be caught in the act of masturbating.

At this point in the treatment one had the definite impression that the patient had acquired real insight and was making progress. He admitted that he was a spoiled brat, that he wanted the whole world to treat him as he had wanted his parents to treat him, that when he did not obtain gratification he used such devices as sulking which was designed to make people feel guilty about the way they treated him.

This led to the subject of the patient's past behavior with women. When he could not get complete love from women, he sulked and stayed away from them, thereby revealing his anger at them. By tying up women, he forced them to give him what he wanted. He always felt intense self-contempt for such an act. The reason why he had not made any sexual attack upon women was revenge (something which he at first did not understand). When he walked away from the woman, he was denying her the satisfaction of her wishes, and simultaneously revealing his complete contempt for her. An additional reason why he coveted the feeling of being treated unjustly was that he wanted to impress people with a sense of obligation to give him everything he wanted.

After more than a year of treatment, the patient was asked whether he had not been able to remember any dreams. He then spoke about having had many nightmares. He recalled one dream where he was standing between two buildings talking very freely to another person. Since associations were sparse, the patient was reassured that in the dream he was engaging in an activity with which he was not familiar. Asked what the two buildings might mean, he mentioned the legs of a woman. However, at the same time, the two buildings obviously also signified two prisons: Elmira Prison from which the patient had been transferred, and Sing Sing Prison. Later in the same session the question of parole came up, and it was suggested that the patient possibly was trying to convince a member of the Parole Board that he was suitable for release.

At this time the patient was preoccupied with his approaching meeting with the Parole Board. At that meeting he was given one more year by the Board, and felt dejected and frustrated. Thereupon he had a dream that he was on a platform and that the view was obstructed. This signified the many obstacles in his way. He was also intensely interested in the new legislation pertaining to sex offenders about which he had read in the newspapers. He said that he could not stand being in prison very much longer. Obviously, at that point he still was afraid of his own hostility which he recognized.

A month later, he felt at last that he was not so preoccupied by the decision of the Parole Board. He discussed how elated he had felt when he had tied up the women. It finally became clear that he repeated the act in order to assure himself that he had the power to do it. After a further month he started to sleep well, and the psychotherapist pointed out to him that the reason for this was possibly that he had stopped fighting authority so forcefully. However, this interpretation the patient did not accept.

Somewhat later he dreamed that he was walking alone in the prison grounds and all the buildings and trees were covered by a thin sheet of ice. To this dream the patient did not have any associations. When it was suggested that the buildings and trees were representatives of women and men, and that the ice on the buildings and trees might mean that he himself was too cold toward them, the patient was again rather skeptical about the interpretation. It was then suggested that in this dream he seemed to be testing himself to see whether or not he was able to communicate with others. It happens as if he himself wanted to "break the ice," but was not yet able to do so.

In the first year-and-a-half of analysis the patient had learned how to deal with submitting to authority and had begun to understand the motives of his attacks upon women. Along with that went a resolution of his feelings of inadequacy and inferiority. His personality make-up had improved considerably. Psychological re-testing at that point showed that he had a more conscious control of his motor impulses than previously. After some twenty months of treatment he stated that he was in good spirits. "I have reached the point where I believe I can go out. I have more confidence in myself. Previously I had a bad opinion of myself, but now it has changed." He dreamed frequently of being out of prison; only once did he dream that the guards were opening the doors of all the cells, but passed his by. He started to scream and woke up. This dream reveals some still persistent fear that he might be passed by and treated unjustly. A little later he had another dream that he was walking with a girl, to whom he was getting married. "We slept together in a bed. As soon as I started to have intercourse with her, I woke up with an ejaculation."

The patient stated that it had seemed very realistic and that it was a pleasant dream. In the following sessions he talked about his previous disappointments; he was at that time particularly anxious about his parole which was coming up soon.

This time the Parole Board gave him three more months in the prison. In the following interview with me he was not so despondent as he had been the year before when he had been given a whole year by the Parole Board. As a matter of fact he talked more freely and was full of confidence that he was going to make it anyhow. Nor was he so self-conscious about things as before. "I now have a better opinion of myself."

The last dream he had was when he dreamed he was fighting in Korea and met a girl he had known back in school. "She was one class ahead of me." Associations: "I was too shy to ask her out because I was afraid of being turned down." His next association was: "I always picked on strangers. I did not want to do it on someone I knew." This indicated that he could make advances toward a stranger, not toward someone he knew. "I don't know against whom it was directed.* It was part of the twisted pattern. So far as I know, I will marry."

In his last session with me he said that previously he would never have thought of asking a girl for a date. "I would rather have walked into a cage full of tigers. I had the ridiculous notion that I either had to be perfect or I was no good at all. The easiest way not to be turned down by a girl is not to ask a girl. When I tied up a girl, she couldn't refuse me. Some time ago I thought it would be terrible to come to a psychiatrist because I thought that the cure would be worse than the disease, but now I know better."

This man will possibly be paroled in a few months and then be given continued psychotherapy on an outpatient basis.

Summarizing, it may be said that this patient is suffering from a severe compulsive-obsessive neurosis with schizoid traits. The original Rorschach test showed him to be extremely narcissistic and infantile, but the last psychiatric and psychological tests showed that he has lost many of his inhibitions, that he is

---

* Unconsciously, the attack was probably directed against his mother.

in closer contact with reality, and that he now has a better and sounder appreciation of himself.

PSYCHOPATHOLOGY OF SEX OFFENDERS

The psychopathology of many sex offenders is revealed partly through the wives they have chosen. Many such wives, in spite of their husbands' cruelty and unfaithfulness, stay with them. On the surface, many of these women showed masochistic traits, which is precisely what the sex offender needs. Several of the offenders spontaneously and explicitly emphasized their need to force their will upon a woman. However, in our treatment of the sex offenders we discovered that their offenses are usually an act of revenge and rebellion against their rejecting and threatening mothers who did not and do not respond to their dependency needs. Interestingly enough, many of the wives showed sadistic and competitive trends underneath their submissiveness. Actually, they threatened their husbands' masculinity. What the sex offenders had done was to seek out wives who were the same threatening and overpowering female figures as they had had in their homes, namely, their mothers.

SUMMARY

The results given here are somewhat scattered, yet despite the many admitted shortcomings of treatment in prison, they justify some guarded optimism. So far, it has been possible to help a few prisoners only. What we do need, however, are specialized units for treatment of all types of offenders, not only sex offenders. Psychiatry has progressed a great deal in many fields; but it is quite possible that the greatest progress within psychiatry is going to take place in the course of the next fifty years in psychiatric criminology. However, this cannot be accomplished until people have revised their attitude toward the offender. If society wants to rid itself of criminals, its emotional attitudes toward crime have to be changed at their roots. Up until the present, society, to a large extent unconsciously, wants to see the offender punished, not rehabilitated. Unless this attitude changes radically, society will continue to have its prisons filled with sick and unhappy human beings. Our research at Sing Sing Prison points to the fact that offenders can be helped even with our present difficult treatment setup, but that the psychiatric facilities have to be considerably expanded if we want to achieve quantitatively worthwhile results. This will be the task of tomorrow.

BIBLIOGRAPHY

1. ABRAHAMSEN, D., "Personality reaction to crime and disease." *Bull. N. Y. Acad. Med.*, XXI, 435, 1945; *J. Nerv. & Ment. Dis.*, CIV, No. 1, 1946.

2. ———, "Psychodynamics in Criminal Behavior." Address delivered at annual meeting of Assn. for Psychoanal. & Psychosom. Med., New York, June, 1944.

3. ———, "The dynamic connection between crime and personality." *J. Crim. Psychopath.*, V, 481, 1944.

4. ———, *Crime and the Human Mind.* 3rd ed. New York, Columbia Univ. Press, 1945.

5. ———, "Psychosomatic Disorders and Their Significance in Antisocial Behavior." Lecture given at Am. Psychoanal. Assn. meeting, Chicago, May, 1946. To appear in *J. Nerv. & Ment. Dis.*

6. ———, "Psychiatric Development of Juvenile Delinquency." Lecture given at Columbia Univ. Forum, New York, 1951.

7. ———, *Report on Study of 102 Sex Offenders at Sing Sing Prison,* as submitted to Gov. Thomas E. Dewey, March, 1950.

8. ———, *Who Are the Guilty?—Education and Crime.* New York, Rinehart & Co., 1952.

9. "After 50 years: an agency looks ahead." *Jewish Soc. Serv. Quart.*, No. 2, Dec., 1944.

10. BENDER, L., "Behavior Problems in the Children of Psychotic and Criminal Parents." *Gen. Psychol. Monograph*, XIX, 1937.

11. OVERHOLSER, W., "Psychiatry and the law—cooperators or antagonists?" *Psychiat. Quart.*, XIII, 622, 1939.

► PSYCHOTHERAPEUTIC TECHNIQUES IN PSYCHOSOMATIC MEDICINE

*By Melitta Sperling, M.D.**

INTRODUCTION

By its discovery of the role of unconscious motivation in human behavior, specifically in illness, psychoanalysis is slowly but fundamentally changing medical thought. This change has led to a new approach in medicine—the psychosomatic approach. Psychoanalysis developed as a method for studying and treating mental and psychic phenomena, yet it stems from the study of somatic manifestations of a psychogenic nature, namely those of conversion hysteria. In addition to Freud, psychoanalysts such as Ferenczi, Simmel, F. Deutsch, and others developed important concepts in regard to the effect of unconscious emotions, thoughts, wishes, and fantasies upon the somatic system. In his pioneering way Groddeck achieved remarkable results in treating severe organic conditions which would today be called psychosomatic, through his intuitive understanding of the unconscious psychologic significance that the particular organ pathology had for the particular patient. In the United States, Alexander and his co-workers are mainly responsible for the growth of psychosomatic medicine.

In the early days of psychoanalysis, interest was focused on delving into the unconscious. Later, it was shifted to the study of the mechanisms of defense against unconscious impulses, of the processes of character formation and symptom formation—in short to the study of the ego as the mediator between the id, the superego, and outside reality. The understanding and correct application of the concepts derived from these studies form

---

* Clinical Assistant Professor in Psychoanalytic Medicine, State University College of Medicine, New York City.

a part of the classic psychoanalytic technique which was originally designed and reserved for the treatment of the psychoneuroses.

At that time the narcissistic neuroses and the psychoses were considered unsuitable for psychoanalysis because they do not permit of the establishment of the classical transference relationship without which a successful psychoanalysis could not be carried out. In the analytic situation, through the medium of transference—that is, through the carrying over to the analyst of the patient's infantile reactions—the patient re-enacts his inadequate attitudes of the past and with the help of the analyst gradually is able to resolve his infantile relationships, attitudes, and reactions. Patients with narcissistic neuroses and especially those with psychopathies and psychoses do not establish these classical transferences, either because their capacity to form object relations is defective or lacking, or because of the extraordinary lability of the object relations when they do exist.

CONTRIBUTIONS OF CHILD ANALYSIS

The development by Anna Freud of a technique for the psychoanalytic treatment of children and the technique of direct interpretation of the unconscious used by Melanie Klein, proved however that it is possible to apply a modified psychoanalytical method, namely child analysis, under conditions which are very similar to those of adult patients with narcissistic neuroses. Today among child analysts the question whether the child is capable of forming a transference is still problematic, and the majority take the negative stand. Other features of the narcissistic neuroses are also present in children. These include a high degree of intolerance of tension, inadequate repression of and inadequate defense mechanisms against unconscious impulses, a consequent tendency to act-out their impulses, lack of control of sexual and aggressive drives together with open display of attitudes which in adults would be referred to as perverse or psychopathic. These qualities are especially characteristic of those children with whom child analysts deal. In many instances the child fulfills those very conditions of the patient with narcissistic neurosis that formerly constituted a contraindication for psycho-analysis. This suggests that on the basis of experience gained from the analysis of children, a modified form of psychoanalysis can be applied to conditions previously considered unanalysable. In my opinion this constitutes one of the most important contributions that child analysis has made to psychoanalysis and indeed to psychiatry.

My work with adult psychosomatics has been greatly enriched and facilitated by the experience I have gained from treating psychoanalytically children of various ages who suffered from severe psychosomatic disorders. In treating children with psychosomatic disorders, particularly very young children, not only can the psychosomatic pattern of response be observed in its beginnings, but there can also be seen in operation the fundamental workings and effects of the mother-child relationship. In young children even severe psychosomatic disorders may still be reversible, especially if it is possible to change the relationship existing between mother and child. This can be seen particularly well where there is concomitant treatment of mother and child, and where a modification of the unconscious needs of the mother manifests itself in a change in the somatic response of the child.

DYNAMICS OF THE MOTHER-CHILD RELATIONSHIP

Let us begin with a brief resume of the psychoanalytic study of the development, course, and response to treatment of a severe psychosomatic disorder, ulcerative colitis, in a child not quite four years old. (A glance at the literature will show that ulcerative colitis is a condition which taxes to the utmost the skills of the therapist who treats it in older children and adults.)

Freddy was referred to me by the hospital in which he had been treated for severe ulcerative colitis for several months. He was at that time nearly four years old. In the playroom he exhibited anxious, phobic behavior. He was anxious about not being able to control his diarrhea and continuously ran from the playroom to the bathroom. He was afraid to touch things, especially clay, and when he did so, had to wash his hands immediately. His mother's reaction to his illness is best highlighted by her remark to me, "I'm such a clean woman and he has such a messy disease." At home he would have diarrhea as soon as his mother finished putting him into clean clothes, would soil himself before she could get his clothes off, or he would soil her freshly washed kitchen floor.

From twice-a-week interviews with the mother, from observation of the child's behavior in the playroom, and from the hospital record, the following developmental history was gradually brought out:

The mother prided herself on the fact that Freddy had achieved sphincter control at the age of one year. At one-and-a-half he showed fears of touching and fear of dirt. He would display signs of anxiety if a speck of food fell on his bib. The onset of his diarrhea occurred at this age. In retrospect it became apparent that neither the mother nor the child had ever allowed themselves openly to acknowledge their anal impulses. Identification with the compulsive mother caused unusually severe and early repression of anal impulses in the child, leading to the formation at the age of one-and-a-half years of an over-severe superego with compulsive features (Ferenczi's "Sphinctermoral"). Freddy could allow himself to soil only at the cost of illness, at the same time that he forced his mother to handle the fecal matter she abhorred.

Freddy's diarrhea became progressively worse. He developed bleedings and high fever, for which he was hospitalized. Since he did not respond to any medication, an infectious origin of the diarrhea was suspected, and a tonsillectomy was performed. No improvement ensued. After several weeks in the hospital he was discharged unimproved, but was hospitalized again after a short stay at home because of an acute aggravation. This time he was admitted to a hospital where there was particular interest in the psychosomatic approach to ulcerative colitis. All types of medication and therapy had already been tried without response. After some time and after he had been taken off medication, Freddy began to improve slightly. During this time he had a psychiatric workup, and the parents were seen by a psychiatric social worker.

The description of the boy's behavior in the hospital confirmed the impression of an early, unduly severe reaction against anal impulses. He remained in the hospital for several months, and the only therapy consisted in letting him play with other children. He was discharged much improved. The parents who had been given some understanding by the social worker were advised to let the child eat and play normally instead of overprotecting him as they had previously done. The child remained well until the age of three-and-a-half years.

At this time during his oedipal phase when the child began to masturbate, the mother threatened his genital impulses just as abruptly as she had earlier suppressed his anal ones. The child responded by an acute repression of his sexual impulses, which found release and expression in a renewed exacerbation of the original symptom of bloody diarrhea.

Freddy was again admitted to the hospital. From there he was referred to me for ambulatory treatment, which the mother accepted after some hesitation. While on the one hand the boy's sexuality was abruptly suppressed by the severe prohibition of masturbation, yet at the same time he was stimulated and seduced by both parents. The father, who had very strong latent homosexual tendencies, had an almost paranoid attitude toward his wife, and suspected her of infidelity. Whenever he quarreled with her, he would take Freddy into bed with him, clearly indicating that he used Freddy as a substitute for his wife.* **

---

* In this connection I refer to my analysis of a case of mucous colitis in a twelve-year-old boy: "Mucous Colitis Associated with Phobias." *Psychoanalytic Quarterly*, XIX, No. 3, July, 1950. In that case, too, recurrence of diarrhea was the result of a masturbatory conflict in a very fearful and overstimulated boy. Here, too, the onset of the diarrhea could be traced back to the anal phase and there was also a recurrence during the oedipal period when the mother had severely threatened him and prohibited his attempts at masturbation.

** The case of Freddy is also described in my paper, "Problems in Analysis of Children with Psychosomatic Disorders." *Quarterly Journal of Child Behavior*, I, No. 1, 13–14, January, 1949.

Such symptoms as the bloody diarrhea serve to gratify the sexual impulses, whose normal outlet has been blocked by prohibition and repression, and they serve also as a release of the aggression against the prohibiting parents, which the child dares not feel consciously and is unable to express directly. The multiple purpose and meaning of the symptoms explain why these conditions resist treatment so stubbornly. The symptoms serve important dynamic functions in the patient's unconscious life. He cannot give them up if he has no more adquate, mature ways of dealing with his needs.

> Freddy would characteristically spare his father and awaken his mother when he had to go to the bathroom at night. This only added to her resentment against him. The mother felt that her husband and son had "ganged up" on her. She told me that she was one of a family of five sisters and two brothers. The brothers had died young, but all the sisters were alive. She had had a son before Freddy was born, who had died in an accident in infancy. Her attitude to Freddy is shown by her remark, "The boys in my family don't live long; Freddy is taking his time."
> In psychosomatic treatment Freddy improved remarkably. However, the mother called up one day, after Freddy had missed a few sessions because of grippe, to let me know that she would not bring the child back for treatment. She said she could not face me and therefore she had to tell me over the telephone. Maybe, she said, she would bring him back at a later time.

In treatment, the child has to be allowed to re-live in a modified form the developmental phases that he has missed in life, and to work-through the pregenital drives in symbolic play activity. Only after this has been done can normal ego development take place. The important thing is the acceptance by the patient of the existence of his oral and anal impulses, not their direct gratification.

The fact that this child developed a condition such as ulcerative colitis so early in life is attributable to the unusually strong and early repression of oral and anal aggressive impulses.

(Freddy was also a severe feeding problem.) His aggression was turned entirely against himself. There had been no manifest display of aggression until play analysis was undertaken at the age of four. The consequent turning outward of the destructive impulses was accompanied by immediate and striking improvement both in the ulcerative colitis and in the child's total behavior. The mother, however, was unconsciously determined upon his complete submission; he had to stay sick and thus be dependent upon her, or not live at all. She could not tolerate any improvement in the boy which threatened to interfere with his dependent relationship to her. Consequently she withdrew both him and herself from therapy.*

In most of these psychosomatic cases the infantile and early childhood setting is very similar. The variations are merely in degree. This particular case has been selected in order to demonstrate the development of the psychosomatic pattern of reaction because I feel that it offered a rare opportunity to observe and treat psychoanalytically such a severe psychosomatic disorder in such a young child, as well as to study the attitudes of parents, and in particular, the mother-child relationship.

It is often very difficult to reconstruct in later life the infantile and early childhood situations which laid down the disposition for the psychosomatic reaction, not to mention the further difficulties of resolving a reaction pattern which was established so early in life. I have had the opportunity to study the same and similar conditions in varying degrees of severity in children and adults of various ages, and I have found it particularly hard to lead the patient back to these early stages and to help him at a late date to discover and to sever his extreme dependent tie to the mother or to mother-surrogates.

The setting up of rigid defenses originating early in life makes the psychoanalysis of people with psychosomatic disorders a very laborious undertaking. Many patients are not suitable for

---

* The further course of this case has been reported in a paper, "Psychiatric Aspects of Ulcerative Colitis," read in April, 1950 during the Symposium on Diarrhea held at the Brooklyn Jewish Hospital. The proceedings of the symposium are to be published in book form.

it because they have never functioned as independent individuals, even though they may have appeared, to others and even to themselves, to do so. Characteristically these patients try to solve their problems by the mechanisms of denial and reaction-formation, and these mechanisms have become ingrained in their character since early childhood. Such mechanisms then become the backbone of their functioning in life, and by the time they come for treatment in adulthood, their reaction pattern is quite rigidly fixed. No matter how independent and self-sufficient a patient's life may appear to be, we find on closer investigation in every psychosomatic case (in some more cleverly concealed than in others) that the patient lives in an emotional symbiosis with one object in his environment, who does not have to be the actual mother but who somehow, in the patient's unconscious, serves the dynamic function of a mother figure.

Let me illustrate how the early origin and rigidity of the defense mechanism make the uncovering of the unconscious causes of the psychosomatic symptoms a matter of great difficulty:

A woman of forty had come for analysis on her own initiative, for a number of severe psychosomatic complaints of many years' standing, which had not responded to medical treatment. Psychoanalysis revealed a very rigid personality with strong reaction-formations, denials, and overcompensations. Her psychosomatic complaints, among which were recurrent attacks of migraine, abdominal cramps with bouts of diarrhea, and chronic constipation, had started shortly after her marriage. It was found that these symptoms expressed her unconscious dependency conflict which she had focused on her husband. She had periods during which she was hyperactive and functioned very well. These alternated with periods in which she suffered either from overt depression or was sick somatically. In the course of her psychoanalysis there was marked improvement in her symptoms and in her relationships.

The analysis of her dependent needs, however, which she had overcompensated by independent behavior, proved to be very difficult. She was very reluctant to recognize any unconscious dependency. The phase of her analysis reported here occurred at a time when she had been in the analysis for a period of almost two years. On the surface she appeared to have a very positive transference, but in reality she had resisted becoming dependent on the analyst. When she felt that she could no longer prevent the analysis of her dependency needs and that the other methods of acting-out these needs had been curtailed by the analysis, she wanted to discontinue analysis by taking a trip abroad. This attempt to break away from the analysis at this crucial point was prevented by interpretation. At this juncture she developed severe epigastric pain. She underwent complete gallbladder and gastro-intestinal examinations with negative results. Thereupon she had several narrow escapes from near-death accidents; for instance, several times she found herself about to drive her car directly into a truck, but, being a good driver, just managed to escape at the last moment.

All these productions were intended to avoid recognition and analysis of a very intense need for a mother. Her strongest resistance was against accepting the fact that she felt such needs toward the analyst. The analysis of this phase helped her to recognize that she was re-living the most traumatic period of her life: the time when she was a year-and-a-half old, and a sister was born who took her mother from her. She had completely denied this early disappointment and reacted to this loss of her mother by devaluating her mother and leaving home very early. She married young, left her husband, and did not form any deep attachment until she met her second husband. In the second marriage she managed to create a situation in which the husband was dependent on her, and whenever this relationship was threatened she became sick.

In such a case it is not possible to achieve a permanent cure unless the basic personality pattern, which has been established very early in life, is changed.

The psychosomatic patient cannot consciously tolerate his pregenital impulses because of his very strong urge to satisfy them in reality; he therefore denies them completely and they are converted into somatic symptoms, and in this way gratified. He has to expend great amounts of psychic energy in maintaining the repression of his pregenital impulses, which are chiefly oral and anal-sadistic ones. The sudden breakthrough of these repressions may result in a flare-up of sadistic, aggressive, and socially unacceptable behavior or, if repressed again, in a dangerous exacerbation of the somatic symptom.

An an example, I may mention the case of an eleven-year-old girl with ulcerative colitis, who, prior to treatment, used to have fits of rage against her younger sister at the times when she was comparatively free from physical symptoms. She would grab her sister so violently that she once dislocated her shoulder, and at another time she pushed her down the stairs, almost killing her. When her anger was repressed, she had her somatic symptoms.

Although the treatment of psychosomatic patients on hospital wards is often inadequate, nevertheless, many patients do improve considerably during their hospital stay. The removal of the patient from the home environment in which he is exposed to intense and specific frustrations is in itself therapeutic. It has been my experience that the improvement of patients in hospitals in many cases is due not so much to effectiveness of medical regimes as to this specific factor of protection from frustration. With the return of the patient to his home environment and specific frustrations, his symptoms usually return. This is equally true of children and adults, but can be better observed in children.

An eight-year-old boy with severe ulcerative colitis would have an intense aggravation of bloody diarrhea and abdominal cramps whenever his mother visited him on the ward. There was always excitement and argument between them about such things as crackers and peanuts which the patient demanded and his mother refused. Each time he was discharged in an improved condition he would have an acute exacerbation after a short stay at home, and be returned to the hospital acutely ill. This cycle was repeated many times until psychoanalytic treatment of the boy and work with his mother was started.*

A girl of twelve who was hospitalized because of recurrent, very severe attacks of dermatitis had to be tied down in her bed during and after visits of her parents because she would become so "itchy" that she would scratch herself until she bled.

Another eight-year-old boy with "cyclic vomiting" would be quite well on the ward without any therapy, but whenever his mother came to visit, he would have a severe attack of vomiting. He had to have innumerable emergency hospitalizations and was unable to maintain himself at home for more than a few days.

SUPPORTIVE PSYCHOTHERAPY

The defenses of the psychosomatic patient should not be analyzed unless the therapist is prepared to use psychoanalytic techniques that enable him to handle the violent resistances that are likely to be provoked by his interpretations. In those cases where the therapist is not prepared to supply such psychoanalytic therapy, the treatment should rather be like the treatment of latent psychotics, namely a form of supportive psychotherapy. Similar to the reaction of the latent psychotic, in whom the removal of neurotic defenses can produce an acute psychotic episode, so in the psychosomatic the analysis of the very strong reaction-formations can bring about the aggravation of the patient's somatic condition. In cases where symptom analysis is done without first analyzing the patient's defenses and thus increasing his tolerance of his impulses, that is, increasing his ego-strength, the sudden breakthrough of the repressed infantile impulses which had previously been released in the somatic symptom, may be expressed in a psychotic episode.

The therapist should therefore make himself an ally to the ego of the patient and appeal to the patient's needs for inde-

---

* Cf. "Psychoanalytic Study of Ulcerative Colitis in Children." *Psychoanalytic Quarterly*, XV, No. 3, 302–311, July, 1946.

pendence by offering himself to the patient as a more suitable object for identification than the mother who helps and protects him only at the price of dependency. In this way the therapist helps the patient to regain his narcissistic equilibrium and protects him from further frustrations from the outside.

The giving of insight should be limited to showing the connection between the occurrence of the symptoms and affects, such as anger, disappointment, resentment, and fear, without any interpretation of specific conflicts. The patient should be encouraged to recognize his feelings and to express them during the therapeutic sessions. The better he is able to recognize the emotions behind the symptoms that give rise to them, the less need will he have of his symptoms.

The patient should be encouraged to turn his interests toward constructive channels of work and play, and should be helped to re-direct some of his aggression to the outside, so that its release will not have to take place through symptoms, nor come out in uncontrolled behavior. His dependency relationships to the therapist and to persons in his environment should not be interfered with, nor should the phenomenon of transference be interpreted to him. The environment must be prepared to create acceptance for the newly released affects, so that these need not be converted again into symptoms. The patient should be helped to develop some of his latent abilities, so that he may dispense with some of the need for secondary gain from his illness. He should be helped to accept himself with his limitations, and see himself more realistically. In other words, the work with the patient should be on the conscious level.

In treating the patient in this way, one does not bring about a change in the patient's need for dependency but only a shift of this dependency to the therapist. As with psychotics, one can work with these patients only in a positive transference, and this is often difficult to maintain due to their hypersensitivity and the fact of the dependency itself. In extreme cases a change from positive to negative transference may lead the patient to psychosomatic suicide. However, as long as no psychoanalytic work is being done, there is no particular reason for the patient to continue seeing the same therapist, once his transference becomes negative.

Here again the similarity to the treatment of psychotics becomes apparent. The technique which Federn developed in the treatment of psychosis, namely to have a third person at hand who can take over in this situation, has proven useful in the treatment of psychosomatics. This may be the general practitioner, or a social worker, or a nurse, or a close relative, who has been included in the treatment plan and who has been thoroughly prepared for this occasion. Since the patient in the negative transference, in order to prove the therapist wrong, does not care what happens to him, there should be no insistence upon continuation of treatment at this point. In the case of a child it is essential that the mother be included in the therapeutic process; without such inclusion, treatment cannot be successful.

From such supportive therapy one should expect only temporary relief from symptoms and mitigation of the severity of attacks. Recurrences should be anticipated whenever the unconscious dependency conflict is re-activated. Aggravations of the somatic condition should be expected if there is a change in the transference or an increase of frustration from other sources.

Collaboration with the medical practitioner and the various specialists is desirable, but such collaboration will be successful with those medical men only who accept the principles of dynamic psychiatry, that is, those who do not support the patient's need for denial of emotional factors by merely prescribing medicine, diets, change of climate, etc. Cases treated for a long time by such a polypragmatic approach often become completely inaccessible to psychotherapy, because the physician actually provides the patient with easy alibis. Like children who are attuned to their mother's unconscious attitudes in their acceptance or rejection of psychotherapy, rather than to the parent's conscious appropriate attitudes and verbalizations, adult psychosomatics are very keen to sense their physician's unconscious rejection of psychotherapy and will react to this rather than to his conscious, encouraging referral.

The psychosomatically oriented physician must understand

that cure has not been effected when the symptom has been removed. Not only is treatment of the disease not finished then; it has actually not even begun. The repressed impulses which had formerly found expression in the symptom may now break through in a behavior problem. The medical practitioner, unless he is familiar with these concepts and processes, will not realize that the behavior problem is only another manifestation of the very same psychic disturbance which originally produced the somatic symptom. He must understand that by clearing up a somatic symptom he has not touched the cause of the disease, and that the disease will break out in another symptom, or in a recurrence of the old symptom, or in a behavior problem, or in some other manifestation, whenever the patient's infantile dependency needs are frustrated, unless these dependency needs are resolved psychoanalytically. In treating psychosomatics this way the therapist should be aware that a lifelong dependency relationship is involved, which supportive psychotherapy will not eliminate but merely shift.

PSYCHOANALYSIS

Only psychoanalytic therapy is capable of resolving the dependency need of the psychosomatic patient by modifying the personality dynamics which produce the symptoms. However, it takes experience and flexibility of technique to treat severe psychosomatic disorders psychoanalytically. The resistance of the psychosomatic patient to interpretation often takes the form of a very severe aggravation of his symptoms and this aggravation must not be permitted to be used as an excuse for breaking off or staying away from treatment.

The preliminary step in the psychoanalytic treatment of the psychosomatic patient is the same as in supportive therapy. As in child analysis there must be a phase of preparation, to encourage dependence on the analyst. Then the analyst, making use of this relationship, carefully introduces interpretations. In the transference relationship, by offering the patient a new and more suitable object for mature identification, the analyst helps the patient consciously to recognize and tolerate his repressed pregenital strivings, and in this way furthers the development of the ego and its strivings for independence.

With children, but to some extent also with adults, it is necessary to allow for some manifest expression of aggressive behavior and to prepare the environment for the transitory change in the patient's behavior. First, the aggressive energy released in the somatic symptom must be liberated, then consciously tolerated by the patient, and next, opportunities for its expression in socially acceptable forms should be provided by the environment. Only then in the course of the analysis can this energy be directed into constructive channels, and eventually sublimated.*

Analysis of the patient's defenses should be carried out with caution, keeping in mind that the resistance of the psychosomatic patient often expresses itself in very severe aggravations of his condition.

Since negative transference must always be analysed very early, its signs should be carefully watched for. It is difficult to work with a psychosomatic patient in a negative transference because such a patient does not verbalize his negative feelings. In fact, he is not aware of them at all. He represses them so completely that the only way they can find an outlet is via his body, that is, in an aggravation or recurrence of the old somatic symptom or in the production of new ones. It is a decided step forward in the treatment of a psychosomatic patient when it is possible not only to re-convert his somatic symptom into the feeling or fantasy that caused it, but to help him to tolerate this feeling without acting it out in uncontrolled behavior. For only if the patient can consciously tolerate his impulses can he achieve control over them. It is then left to the patient whether to suppress them, to displace them, or to transform them and use them constructively.

Negative transference can best be prevented through constant analysis of the patient's resistances, provided one is alert

---

* For a detailed description of the handling of this phase of analysis in the case of a child, cf. my: "Psychoanalytic Study of Ulcerative Colitis in Children." *Loc. cit.*, p. 302 ff.

to recognize their very early signs. Even in acute somatic conditions it is preferable to make the patient come to the office for treatment, if it is at all possible. Certain rationalizations have to be attacked and made understandable very early in the treatment. In working with children it is necessary to work first with the parents and to make sure that they will comply with the needs of the analysis. In working with adults, one must convince them that it is important not to make the very illness for which they are seeking treatment a cause for staying away from treatment.

One of my patients, a young woman suffering from severe migraine, prior to her analysis usually had to stay in bed for several days during her attacks. Although during the first year she still suffered from occasional attacks, she had not missed a single therapeutic appointment because of this. One winter day when the roads were icy and driving was difficult, she came in saying, "I don't think I would have been here on a day like this a few months ago." That morning she had quarreled with her husband and was feeling very frustrated. She had the premonition of an oncoming migraine, scintillating scotomata, and nausea. However she was able to recognize the nature of her impulses and to analyse them for herself: that she did not have to kill her husband (mother) and herself by having an accident. She could and did come to the analytic session unharmed.

When one is treating patients suffering from bronchial asthma, especially children, it is important to convince them (and the parents) that the patient has to come for sessions in any condition and any weather. In these cases, the cold, the heat, the wind, the rain, anything at all—will be used by both child and parent to rationalize asthma. In the considerable number of such cases that I have treated, I have not had a single experience of the child developing an asthmatic attack as a result of coming for the session in bad weather.

In one instance, that of an eight-year-old girl with bronchial asthma, who began treatment in December, the mother called me on the day of the fourth session to tell me that she was unable to bring the child that day because she had never taken her out in such a snowstorm. I had realized that if the child were to be kept home whenever the weather was bad, it would make treatment impossible for this reason alone, aside from the usual use of such rationalizations, and I had already discussed this question with the patient in the previous session. I explained to her that during the analysis it was perfectly all right to be outdoors and to come to the office in any weather, because she was under treatment and nothing untoward could happen to her. Accordingly I told the mother to bring the child in spite of the snow, so that she could convince herself—as she did—that the child's asthma was not affected by the weather.

On the contrary, it is my experience with patients who come to the office for treatment with all the signs of an incipient attack, that it is possible to prevent the attack and to relieve the patient not only from the somatic symptoms themselves but also from the repressed emotions which gave rise to the symptoms, through understanding the dynamics and interpreting them.

The above-mentioned girl with bronchial asthma came for her session on a beautiful summer's day, wheezing heavily and giving all the indications of an imminent attack. During the session she reported that she had been at the movies, that she had felt well all day but had developed the symptoms while watching the picture. The film dealt with a broken marriage and a reconciliation at the end. My young patient had been with her father, who was separated from her mother. He had taken the child to the movies on the day she regularly spent with him. At first she maintained that her wheezing was the reaction to her having had to leave the movies and her father in order to come to me. But this had happened before on many occasions without producing such a reaction, and furthermore her recognition and expression of this feeling did not at all clear up the symptom. When she revealed that she had that afternoon asked her father about a reconciliation and that he had told her "That happens only in the movies," my interpretation that she was very angry at her father and unhappy about his attitude, suddenly relieved her from her difficult breathing and other symptoms.*

If the patient is so ill that emergency treatment in the form of a psychological shock has to be given, then direct, deep interpretation of the patient's unconscious destructive impulses may prove a lifesaving device. But the analyst has to keep in mind first, that only the masochistic aspect of the patient's destructiveness should be interpreted; second, that this interpretation does not produce any change in the basic personality; and finally, that its effect is limited to the acute attack if it is not followed up with psychoanalytic therapy.

The following case offers a good illustration:

The patient, a man in his early twenties, who suffered from ulcerative colitis of one year's duration, came for treatment as a last resort before undergoing major surgery. During the year of his illness he had lost about forty pounds, and had been reduced to a veritable walking skeleton. This was a particularly great trauma for this patient because he had a narcissistic overevaluation of his appearance. Prior to his illness he had spent most of his time and interest in building up his physique. His friends had nicknamed him "the body." Psychoanalytic exploration revealed that he had developed ulcerative colitis when he was confronted with having to make a decision as to marrying a girl he liked. He was unable to decide. Shortly after the girl married someone else, he got sick. He had always been very much interested in food, but now, in addition to following a very limited diet, he suffered from anorexia.

In the third interview he was given the interpretation that what he was doing was a form of suicide (on the installment plan). It was explained to him that he was damaging himself in that very aspect of his personality in which he was most sensitive, namely his physical appearance, and also

---

* Cf. the analysis of a case of bronchial asthma and food allergies in a six-year-old boy, through the prior analysis of his mother and then through analytic treatment of the child, in: "The Role of Mothers in Psychosomatic Disorders of Children." *Psychosomatic Medicine*, XI, No. 6, 377–380, Nov.-Dec., 1949.

that he was depriving himself of a pleasure he had greatly enjoyed, namely eating. It was also pointed out to him that all he was gaining was his mother's concern over him and her preoccupation with his food.

To this he reacted with, "if that's what I'm doing, I'm a fool." There was an immediate and striking improvement in his appetite and his tolerance for previously avoided foods, resulting in a gain of sixteen pounds within a month.

The analysis of the deeper dynamics of his symptoms and of his basic personality structure proceeded only very slowly and met with great resistance, resulting in the production of new symptoms which had the same meaning and effect, namely to keep him dependent on his mother and to prevent his functioning as an independent individual.*

PREVENTION

At best, no matter whether managed by supportive psychotherapy or psychoanalysis, psychosomatic disorders always require long-term treatment. Both kinds of therapy are uneconomic: supportive psychotherapy, because inasmuch as the patient's dependency is not resolved, it is by its very nature a lifelong necessity for the patient so treated; psychoanalysis, because of the specialized skill required and the scarcity of qualified psychoanalysts who are prepared to treat psychosomatic cases.

Many conditions that were formerly not regarded as psychosomatic are now being recognized as such. These swell the number of candidates for the uneconomic and scarcely available therapies. There is today a greatly increasing awareness of those psychosomatic illnesses which incapacitate people, which require repeated hospitalization, and which inflict great losses in emotional, social, and economic terms.

Obviously the most economic way to deal with this problem

---

* For the handling of similar situations in the cases of children, cf. "The Psychoanalytic Study of Ulcerative Colitis in Children." *Loc. cit.*, pp. 302–329.

is by prevention, and the analogy with immunology readily offers itself. Once we know what causes the disturbance, how and when its basis is laid, there is where the problem should be attacked. We have seen that psychosomatic disorders have their source in the early mother-child relationship. Therefore, the work of prevention must begin there. Or better still, the work should begin with the mother before the child is born. There are certain behaviors and symptoms which some women exhibit before and during pregnancy which demonstrate conspicuously that these women have the need to, and inevitably will establish a type of relationship with the child which will be conductive to the development of a psychosomatic response in the child. Prenatal mental hygiene clinics where expectant mothers are screened and treated according to definite indications, would seem therefore to be an important step in this direction.*

SUMMARY

Every case of psychosomatic disorder has its origin in the mother-child relation of dependency. It is found on deeper investigation that the patient lives in an emotional symbiosis with one object in his environment who, whether the actual mother or not, assumes in the patient's unconscious, the dynamic function of the mother figure.

The psychosomatic patient, unable consciously to tolerate his pregenital impulses because of his strong urge to satisfy them in reality, denies them completely, and they become converted into somatic symptoms. In this way these impulses are gratified.

Treatment of psychosomatic disorders may be by supportive psychotherapy or may take the form of psychoanalysis with its phenomenon of the classical transference. In the first case, the treatment is on a conscious level. It does not result in a change in the patient's need for dependency. There is merely a shift

---

* With this in mind I have established a Prenatal Mental Hygiene Clinic at the Brooklyn Jewish Hospital in 1946.
See also: "Psychoanalytic Study of Ulcerative Colitis in Children." *Loc. cit.*, p. 327.

of this dependency to the therapist. Such treatment affords only temporary relief from symptoms and mitigation of the severity of the attacks.

In psychoanalytic treatment, at first dependency on the analyst is encouraged; then interpretations are carefully introduced. By offering a more suitable object for identification, the analyst helps the patient consciously to recognize and to tolerate his repressed pregenital strivings. He thus furthers the development of the ego and its strivings for independence. He helps the psychosomatic patient to resolve his dependency needs by modifying the personality dynamics that produce the symptoms.

The analyst is warned of the dangers of negative transference and the need to watch for its signs. Negative transference is best prevented by analysis of the patient's resistances.

In severe psychosomatic illness, emergency treatment in the form of a psychological shock may have to be given. This may take the form of direct, deep interpretation of the patient's unconscious destructive impulses. However, unless this is followed by prolonged psychoanalytic therapy, its effect is limited.

Prevention is the best method of avoiding psychosomatic disorders. Since they invariably have their source in the early mother-child relationship, that is where the work of prevention must begin. In fact a beginning has been made in preventive work in prenatal clinics, in work with pregnant women who have evinced behaviors and symptoms that would lead to the assumption that their relationship to the child would be conducive to a psychosomatic response in the child.

BIBLIOGRAPHY

1. ALEXANDER, F., "Fundamental concepts of psychosomatic research: psychogenesis, conversion, specificity." *Psychosom. Med.*, V, No. 3, 205–211, 1943.

2. ———, *Psychosomatic Medicine: Its Principles, and Applications*. Chap. V, 34–44. New York, W. W. Norton, 1950.

3. BREUER, J. AND FREUD, S., *Studies in Hysteria*. New York & Wash., D. C., Nerv. and Ment. Dis. Publ. Co., 1936.

4. DEUTSCH, F., "Studies in pathogenesis: biological and psy-

chological aspects." *Psychoanal. Quart.*, II, 225–243, 1933.

5. ———, "Zur Bildung des Konversionssymptoms." *Intern. Ztschr. f. Psychoanal.*, X, No. 4, 380–392, 1924.

6. FEDERN, P., "Psychoanalysis of psychoses, I–III." *Psychiat. Quart.*, XVII, 246, 257, 1943.

7. FERENCZI, S., "The phenomena of hysterical materialization." *Further Contributions to the Theory and Technique of Psychoanalysis.* London, Hogarth Press, 1926.

8. ———, "Disease—pathoneuroses." *Ibid.*

9. FREUD, A., *Introduction to the Technique of Child Analysis.* New York & Wash., D. C., Nerv. and Ment. Dis. Publ. Co., 1928.

10. FREUD, S., "Fragment of an analysis of a case of hysteria." *Collected Papers.* Vol. III. London, Hogarth Press, 1924–1925.

11. ———, "General remarks on hysterical attacks." *Collected Papers.* Vol. II. London, Hogarth Press, 1924–1925.

12. GRODDECK, G., *The Book of the It.* New York & Wash., D. C., Nerv. and Ment. Dis. Publ. Co., 1928.

13. ———, *The Unknown Self.* London, C. W. Daniel Co., 1937.

14. KLEIN, M., *The Psychoanalysis of Children.* London, Hogarth Press, 1932.

15. SIMMEL, E., "Die psychophysische Bedeutsamkeit des Intestinalorgans fuer die Urverdraengung." *Intern. Ztschr. f. Psychoanal.*, X, 1924.

16. ———, "The psychogenesis of organic disturbances and their psychoanalytic treatment." Abstract in *Psychoanal. Quart.*, I, 166–170, 1932.

17. ———, "Self-preservation and the death instinct." *Psychoanal. Quart.*, XIII, 160, 185, 1944.

18. SPERLING, M., "Problems in the analysis of children with psychosomatic disorders." *Quart. J. Child Behav.*, I, No. 1, January, 1949.

19. ———, "Psychoanalytic study of ulcerative colitis in children." *Psychoanal. Quart.*, XV, No. 3, 302–329, July, 1946.

20. ———, "The role of the mother in psychosomatic disorders in children." *Psychosom. Med.*, XI, No. 6, 377–385, Nov.-Dec., 1949.

21. ———, "Mucous colitis associated with phobias." *Psychoanal. Quart.*, XIX, No. 3, 318–326, July, 1950.

22. ———, "Psychiatric aspects of ulcerative colitis." in Symposium on Diarrhea, April, 1950, at Brooklyn Jewish Hospital. To be published.

► DIFFERENTIAL PSYCHOTHERAPY OF BORDERLINE STATES*

By Victor W. Eisenstein, M.D.**

INTRODUCTION

So-called "borderline" patients today constitute a large proportion of those seeking private psychiatric help. They present not only a challenge in differential diagnosis, but a practical problem in differential treatment.

Descriptively, patients of this type appear to function at a neurotic level, that is, they complain of phobias, obsessions, conversions, depression, or anxiety states, with an admixture of abortive paranoid features, transient feelings of reference, or depersonalization. Hoch and Polatin (11) presented illustrative cases of the variety under discussion in a contribution aptly entitled, "Pseudoneurotic Forms of Schizophrenia." The improper evaluation of such patients at the start all-too frequently can lead to misdirected therapy.

The incidence of borderline syndromes that are encountered varies with the setting and the type of individual practice. In private psychiatric practice and agency experience*** I found that, of 250 consecutive consultations, 30 per cent were borderline reaction-types; Piotrowski and Lewis (13) recently

* Reprinted with permission from *The Psychiatric Quarterly*, XXV, No. 3, 379–401, 1951.
** Chief of Psychiatry Clinic and Associate Attending Neuropsychiatrist, Lenox Hill Hospital, New York City.
*** The Consultation Center, Jewish Family Service, New York City and The Family Consultation Service, Eastchester Neighborhood Association, Tuckahoe, New York.

reported that almost 50 per cent of patients (20 out of 41) who had been discharged from the New York Psychiatric Institute with a diagnosis of psychoneurosis, developed definite signs of schizophrenia in the interval between discharge and the follow-up some years later. Rorschach test criteria also suggest a high incidence. In a random sampling of fifty psychodiagnostic referrals of private adult patients, Woltmann (19) found that 32 per cent fall into the borderline category.

Many therapeutic failures of classical analysis belong in this group (12). This fact may appear paradoxical in view of the major contribution of psychoanalysis to the understanding of borderline neuroses. However, the paradox lies in the fact—which can be ascertained at almost any clinical conference—that techniques of therapy in general application have not kept pace with the theoretical understanding of these disorders. To treat borderline states as "transference neuroses" is an error, fraught with disappointment and the danger of precipitating psychotic episodes. In regard to this Federn (5) cautioned: "The most important self-defense against schizophrenia is the neurosis which is usually of the hysterical or obsessional type. No latent schizophrenic should be 'cured' of his neuroses, and he definitely should not be treated by the standard form of psychoanalysis."

Various technical considerations involved in the intensive psychotherapy of borderline states have been the subject of recent articles, notably those of Stern (17), (18), Federn (5), Schmideberg (16), and Fromm-Reichmann (9).

This paper aims at outlining a comprehensive plan of treatment that may be utilized by psychiatrists of varied theoretical orientations, and at presenting certain specific procedures appropriate to each phase of psychotherapy. As the treatment of borderline states differs appreciably on the one hand from methods in use with psychoneurotic patients, and on the other with deteriorated schizophrenics, the differential handling and the reasons therefor will be stressed.

Since the premises on which the plan of treatment is based determine the nature of the therapist's relationship with the patient, the nature of the interpretations, and the goals of treatment, these will be briefly stated. The major premise, as determined by psychoanalytic investigation (6), is that the ego or integrating apparatus of the borderline patient is itself severely involved. The minor premise is that the individual, in spite of relatively normal function and manifestly neurotic appearance, is suffering from the scars of early and very deep narcissistic injuries.

When such individuals come to treatment, emotional contact with the therapist is as much feared as sought. Borderline patients are made anxious by aloofness of manner, yet they tend to be suspicious of warmth. If they feel negative or anxious, they are apt not to show up for the next interview, being too frightened even to telephone to cancel the appointment. The therapeutic approach in such cases is necessarily focused on the treatment of the weak and narcissistically regressed ego-structure (2). In these disorders the therapist must, therefore, assume the active and benevolent role of a parent, rather than the customary neutral position of an impersonal analyst; yet he must provide more than supportive or educational help, if the patient's inner situation is to be changed.

The treatment of borderline cases may be outlined in three phases: the initial phase of establishing affective contact; the actual therapeutic working alliance; and the period of weaning and adjustment. Each phase has its own set of technical problems and each calls for a specific therapeutic attitude.

THE FIRST PHASE OF TREATMENT

Unlike the true psychoneurotic patient, the borderline patient does not, as a rule, have sufficiently good emotional contact at the start to join in a therapeutic endeavor aimed at producing inner change. A preliminary period, oriented toward the establishment of contact through discussion of the patient's current problems and through active support from the therapist, is invariably required. This period may last from several weeks to many months. In view of the adverse reality situation and the psychopathology generally existing in other members of the family, one has to be prepared, with this type of patient, literally to become the "family psychiatrist." Yet the patient must always be made to feel that he is the focus of our total interest.

Borderline cases unconsciously have a strong receptive and dependent orientation in their relationships. To them, literally, actions speak louder than words. Therefore, the primarily "giving" attitude on the part of the therapist has its psychotherapeutic rationale. The patient should, from the start, feel the therapist's attitude of friendly understanding; and the latter should say only what can support the patient in his occasional spontaneous comments during initial contacts.

Initial Negative Attitudes

Since the diagnosis of borderline states carries the certainty that we are dealing with a highly ambivalent person, reduction of negative feelings becomes the first item on the therapeutic agenda, no matter what the theoretical orientation of the psychiatrist may be. The more consistently attitudes of fear, distrust, disappointment or resentment with previous therapists and related figures are ventilated at the start, the greater the probability that the patient will be brought into a more trusting and favorable relationship, and the greater the emotional contact that ensues.

An apprehensive or suspicious attitude toward the treatment is handled, in the borderline patient, quite differently from the way it would be handled in an ordinary neurotic patient. For example, if the patient asks, "Is that a dictaphone on your desk?" the therapist fosters reality-testing by inviting the patient to see how the machine works, rather than risk stirring up paranoidal fears in the interest of obtaining material through free association to the question.

Activity in Approach

The approach to the borderline patient may be characterized as "active." This activity refers to the therapist's initiative in, and direction of, interviews. It is not to be confused with the type of activity used by some in making direct interpretations of psychotic content (ordinarily unconscious content) for the purpose of establishing contact with an uncommunicative or deteriorated schizophrenic (14). Rather, the preliminary activity refers here to a discussion of the patient's reality-situation and his reasons for wanting to escape from it.

For example, in the highly anxious type of borderline case, with tormenting obsessive fears of hurting his own children, it is mandatory to reduce the underlying guilt early, in order also to reduce the extreme agitation. Our initial inquiry, then, is shaped by the inner question, "Against whom is this illness really being directed?" This generally involves the husband or wife, and the expression of grievances in the current marital relationship soon affords the possibility of inquiring, "When did you feel like this before?" The transition from the first phase of treatment to the therapeutic relationship can also be made at a time when the patient expresses a request for help at a period of indecision. Where sufficient material has been obtained about the developmental history, such requests for advice can be used in a manner that links them up with the patient's past. Thus, an anxious patient, presenting fears of suicidal impulses, one day asked impulsively, "Do you think I ought to annul my marriage? I can't stand my husband sleeping near me!" It was suggested: "If at this time instead of discussing dissolving your marriage, we could discuss your present and previous sleeping arrangements, we might help you find out exactly why you want to withdraw." She then reluctantly related her embarrassment and resentment at having to share a bed with her brother, from the time of early childhood to late adolescence. Then followed the favored position of the brother in her parents' estimation; and her own guilt-laden hostility to this brother, whom she also admired, occupied the discussions for some time. Thus, the burden of self-destructive guilt which she had first presented began to subside.

Directed early interviews, based on the therapist's estimate of the dynamic problem, tend to avoid those situations of anxious silences which are very apt to occur in such cases, and they open the way for interpretative psychotherapy.

SECOND PHASE: THE ACTUAL
THERAPEUTIC WORKING ALLIANCE

Interpretation having been made feasible, the focus of treatment remains on the actual weak ego-state of the patient and on measures to improve its strength, rather than on material for interpretation. Reduction of the patient's guilt and anxiety is one of the available resources; raising the patient's self-esteem through the positive comment on some actual aspect of his work or other accomplishment, is another desirable feature. However what is therapeutically decisive is the interpretation of the patient's adaptive difficulties as a reaction to hurts, and to early and real deprivations of legitimate emotional needs.

The therapeutic utilization of the preverbal portion of the ego helps the patient to put his feelings into words instead of actions (that is, it reduces the tendency to acting-out). Certain defensive bodily attitudes can be safely demonstrated to the patient, and his curiosity engaged regarding their meaning and function. The material for such demonstration is always at hand in the expressive movements of the patient—a grimace or a gesture, such as putting the fist in the mouth, tearing at his nails, gnashing his teeth, biting his lips, etc. Such bodily attitudes, when tactfully inquired into and judiciously handled, mobilize the affect involved in this bit of dissociated behavior and, when successful, show the patient that all is not forgotten, even from that time of life when he could not yet speak.

The patient's use of stereotyped phrases, such as "maybe" or "I think" or "I don't know," or similar mannerisms of speech, indicating an underlying indecisiveness or ambivalence, may be demonstrated in relation to his underlying fear of aggressiveness. His own facial expression, or the lack of it, may also interest the patient from the standpoint of understanding its cause. In many borderline cases, lack of facial expression more often reflects an actual lack of contact than it does the repression of feelings, and calling attention to this lack often succeeds in thawing out some of the frozen affects.

On the contrary, obvious erotic gestures, finger play, repetitive rhythmic movements, etc., if brought to the patient's attention, only embarrass him and evoke his further defensiveness. The patient should not feel ridiculed, lest he increase his defensive withdrawal. Properly handled, such procedures as duplicating the patient's expression or movement may help the patient realize his defensiveness as expressed in his manner, rather than in his words.

It may be relevant at this point to indicate the essential yet subsidiary role of early memories in discussing with the patient his reactions and attitudes. This can be illustrated as follows:

An extremely anxious young woman, given to violent acting-out, who appeared "hysterical," but whose history was marked by a definite acute schizophrenic episode, recalls as her first memory (at two-and-a-half years) a situation of abandonment: "I was on the porch crying. My mother watched from a distance, but didn't come over." This memory became the symbol of the coexisting early ego-state, which repeatedly sought to reproduce the present reality in the traumatic early masochistic form. In the sessions she frequently showed cringing and jerking movements which denied the wish to be touched—out of a fear of being frustrated again. These sudden bodily movements lessened as she verbalized her cravings as appropriate to her earliest history.

In ordinary psychoneuroses, where free associative material is abundant, the first memory is ordinarily of no unusual importance. In borderline cases, however, this first conscious remembrance (4) often provides a springboard for fruitful discussions of early feelings in relationships.

INTERPRETATION OF EMOTIONALLY-CHARGED CONTENT

Interpretation of content is limited by the precarious state of integration in borderline patients. With this limitation in mind the specific material presented refers to: dreams, hostility and ambivalence, homosexual material, acting-out, and suicidal impulses. These are probably the most frequent situations where the technical handling may spell the difference between precipitating or avoiding panic, an acute psychotic episode, or even suicide.

Conscious Fantasies

If the focus of our treatment remains as it should on the patient's reality adjustment, we show a minimum of interest in his fantasies and a maximum of interest in his life situation, from which the fantasy is a withdrawal. An instructive example will illustrate this:

> A woman who appeared "neurotic" in most particulars but was actually a borderline psychotic, one day reported a fantasy in which she rode into the woods on a horse, dismounted, put on a rubber penis and had intercourse with another girl. She continued to disclose other homosexual fantasies but this release only alarmed her to the point of panic. The massive anxiety evoked by her discussion resulted in attacks of diarrhea which lasted for many weeks.

Now, assuming that this material had been brought in by an ordinary neurotic patient who had been prepared for the affects by a preliminary working-through of her anxieties, the ventilation of such a fantasy would have had a further cathartic effect and would have been integrated through the patient's further free associations. On the other hand, in a frankly psychotic patient, such a fantasy might be temporarily accepted as the legal tender of the patient's psychotic reality, that is, "What do you want with the penis?", by which the therapist becomes, as it were, temporarily the delusional partner of the patient. In borderline patients, however, the fantasy is best utilized for the verbalization of the patient's actual discontent with the reality of her femininity. For example, the patient could be asked, "What caused you to be so dissatisfied with being a girl?" This would not only stem the flow of homosexual anxieties, but would lead to genetic elements that would help the patient see and feel the reason for her withdrawal into such fantasies.

Dreams

Borderline patients tend to bring in dreams as a sort of mute plea for help and approval, depending on their relationship to the therapist. In many such cases, there is a tendency for the patient who is somewhat familiar with the relationship of dreams to psychotherapy to bring in dreams of isolation, as it were, saying almost, "Here, analyze this." It is a vicarious sacrifice; frequently it is diversionary from the fear of having some deeper feelings laid bare. When such a patient brings a dream it is often helpful to ask, "Why did you dream this?" or "What do you understand about it?" Attempts at analysis beyond this point are better postponed to a much later stage.*

There is much less personal responsibility for dreams than for current reality-material. Therefore, the patient is eager to bring in such material; or his interest in fantasy may be actually greater than it is in reality. Nothing is gained, and much lost, by trying to make unconscious phantasies vividly conscious in these particular cases. The only advantageous uses of dreams in borderline cases are the following: They are invariably useful for demonstrating hidden negative attitudes toward the treatment; portions may be selectively linked up with those problems currently under discussion, as for example, hidden fears or guilt feelings regarding sex (3). Dreams of self-destruction are frequently reported by this type of patient and, if discussed from the self-punishment aspect, dangerous acting-out may be prevented.

In more serious cases, the reality-situation is often more accurately perceived by the patient in his dreams than in his waking state. (Freud notes, for example, certain cases of schizophrenia in which the delusion was corrected by a dream [10].) One of my patients isolated in dreams the portion of the ego which was split off from reality. That portion frequently appeared as a hostile trouble-maker who was bent on destroying himself

---

* The suitable utilization of dreams in schizophrenic disorders has recently been described by D. Noble in: "A Study of Dreams in Schizophrenia and Allied States." *American Journal of Psychiatry,* CVII, 8, 612–616, Feb., 1951.

and everybody else, while the other portion expressed horror, shouted denials, or was aligned against the trouble-maker in the dream.

Hostility and Ambivalence

The capacity to love of the borderline patient has been crippled by ambivalent conflicts in his earliest years. In these cases hostility is not a matter of defusion of instincts, as in the severely destructive and frankly psychotic patient for whom the environment, stripped of libido, has become overwhelmingly menacing. What has to be identified in a borderline patient is the struggle between hostile and dependent attitudes. This struggle can often be interpreted along the line that the patient hates certain people because he really fears them—fears that they can hurt his pride and dominate him, ignore him, or somehow take advantage of him. Discussions of hostility against the parents may generate too much guilt if they are related too early, or if a certain degree of realistic financial or other dependency exists simultaneously. For this reason it is preferable to focus on current authorities such as employers, teachers, etc. The working-through to the primary situation in which the hostility is rooted, is contingent upon the establishment of a positive transference relationship in which such analysis is possible.

HOMOSEXUAL MATERIAL AND MASOCHISM. Homosexuality is usually brought up by the patient in connection with a fear component. One type of preliminary discussion is almost invariably called for in these cases, namely, to point out the realistic difference between the mere fear of being a homosexual and the actuality of being a homosexual. Failure to observe this precaution may sometimes precipitate a panic reaction or a florid paranoid state. In many patients, the homosexual and masochistic attitudes often coexist. One way in which a narcissistically wounded ego attempts to protect itself is by masochistic deformation. Like a detached or withdrawn attitude, it is a defensive adaptation to early situations of helplessness. Masochistic attitudes may be advantageously demonstrated as a protection in dealing with those whom the patient considers more powerful (or even omnipotent). In this connection it is perhaps relevant to mention that this is one of the reasons why lying down on the couch is contraindicated in these cases. For such patients to lie down during the interviews only accentuates the masochistic and dependent attitudes and exaggerates in their minds the doctor's fantasied and projected omnipotence. The result is that the therapist is not seen or felt as the representative of reality that he should be.

Acting-Out

Fenichel (7) has pointed out that in patients regressed to, or fixated at, the preverbal infantile level, acting-out serves as a reassurance against a fantasy danger, a denial of that danger, or an escape from it. With both the ordinary neurotic patient and the borderline patient, nothing short of accurate affective interpretation linked with specific episodes in the past will entirely eliminate tendencies towards acting-out. This acting-out may take specific forms depending upon the nature of the conflicts, such as running away from the treatment, leaving town, joining the army, certain types of sexual promiscuity, or self-destruction. In actual practice, the preventing of acting-out in borderline patients depends upon a total lessening of pressures on them through a trusting transference relationship, and through interpretations of guilt, reinforced by advice and often by direct help that modifies the external situation.

Suicide

This danger is ever-present in a large percentage of borderline patients. It is generally discussed in relation to unconscious or deeply emotionally-charged material, from which the patient seeks to escape. The patient may be aware or unaware of the fact that this tendency exists at the point where he feels that difficult demands for change are being made on him. This should be pointed out if the patient fears that he is not progressing or satisfying the doctor's or relatives' assumed expectations. Interpretation of the underlying guilt and hostility is invariably necessary, such as, "What has caused you to be so

extremely angry at them and at yourself?" Or, "Who would suffer
if you did do away with yourself?" It is often relevant to point
out, as related to developmental material, the fear of abandonment by the therapist, or the patient's giving up hope of ever being loved. The working-through of hostile identifications on a
long-term basis reduces the self-destructive drive, and is useful
in an emergency only when it has already been the topic of previous discussions. Obviously, a positive transference, or what
there is of it, is the best resource at the command of the therapist in this connection; for, on the basis of this alone he may
consider with the patient the postponement of any life-or-death
solution until the psychotherapy has had a trial at alleviating
the present desperate feelings.

TRANSFERENCE AND
COUNTER-TRANSFERENCE

The quality of the relationship with borderline patients
might be designated as tangential contact. The aim of treatment
is to merge these areas of tangential contact into a more co-
hesive and less regressive transference. The transference relations of these patients, though less reliable than in ordinary
psychoneuroses, are more intense and may reach passionately
childish levels of expression in either hostile or erotic phases.
One may expect more unpredictable reactions than in ordinary
psychoneurotic patients. A bid for approval and love is ever-
present and ever-ready to be disappointed. Withholding a
word of approval in these cases is usually not justified. The
frankly dependent and masochistic needs are easily thwarted,
and running-away from the treatment without serving notice is a
common occurrence, as emphasized by Stern (17). In view of
what has been stated regarding the traumatic ego-warp of these
cases, the therapist expects the patient to react like a hurt child
coming to mother with his grievances. This pre-oedipal type
of transference should therefore not be interpreted, but should
be nurtured until the treatment is very far advanced.

Nevertheless, what aspect of transference should be brought

to the patient's awareness? Without the analysis of transference the patient can have no emotional conviction of his misreading of the past into his present situation. Positive transference is of advantage in offsetting the strong egocentric preoccupations existing in such cases; yet the regressive aspects must be interpreted. Analyzing the thwart-reaction and the dependency upon the fancied "omnipotent" therapist, may bring the relationship to a more realistic level. Similarly, when the dependent attitude is an overcompensation for sadism, the guilt connected with the latter may be brought out, in order to reduce the patient's need for "protection" from the therapist. Since regression may be activated by erotic temptations implied in a treatment setting, such sexual or homosexual anxieties, when they interfere with the treatment, can best be countered by inquiring into the fear rather than by pointing up any positive manifestations.

The patient's intense hostility is a great obstacle to progress, and his fears of therapeutic retaliation must be brought out. Flescher (8) has pointed out that the latent psychotic patient's destructive urges and his fears of them are "probably responsible for more of his social withdrawal than is the narcissistic position of his libido." The fear of aggressive impulses mobilized in an intimate relationship may make for difficulty in treatment, or may lead to actual interruption of treatment by the patient.

Because of the early masochistic deformation that exists, the transference reactions of borderline patients are apt to be dominated by such attitudes. Commonly, the patient tries to maneuver the therapist into the position of refusing, that is, into the image of the mother refusing food or love to the child. Interpretation of the wish to be refused as outlined by Bergler (1) is often a helpful expedient, particularly with borderline patients who constitute many of the so-called "oral" types.

The element of narcissistic identification with the therapist plays a considerable role in such cases, and is a matter calling for some discretion regarding the precise moment at which to call it to the patient's attention. As long as the manifestations are relatively innocuous, nothing need be said. However, when the patient endangers his personal relationships by indulging in gratuitous "analyses" of his friends, the identification should be pointed out for its real danger rather than on the basis of competition, or gratification of libidinal desires.

With few exceptions it may be said that the analysis of negative attitudes, disappointment, distrust, resentment, etc., in practice engenders less danger of regression and relapse in general than does the exposure of hidden erotic attitudes towards the therapist. The whole orientation, unlike that which obtains in transference neuroses, is to keep the patient as far as possible in a favorable and trusting relationship with the therapist. Under the influence of this relationship, some of his egocentric interest is directed into reality-oriented channels.

Counter-transference Problems

From what has already been said of borderline cases, it is evident that they are, as a rule, difficult patients. Emotionally they demand a great deal more from the therapist than do ordinary neurotic cases. Their therapy, calling as it does for a more active role on the part of the psychiatrist, is subject to difficulty from the latter's counter-transference attitudes. The therapist constantly has to examine his feelings and reactions in order to be aware of influences at work emanating from his own direction. Work with these patients demands a lookout for attitudes of irritation with the patient and for discernment of the cause, whether rooted in frustrations of one's therapeutic efforts, hurt to one's narcissism, or one's own unresolved anxieties. If from his own previous analysis the therapist is not aware of the significant attitudes, the therapeutic situation is apt to suffer. One must observe whether, in shifting one's schedule, the borderline patient is apt to be the one chosen for cancellation or for shifting hours. Such an attitude is readily transmitted to the patient and indicates to him that he is less valued, or more difficult, hence rejected. The patient's subtle discernment in these matters is not always a matter of projection.

Positive attitudes of counter-transference may be less troublesome from the standpoint of management; nevertheless, they can interfere with a dispassionate appraisal of the situation presented by the patient. For example, this may be evident at the start, where one is inclined to favor a diagnosis of psychoneurosis, rather than borderline schizophrenia, because the patient is an articulate young man, or an attractive or intelligent young woman. Intellectual or aesthetic contact however is not emotional contact. The ready flow of material in these cases may deceive one into making technical errors that would militate against the patient's best interests. If we fail to assess the true situation, there is an ever-present danger of precipitating a frank psychotic reaction through psychotherapeutic endeavor.

CASE-WORK WITH PATIENTS AND RELATIVES

Importance of Work with the Family

In the treatment of transference neuroses, one rarely has to work with members of the patient's family. In borderline cases, on the other hand, it is almost mandatory to do so, either directly, or through the mediation of a social worker. The prognosis generally varies with the life-situation, and the worse the level at which this is maintained, the less probability there is of rehabilitation. One encounters almost as much resistance in dealing with the families of these patients as with the patients themselves. It is technically almost always better to ask the patient's permission to see his relatives. Because of financial or other dependency of this class of patients on the home situation, it is the family rather than the patient who all too frequently may interrupt the treatment.

For this reason, although our alliance is with the patient, the parent or relatives must be brought into more positive relationships before we can hope to lessen the external pressures on the patient. Generally, much time must be spent in working through the parents' resentment of the therapeutic need and interference. It may be assumed that most parents of such patients feel guilty and defensive, and their denial of their role in contributing to illness may be expected as a natural matter of course. The family generally responds to requests for certain details of the patient's developmental history and this affords the opportunity for checking events given by the patient, or forgotten by him, and the members of the family may thus be helped to appreciate the patient's difficulty through this indirect focus on developmental history. The relatives must be prepared for expressions of hate by the patient in the course of treatment, and for the fact that the patient may temporarily get worse before he gets better. (Especially is this true because of the possibilities of negative therapeutic reactions.)

Case-Work

Work with the family is not merely an auxiliary to the psychotherapy of borderline states; it is an integral part of the treatment. The change of parental attitudes is not merely a matter of instruction, but one of therapy on a near-psychiatric level. The psychiatric social worker is often in better position to work with the family than is the psychiatrist who is treating the patient. Moreover, the case-worker can serve an important purpose in the direct social and occupational rehabilitation of borderline patients. Consistent analytically-oriented work in these directions has been described by Ryerson and Weller (15).

FINAL PHASE: WEANING FROM
TREATMENT CONTACT

The reduction in the intensity of treatment and the preparation for separation constitutes the third phase of the treatment of borderline patients. This phase is considerably more extended than with ordinary neurotic patients. A new adjustment, which would take days or weeks in a true psychoneurotic patient, usually takes months in a borderline case. Abrupt termination or failure to observe each new adjustment over a considerable period invites relapse.

In the psychoneuroses, the aim of the analyst is to remake the personality into a relatively independent one; ideally, then, all vestiges of dependency transference are fully analyzed. In the case of the borderline patient, the average goal is that of helping a person with severely damaged ego to function at a higher level of integration.

While continuous therapy to completion is ideal in ordinary neuroses, it is not ordinarily attainable in borderline cases. Discontinuous analysis in periods, to the limit of current adjustment possibilities, has been recommended by Bychowski (2), Flescher (8), and others. If the therapist does not arrange for this, in actual practice, the patient does so after he achieves a certain degree of symptomatic improvement. This consideration makes the third phase of the therapy of borderline cases a long-term, if not a lifelong matter.

The best results can naturally be expected in younger patients who are accessible to the above-described modified analytic effort; however, even patients of middle age can benefit considerably from interpretative psychotherapy where neurotic traits predominate and where the life-situation is favorable.

SUMMARY

The class of patients who are descriptively neurotic but dynamically psychotic nowadays make up a large proportion of those seeking psychiatric treatment.

This paper considers the special therapeutic problems of the borderline group; illustrates differences in the technical handling of given material in these cases, as against true neurotics on the one hand and frank schizophrenics on the other; and outlines the rationale for a comprehensive plan for differential treatment. The premises on which the outline of psychotherapy is based are discussed in relation to the nature of the therapist's relationship, the kind of interpretations given, and the goal of treatment.

Attention is called to selective measures required in regard to fantasy, hostility and masochism, homosexual material, acting-out, and suicidal impulses. Specific auxiliary measures are presented in relation to work with families of such patients.

The differential psychotherapeutic procedures outlined in this plan can be utilized to a large extent by therapists of diverse theoretical orientations.

BIBLIOGRAPHY

1. BERGLER, E., *The Basic Neurosis*. New York, Grune and Stratton, 1949.

2. BYCHOWSKI, G., "Therapy of the weak ego." *Am. J. Psychother.*, IV, 407, July, 1950.

3. EISENSTEIN, V. W., "Dreams following intercourse." *Psychoanal. Quart.*, XVIII, 154–173, 1949.

4. ———, AND RYERSON, R., "Psychodynamic significance of the first conscious memory." *Bull. Menninger Clinic*, XV, 213–220, Nov., 1951.

5. FEDERN, P., "Principles of psychotherapy in latent schizophrenia." *Am. J. Psychother.*, I, 129–145, April, 1947.

6. FENICHEL, O., *Psychoanalytic Theory of Neurosis*. New York, W. W. Norton, 1945.

7. ———, "Neurotic acting-out." *Psychoanal. Rev.*, XXII, 1945.

8. FLESCHER, J., Discussions at Psychiatric Forum-Group, New York, March, 1950.

9. FROMM-REICHMANN, F., *Principles of Intensive Psychotherapy*. Chicago, Univ. of Chicago Press, 1950.

10. FREUD, S., *An Outline of Psychoanalysis*. New York, W. W. Norton, 1949.

11. HOCH, P. AND POLATIN, P., "Pseudoneurotic forms of schizophrenia." *Psychiat. Quart.*, April, 1949.

12. OBERNDORF, C. P., "Failures with psychoanalytic therapy." Chap. II, *Failures in Psychiatric Treatment*. Paul Hoch, ed. New York, Grune and Stratton, 1948.

13. PIOTROWSKI, Z. AND LEWIS, N. D. C., "An experimental Rorschach diagnostic aid for some forms of schizophrenia." *Am. J. Psychiat.*, CVII, 362, Nov., 1950.

14. ROSEN, J. N., "The treatment of schizophrenic psychosis by direct analytic therapy." *Psychiat. Quart.*, XXI, 3–37, 1947.

15. RYERSON, R. AND WELLER, E., "The private practice of psychiatric case work." *News Letter of the Am. Assn. Psychiat. Social Workers*, XVI, 1946.

16. SCHMIDEBERG, M., "The treatment of psychopaths and borderline patients." *Am. J. Psychother.*, I, 45–71, Jan., 1947.

17. STERN, A., "Psychoanalytic therapy in borderline neuroses." *Psychoanal. Quart.*, XIV, 190–199, 1945.

18. ———, "Transference in borderline neuroses." *Psychoanal. Quart.*, XVII, 527–529, 1948.
19. WOLTMANN, A. G., Personal communication on 50 cases examined between June, 1949 and March, 1950.

► THE EMERGENCY PSYCHOTHERAPY OF DEPRESSION

*By Leopold Bellak, M.D.**

GENERAL FORMULATIONS

As used in this paper, "psychotherapy" is to be considered psychoanalytic psychotherapy: an attempt by the therapist to modify behavior by means of verbal operations, predicated upon psychoanalytic hypotheses. The term "depression" is used to denote psychogenic depressions. However, it includes manic-depressive psychosis, depressive type. I have formulated a "Multiple-Factor Psychosomatic Theory of Manic-Depressive Psychosis" (2) in which I suggest that this disorder is a syndrome related to both somatic and psychogenic etiologic factors. I believe, however, that psychoanalytic hypotheses permit better understanding, prediction, and therapeutic control than any other conceptualization.

In psychoanalysis proper, each analysand is a new phenomenon; a large area of investigation may on the whole be well-known ground, yet the individual nuances are carefully traced by the day-to-day study of associations. Thus, each therapeutic session is at the same time an instrument of research invaluable for validation and new discovery.

Psychotherapy as compared to psychoanalysis is more in the nature of an applied science: a skill based upon the fundaments of psychoanalytic hypothesis. Needless to say, basic science and applied science interact and are both necessary. For psycho-

---

* Clinical Assistant Professor of Psychiatry, New York Medical College; Lecturer in Psychology, New School of Social Research; Consultant Psychiatrist, Altro Health and Rehabilitation Services.

analytic psychotherapy the therapist must attempt to concep-
tualize his patient's problems in advance, weigh the liabilities
and assets and, at times, proceed with interventions with only
minimal cues to check his bearings. In this respect, psychotherapy
can be a more difficult job than psychoanalysis, demanding not
only knowledge but also a great flexibility.

"Psychoanalytic psychotherapy" is differentiated, for the purposes of this paper, from the classical psychoanalysis proper in
a number of important ways.*

Goal

The goal of classical psychoanalysis is the change of personality structure in all metapsychological aspects. In psychotherapy, the goal is primarily symptom removal, without the
hope of a profound restructuring.

Time

In psychoanalysis proper, time per se and transitory conditions can be of only secondary importance. The generally expected duration of psychoanalysis is measured in years; in psychotherapy the average duration is measured in months (less, of
course, in emergency psychotherapy wherein at least the most
urgent changes are hoped for within three to six sessions).

Method

Psychoanalysis proper uses as its main tool the patient's
free associations. From these free associations the analyst will
proceed at first to interpret the defenses, and in due course go
on to ontogenetically earlier and more deeply repressed material.

In psychotherapy, free associations may or may not be used,
or may be used intermittently. Frequently, id impulses are directly interpreted instead of the defenses against them.

---

* These differences are presented here only schematically and in
a sketchy way, as a minimal delineation of the term "psychotherapy" as used in this paper.

The Transference Situation

In psychoanalysis, the interpretation of the transference is one of the main vehicles of the treatment. "Negative transference" is as useful a vehicle as "positive transference."

In psychotherapy on the other hand the transference situation may or may not be interpreted. Negative transference is almost always an obstacle. It is most important in psychotherapy to terminate treatment with a positive transference continuing, since it may be a satisfactory basis for years of continued well-being in the patient.

Indications

Psychoanalysis proper is indicated in the presence of good ego strength, the absence of immediately pressing issues, and the presence of chronic, widespread and deep-going disturbances. Psychotherapy is indicated in problems which, because of their milder or more circumscribed nature, do not necessitate psychoanalysis proper, or because psychoanalysis might be too great a burden, or because immediately pressing issues and symptoms necessitate an active intervention.

Basic Steps

There are certain basic steps which are common to all analytic psychotherapy; namely, communication, interpretation, insight, and working-through (3).

COMMUNICATION. In communication, the patient informs the therapist of his problems, his history, and his contemporary life. This may be accomplished by free association or other means.

INTERPRETATION. In interpretation, the therapist listens and perceives the structure and pattern of behavior in the patient and/or a misinterpretation of events. When this has become clear, and when he believes the timing appropriate, he brings this pattern to the attention of the patient. This pointing out of common denominators in behavioral patterns and apperceptive distortions is called "interpretation." (There are a number of interventions the therapist may make which are related to or preparatory to interpretations—such as simply pointing out details and permitting the patient himself to perceive the pattern; actual teaching, reconstructing historical events, and the like—which need not be discussed here in detail.)

INSIGHT. We speak of insight if the patient perceives a pattern (configuration) in his behavior and thinking. In another paper (3), I have discussed how this insight needs to be both intellectual and emotional, and how it may pertain to the understanding and interrelating of patterns as they exist in the contemporary life situation, in the transference situation, in earlier life situations, and particularly as they pertain to the relationship between conscious and unconscious motivation.

WORKING-THROUGH. Working-through is a process whereby the patient applies the newly acquired insight to a variety of situations for which the same patterns hold true, in the contemporary life situation, in earlier history, and in the transference relationship. His awareness is thus increased. By means of a learning process, his behavior is changed, and by metapsychological restructuring therapeutic changes are brought about.

SPECIFIC FORMULATIONS

Emergency psychotherapy, then, is a method of treatment for symptoms demanding quickest possible relief because of their crippling or endangering nature. Its goal is limited to the removal of specific symptoms; the time is limited to the absolute minimum. Emergency psychotherapy is therefore indicated when the time of either the patient or the therapist is greatly limited. This implies that sometimes such emergency steps may be directed solely toward the depression, while a more conventional psychotherapy may be carried on later by the same or another therapist for more basic problems. Such emergency measures have actually been used, for instance, in a social-agency setting where, in such cases, a psychotherapist will do the emergency therapy and, after that, turn the patient over to the case-worker for support and other measures. It also occurred, for example, while the Veterans Administration authorized private treatment

—on a contract basis—often for only six hours (at least, there was no certainty as to whether extensions would be granted).

Procedures

For the emergency psychotherapy of depressions specifically, I suggest the following procedures:

HISTORY-TAKING. Get as exhaustive a history of the onset of the chief complaint (depression) as possible. Such history-taking is not, or need not be traumatic. To the contrary, if accomplished tactfully, the most persistent and detailed questioning will afford the patient narcissistic gratification (indicating as it were the interest taken in him) and will increase his rapport, rather than upset him. The aim of this history should be to gain a complete understanding of the precipitating factors and of the entire contemporary life situation.

Get an exhaustive developmental history. The purpose is not to obtain data to be filed away ("which month did you get your first tooth?") but to understand the development of the patient in a given family environment: relation to parents, to siblings according to relative ages and impact upon each other, cultural and socio-economic setting, etc. We want to know whom the patient identified with at different times, whom he loved, and by whom he was frustrated, whom he imitated, and with whom he competed. To a large extent the personality is the reflection of the history of the personality.

The history-taking is complete only if as a result of it, the onset of the present illness can be thoroughly understood in dynamic terms. Freud has said that an adult neurosis breaks out when a contemporary situation repeats a traumatic infantile situation. The present illness is understood if the precipitating life situation can be clearly perceived as a pattern repetitive of an earlier one, and if the significance of each contemporary factor is clearly seen.

APPRAISAL. If the onset of the illness has been understood as stated above, one must appraise carefully the liabilities and assets of the patient's entire situation, internal and environmental. Then one either suggests environmental changes with the hope of altering specific dynamic situations* and/or proceeds to well-planned psychologic interventions. The limitations of time, and of all assets of the patient, must be kept clearly in mind.

PSYCHODYNAMIC PICTURE. Certain specific statements can be made about the psychodynamic picture of depressions, on the basis of the classical psychoanalytic investigations (1), (10), (14), (15), (12), (17), (16), (11), etc. The depressed patient has internalized and cathected love objects against whom he harbors great hostility. A severe superego prohibits expression of this hostility, and all the anger is thereupon directed against the ego: in short, the depression is the equivalent of intra-aggression.

The hatred against the love-object is one part of an ambivalent attitude which is related to disappointment and frustration of oral wishes, by the love-object. These oral wishes are of both an oral-receptive and an oral-aggressive nature.

INTERPRETATION. Predicated upon this psychodynamic picture are the following operations: making conscious, in as cautious a way as possible, the anger which the patient feels, and which may manifest itself symptomatically as self-reproach. The patient must be steadfastly reassured that this anger is quite acceptable: that is, an attempt at the decrease in the severity of the superego must go hand in hand with the increasing awareness of the anger. The therapist, representing the authority and the superego at the moment, must be permissive and reassuring. Slowly, the patient may be made aware not only of his feeling of anger, but also of the target of his anger, of the person it is meant for in the contemporary situation, and if suitable, this may be related to the person for whom the anger was meant in the infantile situation.

Such direct interpretations may have cathartic value:** the

---

* As G. Bibring (9) has most lucidly discussed in relation to case-work.

** I am greatly concerned that much in this paper may be misconstrued as a recommendation of overactive interpretation—the pitfall of the novice. Let me remind the reader that the psychotherapist's words are his scalpel and that no intervention should be made without knowing precisely why it is made.

intrapsychic "pressure" is decreased, the severity of the depression and the danger of suicide are decreased by deflecting the intra-aggression. Immediate relief may follow interpretations, marked by a symptomatic smile or some other response. If the patient does not respond in such a way, one must ask oneself if the interpretation was wrong, or poorly timed, or poorly formulated.

Aside from the aggression, the passive oral wishes have to be tactfully pointed out. Again, the patient needs to be reassured as to the acceptability of such oral wishes, and examples of everyday life (common feelings about getting up on a rainy morning) might be given for this purpose. The therapist must be supporting and giving and at the same time must interpret the patient's need for support. (Occasionally, offering the patient a cigarette, or a candy, or a drink may be indicated.) The patient must have the feeling that he can rely upon, and call upon, the doctor any time it should be necessary, and in any way reasonable. Steady references may be made to the relationship between the current situation and the infantile traumatic situation.

Dreams, of course, may play a very useful role in emergency psychotherapy. If they occur regularly enough they are the best guide to the current unconscious problems of the patient. Here, as in all other areas, it is the task of the therapist to know as much as possible of what goes on in the patient, and to interpret only that small segment of this information which is calculated to have a beneficial effect at a given time.

I have found it very useful to ask for the last two or three dreams (if the patient is seen only once or twice a week), and to choose for interpretation those portions which contain superficially and manifestly discernible features of a recurrent pattern. That is, I may point out that in all three dreams the patient dreams of herself as a little girl in her mother's house, and that this probably expresses her wish to be a little girl again and to be cared for instead of her having to be a mother herself and to care for and toil for her own child. In this way, for instance, I may bring out both the oral longing and the anger over its frustration, as well as the anger directed at the child who demands attention, and who may be an identification figure for the younger sibling of the patient (which younger sibling was the original rival).

Special Situations

Special situations may exist where the depression is reactive to severe bodily injury, illness, or loss. Experience with cardiac and tuberculous patients (4), (5) has shown that such depressions are superficially related primarily to changes in the body image and in the self-image; the loss of competent functioning is experienced as a narcissistic injury. With increased dependency upon the environment goes the usual increase in oral demands and the anger related to the supposed disappointments and frustrations.

Much good can be done if the patient's unconscious, or preconscious, or even conscious notion of his injury can be examined and freed of its neurotic exaggerations. The misconceptions are at times facilitated by intellectual misinformation. For instance, a discussion of the anatomy of a coronary and the anastomotic repair (with a comparison to the healing of a fractured armbone) may vastly improve the patient's body-image and the related depression.

On the other hand, misconceptions on the basis of, say, one male patient's identification of his own illness with the illness of his mother, may lead to false conscious expectations and pathogenic female identification.

Again, not infrequently, it is fairly simple to show a tuberculous patient how his conception of the bleeding hole in the lung actually reveals childhood conceptions of female genitality and castration. Simplicity of language and a light touch may make such an interpretation, which one ordinarily would make only much later in the course of a regular psychoanalysis, acceptable (or at least not harmful) to a patient.

INDIRECT CATHARSIS. Particularly in patients with psychosomatic involvement, but also in all depressed persons, a procedure may be useful which one might call a "method of indirect catharsis." It consists simply of the therapist putting the patient's feelings into words for the patient in a very strong and dramatic way. It has been helpful to use strong vernacular expressions for aggressive sentiments, for example, "I bet you really wished the goddamsonofabitch would drop dead!" This method permits the patient vicarious gratification without his quite having to take the responsibility for these feelings. At the same time, it is reassuring for him to hear that the doctor, as an authority, would dare to express such feelings. Reassurance to the effect that everybody feels that way at times, even about people whom one may basically love, is also necessary. *It is important that every disclosure of an inacceptable feeling or drive must be accompanied by reassurance of this kind.*

TEACHING. To a certain extent, teaching is part of psychotherapy, as Freud reports for early psychoanalysis. Not only must the patient actually learn to report dreams, daydreams, and fleeting thoughts, but he must be told at appropriate occasions how aggressive and dependent wishes are part of every person and that his own happen to be both extra-strong and extra-inhibited. Pat examples and little stories are of great teaching value (for instance, I often introduce—apologetically, because of its naivete—the example of the teakettle that boils over, as a simile to inhibited emotions, and it rarely fails to produce some affirmative response from the patient).

PROBLEM OF SUICIDE. In the treatment of depressions, the problem of suicide must always be uppermost in the therapist's mind. The diagnostic appraisal of suicidal liability belongs, of course, to the most difficult and, at the same time, to the most important tasks. Projective techniques, notably the Rorschach, for example, in the hands of Hertz (13), may be able to make some contributions to this difficult problem.

Clinically, the expression of the wish to die is most often an oral wish to sleep without cares, as Lewin has pointed out (16). By themselves, such oral wishes are probably responsible for the frequency of such thoughts in the general population, especially in adolescence, and they are usually of no clinical consequence. However, when such oral wishes are accompanied by a great deal of unexpressed hostility in people with little ego-strength and with great anxiety, then there is reason for worry on the part of the therapist.

In the emergency psychotherapy, it is of the utmost importance to unearth any existing suicidal fantasies and to find out to whom they are addressed, consciously and/or unconsciously. If there is a conscious fantasy, it should be analyzed. For example, "I bet you feel 'I'll show her—she'll be really sorry when I'm gone'." If there is no conscious fantasy, it must be found out whom the aggression is meant for, as discussed earlier in the history-taking, and these sentiments should be vigorously brought out. The concept of "self-harm to harm another" must be dramatically illustrated; the saying "to tear one's hair out" when one is really exasperated at someone else, may serve as an example. A story I have found useful is the one about the man who stands in front of his burning house, holding his sides with laughter. When asked by the neighbors what he is so happy about he says: "Oh boy! Are those mice getting it!"

If the suicidal danger seems acute, it is, of course, better to safeguard the patient by institutionalizing him or arranging nursing care. Adjuncts of psychotherapy, such as the mixture of sedation and stimulation mentioned below, or electric shock treatment, may also have to be instituted.

Adjuncts to Psychotherapy

DRUG THERAPY. In psychotherapeutic work there are certain drugs that may be helpful. The sodium amytal interview for catharsis and for the gathering of information has been amply described in the literature. Oral barbiturates in proper mixture with stimulants such as desoxyephedrine have also been described (6): one-grain-and-a-half of nembutal together with 2.5 mg. or 5 mg. of desoxyephedrine hydrochloride, taken by the patient one-half hour before the appointment, may greatly facilitate the ability of the patient to communicate without the interference with locomotion and without the disadvantage ensuing from intravenous medication. Such medication twice a day (upon arising and at noon), may be of considerable symptomatic value in the relief of depression.

THE THEMATIC APPERCEPTION TEST. The Thematic Apperception Test (TAT) has suggested itself as a valuable adjunct to psychotherapy (7), (8). The TAT consists of a series of ambiguous pictures of life situations. The subject is asked to tell a story about what is going on in the picture, what went on before, and what the outcome will be, permitting himself a free flow of his imagination. In telling the story, the subject apperceptively distorts and structures the situation in terms of his own problems. This technique was originally devised primarily as a method of appraisal and diagnosis. As such, it is useful for the understanding of the patient's dynamics before therapy is actually begun. The pictures relate to parental figures, to contemporary ones, and so on, highlighting the interpersonal problems of the subject.

In therapy, the stories the patient tells may be used as vehicles of communication; the patient may be handed his own typed-out story and asked to comment about it, or free-associate to it. In selecting specific stories, the therapist has an opportunity to focus the patient's attention on a given area. While a naive subject may at first maintain that he simply described the picture, it will not be difficult to show that other people see different events in the pictures. By this means it is relatively easy to induce—in otherwise naive subjects—an awareness of the subjectivity of their notions and emotions: it is a basic step of therapy to make the symptom—in this case, the depression—*ego alien* to the patient. He must learn to ally part of his ego and its reality-testing with that of the therapist, and together they must be able to stand off and watch his subjective reactions.

The TAT facilitates this step by showing the subject that seemingly objective productions of his are, in reality, highly subjective ones. What one might call a "psychotherapeutic attitude" towards the self, is thus introduced.

The same point can be further reinforced, and the subjective distortions clearly demonstrated, if one can show the patient a repetitive pattern in his stories: for instance, one may impress the subject with his latent aggression by demonstrating that all or many of his stories concern violence when the picture on the whole lends itself as well to nonviolent interpretation.

Or, one may be able to point to the severe conscience as it may manifest itself in quick and overly severe punishments of culprits in the story, or may be able to show the oral longing and feelings of disappointment in the outcome of the stories, etc.

ELECTRIC CONVULSIVE THERAPY. Electric Convulsive Therapy (ECT) may be combined with psychotherapy, if the suicidal danger is too great or if the depression is too deep for communication. In that case, psychotherapy is probably best restricted to a suggestion of such environmental changes as seem advisable on the basis of dynamic insight; or therapy has to be limited to directive help for the patient in dealing with his immediate problems.

SUMMARY

Emergency psychotherapy of depression is a method of treatment for symptoms demanding quickest possible relief. Its goal is limited to the removal of specific symptoms; the time is limited to the absolute minimum. Procedures include the taking of a comprehensive history, appraisal of the psychodynamic picture, and interpretation, in as cautious a way as possible. The aim of interpretation is to help decrease the severity of the superego, to decrease (and deflect from the ego) aggressive drives, and to lessen the pressure of oral demands. Dreams and fantasies are valuable material for interpretation in depression because of their cathartic value.

There are special situations in the therapeutic management of depression due to bodily injuries, illness, or loss. Here the method of indirect catharsis is of value, as well as direct teaching.

The problem of suicide is an ever-present danger; and the diagnostic appraisal of suicidal liability is one of the most difficult and important tasks of the therapist. In depression it is of vital importance to unearth any suicidal fantasies and to find out against whom they are addressed. If the suicidal danger is acute, it is better to safeguard the patient by institutional and/or nursing care.

Adjuncts to psychotherapy in depression include drug therapy, the Thematic Apperception Test, and Electro Convulsive Therapy.

BIBLIOGRAPHY

1. ABRAHAM, K., *Selected Papers on Psychoanalysis*. London, Hogarth Press, 1942.

2. BELLAK, L., "A multiple-factor psychosomatic theory of manic-depressive psychosis." Preface in L. Bellak, *Manic-Depressive Psychosis and Allied Disorders*. New York, Grune & Stratton, 1951.

3. ———, "Some basic concepts of psychotherapy." *J. Nerv. & Ment. Dis.*, CVIII, No. 2, 137–141, 1948.

4. ———, (with HASELKORN, F.), "A multiple-service approach to cardiac patients." *Social Casework,* July, 1950.

5. ———, "Psychiatric aspects of tuberculosis." *Social Casework,* May, 1950.

6. ———, "The use of oral barbiturates in psychotherapy." *J. Psychiat.*, CV, No. 11, 849–850, May, 1949.

7. ———, "The Thematic Apperception Test in clinical use." *Projective Psychology.* L. A. Abt and L. Bellak, eds. New York, Alfred A. Knopf, 1950.

8. ———, PASQUARELLI, B. AND BRAVERMAN, S., "The use of the TAT in psychotherapy." *J. Nerv. & Ment. Dis.*, CX, No. 1, 51–65, July, 1941.

9. BIBRING, G. L., "Psychiatric principles in casework." *Social Casework*, XXX, No. 6, 230–235, 1949.

10. FREUD, S., "Mourning and melancholia." *Collected Papers,* Vol. IV. London, Hogarth Press, 1925 (1915).

11. GARMA, A. AND RASCOVSKY, L., eds., *Psicoanalisis de la Melancolia.* Buenos Aires, El Ateneo, 1948.

12. GERÖ, G., "The construction of depression." *Intern. J. Psychoanal.*, XVII, Part 4, 423–461, 1936.

13. HERTZ, M., "A further study of 'suicidal' configurations in Rorschach records." *J. Proj. Techniques*, XIII, No. 1, 1949.

14. JACOBSON, E., "Depression. the oedipus complex in the

development of depressive mechanisms." *Psychoanal. Quart.*, XII, No. 4, 541–560, 1943.

15. ———, "The effect of disappointment on superego formation." *Psychoanal. Rev.*, XXXIII, No. 2, 129–147, 1946.

16. LEWIN, B. D., *The Psychoanalysis of Elation.* New York, W. W. Norton, 1950.

17. SPITZ, R., "Anaclitic depression." *The Psychoanalytic Study of the Child*, II. New York, *Intern. Univ. Press,* 1946.

► RORSCHACH PERCEPTANALYTIC MEASUREMENT OF PERSONALITY CHANGES DURING AND AFTER INTENSIVE PSYCHOANALYTICALLY ORIENTED PSYCHOTHERAPY[*]

By Zygmunt Piotrowski, Ph.D.,[**]
and Martin Schreiber, M.D.[***]

PURPOSE AND SCOPE

This study had its inception twelve years ago (1939) with the psychotherapist's (M.S.) dissatisfaction with the usual criteria for evaluating psychotherapeutic results and for discriminating between improvement based on symptom change and

[*] Prepared with the aid of a research grant from the National Institute of Health, Public Health Service.
[**] Associate in Psychiatry, Columbia University; Adjunct Associate Professor of Psychology, New York University; Attending Clinical Psychologist, Kingsbridge V. A. Hospital, New York City.
[***] Instructor in Psychiatry, Columbia University; Adjunct Psychiatrist, Mt. Sinai Hospital, New York City; Assistant Attending Psychiatrist, Presbyterian Hospital, New York City; Attending Psychiatrist, Hillside Hospital, New York City.

improvement based upon character change. Since symptom improvement, or symptom change (whether noted and reported by the patient, by relatives, by the family physician, or by the therapist himself) are, perforce, all heavily weighted with subjectivity, and since symptomatic changes have, in the past, constituted the major common criterion for evaluating psychotherapeutic results, a more objective and more accurately verifiable criterion was sought. It was felt that the comparative, or serial, Rorschach method might furnish the sought after means for validating clinical impressions of basic and deep characterological changes resulting from psychotherapy.

This study has a twofold purpose. First, it should indicate that the multiple or serial Rorschach is a valuable tool for revealing the directional trend of therapeutic improvement at the characterological process level. Secondly, by the application of this method to two different groups of patients, we have been able to objectively demonstrate the difference in the characterological therapeutic results of psychoanalytically oriented psychotherapy in contrast to non-analytic (eclectic) psychotherapy.

Because of limitations of space and our desire to focus entirely on the Rorschach findings, we are deliberately omitting from this paper otherwise germane and pertinent material relating to the following subject matters: detailed discussion concerning clinical diagnostic evaluations and impressions vis-a-vis Rorschach diagnostic formulations; clinical details and criteria of clinical improvement; details of treatment procedures; differential criteria for discriminating between psychoanalysis, intensive analytically oriented psychotherapy, and non-analytic or eclectic psychotherapy.

Our subject material comprises 23 cases in all, divided into two groups which will hereafter be called "Group A" and "Group B".

Group A, 13 cases, have all undergone "successful" (from the subjective and clinical standpoint) psychoanalytically oriented psychotherapy. All were treated by the same therapist, and all underwent intensive and deep psychoanalytically oriented psychotherapy with three to five sessions per week, eleven months a year, over a period of two to six years. All had serial Rorschach examinations at intervals varying between six and eighteen months. The primary or "basic" (pre-therapeutic) Rorschach was usually carried out after the second or third visit following the completion of the primary clinical diagnostic summation based upon the comprehensive psychiatric interview. In this group we have a minimum of three Rorschachs per patient with a maximum of six per patient.

This study consists primarily of a comparison of the first Rorschach record, taken at the beginning of psychoanalytically oriented psychotherapy, hereinafter designated as POP, with the interval and last Rorschach records of the same patient taken at the termination of POP. These 13 POP patients (marked by letters in the table) were treated by one of us (M.S.) and their Rorschach records were interpreted by the other (Z.P.). Patients A to J were psychoneurotics and all except one had intense compulsive obsessive character traits; the exception was a case of anxiety hysteria with phobias. Patient K suffered from epilepsy with organogenic and psychogenic convulsive seizures and was an obsessive character; he was treated with anti-convulsant drugs and with POP. Patients L and M were schizophrenics; the former was a relatively mild case of ambulatory schizophrenia, with hypomanic acting out and with drug addiction, while the latter was a case of early schizophrenia with very marked schizoidism and paranoid trends. These POP patients were of superior intelligence and education. All were adult private patients, 10 men and 3 women. The detailed clinical diagnostic formulations for these 13 cases, A to M, will be found appended at the conclusion of this paper (Table III).

The analytic psychotherapy in each specific case varied in its distance from the psychoanalytic standard. The standard psychoanalytic procedure centering upon free association, dream analysis, the analysis of transference phenomena, the analysis of the repetitive compulsive behavior pattern in the patients' contemporary productions relating to daily life problems, the recovery of repressed and forgotten infantile material through the reversal of layers of unconscious ego defense (resistance), was carried out in relatively pure form in 6 (B,C,E,F,H,J) of these 13 cases. Thus, the psychotherapy of these 6 was the least removed or deviant from the standard analytic procedure.

On the other hand, in cases A, D and G, the standard psychoanalytic procedure was preceded by two to four years of preliminary intensive POP therapy. In case K, one and a half years of standard psychoanalysis was followed by six months of POP.

Three cases alone, I, L and M, were purely POP. These 3, therefore, are those where the therapy was farthest removed in the scale from the psychoanalytic standard.

Group B, the non-POP or control group, consisted of 10 patients, 6 men and 4 women. Each of them was diagnosed by more than one psychiatrist as a psychoneurotic of the obsessive-compulsive type. On the average, they were treated approximately over the same period of time as the POP patients. The interval between their first and last Rorschach records was similar to that of the POP group. However, they differed crucially from the POP group in the type of psychotherapy. Each of the non-POP patients was a clinic patient, was treated by different psychiatrists successively, and was given sporadic psychotherapy, mainly of a ventilating and supportive nature. This psychotherapy could not be either persistent or consistent; it was varied and intermittent. Although both groups had different psychotherapists, their Rorschach records were taken and interpreted by the same psychologist (Z.P.). The non-POP patients (marked by numerals in the table) were of similar age and intelligence as the POP patients, but not of the same educational level. Both groups appeared clinically improved but the degree of improvement was clearly greater in the POP group (except in the case of M). The main sign of improvement in the non-POP group was alleviation of anxiety. In the case of nearly all POP patients, the difference between the first and second Rorschach examination was usually striking and was quantitatively much greater than between any other consecutive examinations. The increase in the number of responses, especially of the most important responses (movement, color, whole), was correlated with a marked decrease in depression. The qualitative changes (improved quality of the movement and color responses) required more time to appear and were much more gradual.

MAJOR RORSCHACH CHANGES

Increase in Number of M.

The perceptanalytic component which is of the greatest importance in psychotherapy is the human movement response (in brief, M). It denotes a definite tendency, deeply embedded in the individual, to assume an unchanging attitude or attitudes when dealing with others in matters recognized by the individual himself as vitally important to him (3). This conception of role in life is not easily modifiable. While people can and do act in a manner incompatible with their basic conceptions of role, they do it at the expense of productivity, inner security, and freedom. According to Rorschach (5) the human movement response is a measure of creative imagination. A conception of reality and one's role in it cannot be formed without some creative imagination.

All of the POP patients, but only four of the non-psychoanalyzed patients, showed an increase in the number of M. In the POP group the average M was 3.8 at the outset and 9.8 at its termination. For the non-POP group, the group average remained the same, being 2.9 both times. The marked increase of the M in the analyzed group is a numerical expression of the greatly increased creative imagination, of greater insight into the nature of interpersonal relationships between the patient and his environment. Also, persons with many M are more aware of the different ways in which people relate to each other than those with few M.

Changes in Quality of M.

There are at least two main types of M. One is of an extensor, or expansive, nature in which the acting human beings expand in space or overcome the force of gravity. Examples of extensor M are: dancing, running, lifting, etc. Self-assertiveness, a need for leaving an imprint of one's personality on others, and a desire for self-reliance and spontaneous activity are indicated by the extensor M. The other main type of M is the flexor M, in which humans shrink in space or give in to the force of gravity. Examples of flexor M are: bending, bowing, falling, resting, etc. Compliance, a need to lean on a psychologically stronger person in whose protective and benevolent atmosphere alone the compliant individual can display his full initiative, activity, and imagination, are signified by the flexor M.

In our study, all of the POP patients showed some increase in the number of the extensor M. In the final records of seven of these patients all of the new M were extensor, while the number of compliant or passive M had decreased. In the remaining six cases at least the majority of the new M was of the extensor type. On the other hand, only four of the non-POP patients increased the number of their extensor M. Three of these patients actually lowered the number of their extensor M. These changes imply that the POP patients have decidedly improved their capacity to assert themselves and to think of themselves in terms of a freer, more spontaneous and more nearly complete self-expression, and that in the non-analyzed group this improvement occurred only in a minority of patients, and to a smaller degree, even when improvement did take place.

Ordinal Place of M.

Rorschach stated that the ordinal place in which a component appears during the examination is one of several measures of the freedom with which the individual is inclined to express overtly traits indicated by that component. If the M appear at the beginning of the examination, they are considered uninhibited, while their appearance solely in the later part of the examination is ascribed to inhibition. Six of the POP patients had produced their M in the first three Rorschach plates during the first examination; they did the same during the last examination. The remaining seven patients, at the last testing, advanced their first M to an earlier plate. There was no change in the ordinal places of M in the non-POP group.

Increase of ΣC.

ΣC is the sum of color responses. The chromatic color responses measure another very important part of personality. They indicate the individual's desires to associate with, or dissociate from, another person, with the intent of a voluntary or forcible exchange or discontinuance of pleasures or displeasures between them (3). The larger the ΣC, the greater the emotional interest in the environment. In the POP group, the ΣC increased from an average of 5.5 to an average of 9.4, while in the non-POP group the ΣC dropped slightly, from 3.0 to 2.7.

Increase of FC.

Three types of color responses are differentiated: FC, CF, C. The more dominant the F, or form element, the greater the conscious control exercised over the emotional impulse. The FC indicate a capacity for an effortless and adequate emotional adaptation to at least the conventional and usual social situations. The C point to emotional impulses in which no regard is given to the rights and wishes of other people, and in which the self-centeredness and lability are highest. The CF are indicators of reactions between those two extremes (5). It is desirable that an adult produce more FC than CF and C. Twelve of the 13 POP cases produced more FC at the last examination than at the first, the group average rising from 2.0 to 5.1. In the non-POP patients the FC group average dropped from 1.1 to .2, with only two members of this group augmenting their FC in their last records. Moreover, 9 POP patients initially had fewer FC than CF and C combined. At the end of treatment, however, the FC exceeded the sum of CF and C in 8 POP cases, and this happened despite the fact that 7 of these 8 patients had increased also their CF and C. In 3 additional POP patients the FC increased relative to the sum of the CF and C without exceeding the latter. The only POP patient, patient M, who failed to show an improvement in any of these three measures of desirable change in affectivity, was a schizophrenic who had found it increasingly difficult to function successfully in his highly competitive business field. Of the 10 non-POP patients, only two showed improvement in terms of shift in the absolute or relative distribution of color responses.

Ordinal Place of Color Responses.

The principle of the significance of the "early appearance" during the examination applies to color responses as well as to human movement responses. When color responses occur earlier, we assume that the subject becomes aware of his emotional drives more easily than when the color responses appear later in the Rorschach record (5). There was no change in the position of the initial color response in the non-POP group. In the POP group, 9 patients produced a color response to the first colored plate both in their first and last records. The 4 POP patients who failed to respond with a color response to the first two colored plates during their first examination, did so during their last test. There was no consistent trend in the color responses produced in the last three fully colored plates.

Diffusion of Color Responses.

With improvement in psychotherapy the color responses tend to be more equally distributed over the five chromatic color plates. This change is more pronounced than the absolute increase in the sum of color responses.

Increase in Warm Color Responses.

Furthermore, in 10 of the POP patients the increase in ΣC was due to warm color (red and yellow) responses. In the only 3 non-POP patients whose ΣC increased, the increase was due to cold color (green and blue) responses. The growing preference for warm colors by POP patients may be interpreted as a weakening of timidity in affective life and a strengthening of emotional drives, the warm colors being signs of a more intense emotional interest in people than the cold color responses. When appraising the modifications of human movement and color responses, it should be remembered that these two kinds of responses are more intimately associated with specific character traits than is any other Rorschach component (5).

Equalization of Bright Shading and Color Responses.

The most significant meaning of the bright shading responses and of their sum (Σc) is that they point to a capacity for a conscious, self-regulating, and instantaneous control over the motor impulses, the latter being measured primarily by the color responses (3). Contrary to a widely held view, anxiety does not increase with Σc, but increases with the difference between Σc and the number of other perceptanalytic components, particularly with the difference between the Σc and the ΣC (4). In the record of 9 POP patients the Σc and ΣC became more even at the end of the treatment. The remaining 4 POP patients displayed no significant discrepancy between the Σc and the ΣC in either the first or last record. Only 2 of the non-POP patients showed a trend toward an equalization between the Σc and ΣC.

Relative Increase of "Good" to "Poor" Whole Responses.

The significance of the W, or whole response, depends on its close association with drive for difficult accomplishment (5). The greater the number and the structural differentiation of the W, the stronger the tendency to leave nothing to chance or accident but to plan one's life so that all one's activities would contribute to the realization of a paramount and all-embracing goal of life, and the stronger the readiness to exert oneself to achieve something difficult and complex, recognized as a praiseworthy achievement by those whose approval is sought (3).

In the study, the average number of W did not change significantly. It was high in the POP group from the beginning, indicating that—as a group—these patients possessed a readiness for difficult achievement, worthy of notice, even before they had begun psychoanalytic treatment, and that their planning of future activities had not been below that of most individuals of superior intelligence and high education. All of the POP patients belonged to the intellectually and educationally superior group. However, although the number of the W did not augment, their quality improved. The "good" W are sharply conceived, that is, they contain a well-constructed and exact visual image of an object which has a definite shape (butterfly, human being, etc.) and which fits very well the blot area to which it pertains. The "poor" W are either vague (landscapes, formations of clouds, flowers, etc.), containing images of objects with indefinite shapes, or inaccurate, that is, they contain images of objects with definite shapes, but these shapes do not correspond to those of the blot areas to which they are related by the subject. The good W manifest a more precise intellectual grasp of problems and planning of better quality than do the poor W. The relative increase of the good W with no significant change in the total number of W is a sign of an improvement in the quality of planning for difficult and constructive achievement. Our study revealed that at the beginning of treatment, 7 POP patients showed a difference of at least 4 between the number of good W and the total number of W. At the end of treatment, no POP patient, except patient M, displayed this high degree of difference. In the non-POP group there was no significant change in the ratio of good whole responses.

Increase or Decrease of F+%.

The percentage of sharply conceived forms, or the F+%, is obtained by dividing the sum of the good F, Fc, and Fc' responses by the sum of all F, Fc, and Fc' responses (3). The F+% is considered to be a measure of the capacity for a prolonged and conscious control over thought processes. In the study there was no significant improvement in this respect, either in the POP or in the non-POP group. The patients had satisfactory F+% from the beginning, as is usually the case with non-psychotic obsessive-compulsive individuals. In the POP group only two patients initially had a F+% below 70 (one of them was patient M), the majority producing F+% above 80. No POP patient but one reduced his F+%; the exceptional case produced initially the highest possible F+% of 100; at the last examination this was reduced to 91%. The extreme F+% of 100 is not desirable, indicating pedantry rather than reasonable precision. The non-POP group showed the same small and insignificant improvement in the F+%. The F+% is an extremely important perceptanalytic component and it rarely drops below 70 in psychoneurotics and normals. It can be high even in schizophrenics provided their psychosis is mild or incipient.

PSYCHOLOGICAL IMPLICATIONS OF HUMAN MOVEMENT RESPONSES

The complete and best perceptanalytic technique of personality evaluation consists in interrelating all the Rorschach components with one another. Such an evaluation is a difficult, complex, and long procedure. In this communication we are employing the simpler and easier method of describing personality changes in terms of single components, studied in isolation from the other perceptanalytic components.

We have found that, when components are investigated singly, the M occupies the top position. Our data show that during a successful psychotherapy the M change more gradually and more slowly but more consistently than any other perceptanalytic component. Therefore it might be worthwhile to discuss in greater detail the psychological implication of the M. Rorschach emphasized the view that the M is an inhibitor of overt motor activity. As the M increase, the overt motor behavior diminishes, and fantasy life intensifies (5); in other words, the creative fantasy develops at the expense of overt action. Beck (1) paraphrased this definition when he said that the M indicated "mental activities in which we should like to engage in the outer world, but can not or dare not; they are our wish fulfilling activities."

According to these conceptions, the content of the M would never be reflected directly in the individual's external conduct. However, observations on treated neurotics prompted Rorschach to alter his conception of the M: "Subjects who interpret extension kinaesthesias are active individuals with strong drives toward importance and activity although they frequently show neurotic inhibitions. Those who see flexion kinaesthesias have passive and resigned natures" (5). In the same supplement to the *Psychodiagnostics* (5), Oberholzer put it even more plainly: "The M series is what is 'lived.' I purposely avoid saying 'experienced' in order not to imply that the patient knows the nature of this experience. M is the compulsion determining what is lived and how it is lived." The Oberholzer and the revised Rorschach concept of the M do not exclude the possibility of the M being manifested directly in outward conduct. On the other hand, Beck's definition of the M as unfulfilled and unfulfillable wishes, excludes the possibility of the M ever being expressed in overt behavior. Facts do not warrant this extreme tenet. There is a fundamental difference between "sometimes" and "never."

The chances of the M being expressed immediately and directly in overt behavior can be estimated by taking into consideration the bright shading and the whole responses, the color and the dark shocks, the percentage of sharply conceived forms, etc. Therefore, in our view, the tendencies represented by the M press for direct and immediate outward manifestation, but this manifestation is sometimes delayed or indirect. This view is supported by our data in this study. If M is defined as a tendency to act upon the environment in a definite way when personally vital matters are involved (3), the M implies a tendency to act in an individual manner. Here we have a hall-mark of character.

Another concept is that of Klopfer (2) who used Rorschach's definition but supplemented it by saying that the M also signified "the acceptance of one's inner promptings, i.e., how much one is at home with oneself." However, there exists a phenomenon called movement shock which indicates that the subject is not at home with himself. The two most frequent forms of movement shock are the shock occasioned by plate III, which elicits M more easily than the other plates, and the postponing of the M to the latter part of the Rorschach record. The movement shock may be found in records with any number of M. Any perceptanalytic shock points to a deep-seated ambivalence toward one's own attitudes, drives, or impulses. One cannot assume that the presence of M indicates "being at home with oneself," even when there is no movement shock. The M themselves may reveal great inner tension and fear of one's promptings, as do the following M: "men

fighting with legs tied together," and "women trying to free themselves from their bonds." Individuals producing such M may
explode into violently aggressive behavior under certain circumstances. Frustrations and inhibitions shown in the M themselves
are more serious and less modifiable than frustrations indicated
by neurotic shocks, color, shading, and movement shocks, and by
a disproportionately large number of light shading responses (3).

The psychological roots of the mental processes represented
by the M are regarded as deep and apparently unconscious, for
the M are assumed to have originated in basic tendencies, stirring experiences, strong feelings about people, and ardent expectations regarding the future. Rorschach (5) reproduced two
records of an obsessive neurotic of superior intelligence and education, taken at the beginning and at the end of a five-month
psychoanalysis. The patient improved in many respects, but a
comparison of the records reveals no essential change in the
quality of the M, despite a great rise in their number from 10
to 24. A real character change would not be expected in five
months. Incidentally, not every increase of the M is desirable.
Increasing M beyond an optimal number may hamper rather
than aid the successful handling of interpersonal relationships.
Too great a variety in the types of M tends to be correlated
with too great a diversity of intellectual activities, and thus tends
to interfere with directness and efficiency of action.

The serial study of the Rorschach records of our POP patients disclosed that any changes which occurred in the M were
directional in trend and approached gradually what might be
described as the "M ideal." In brief, the more assertive the movement, the greater the spontaneity and freedom of the movement,
and the larger the number of body parts (ideally: the entire
body) performing the movement—the more any specific M approaches the desirable M ideal. Full, friendly, constructive, and
easily assertive actions performed by entire human beings of the
same sex as that of the examined subject, without any suggestion
of hesitation or effort, would signify the most desirable M and
would mark one end of a measuring scale of M. At the other
extreme of the scale would be the most undesirable M, with a

complete restraint, without freedom or overt movement, representing parts of human beings or mutilated people, incapable of any purposeful action.

All methods which reveal valid and significant personality traits must have something in common. Rorschach compared the significance of the M to that of dreams. However, there are striking methodological differences between the two. In the first place, the dreams are many and vary a good deal, while the M are few, repetitive, changing seldom and slowly. The M indicate basic personality trends. Such trends are present also in all dreams, but, as a result of the distorting effects of dreamwork, those basic character traits are not fully apparent to the same degree or with such direct clarity in the dreams as they are in the M. Methodologically the most important point is that hardly a dream can be interpreted adequately without the intermediary of free and extensive associations, while the interpretation of the M requires no additional data. Thus, despite a theoretical similarity between dreams and the M, there are essential methodological differences.

The gradual change taking place in the M becomes evident when M produced in consecutive Rorschach records are scrutinized. Rorschach pointed out that minute perceptanalytic changes may be correlated with great changes in overt behavior, a statement which our data substantiate. One of our POP patients modified one of his M slightly from examination to examination, although his capacity for successful assertiveness was increasing quite noticeably. At the onset of treatment he interpreted plate VII reversed as: "Some one-legged dancing girls, maybe; slim waist, one arm; they are back to back and this black spot may be an eye with hair above it. You would have to add to it, of course." On second examination he said: "It looks like two dancing girls. Spinning around on this foot; a ballet." Third examination: "There is a dancing girl. Two, with their heads together." Fourth examination: "Some dancing girls." Fifth and last record: "We have a lot here. Two girls dancing, back to back." The basic percept, girls dancing back to back, was the same in all five records. However, in the first record

TABLE I.

CHANGES IN RORSCHACH FROM BEGINNING OF TREATMENT TO END OF TREATMENT—IN A GROUP OF 13 PATIENTS TREATED WITH INTENSIVE PSYCHOANALYTICALLY ORIENTED PSYCHOTHERAPY (A TO M) AND IN A GROUP OF 10 NON-PSYCHOANALYZED PATIENTS (1 TO 10).

Patient	Sex	Increase no. responses by more than 5	Increase no. M	Increase no. extensor M	Increase no. FC	Relative increase FC to (CF+C)	Equalization of ΣC and Σc	Increase no. good W	Relative increase good M to good W	Decrease time per response	Increase % human responses
A	m	+	+	+	+	+	+	O	+	+	+
B	m	+	+	+	+	+	O	+	+	+	+
C	m	+	+	+	+	+	+	+	O	+	+
D	m	+	+	+	+	O	+	+	+	+	+
E	m	+	+	+	+	+	+	O	+	+	+
F	m	+	+	+	+	+	O	O	+	+	+
G	f	+	+	+	+	+	+	+	+	+	+
H	f	+	+	+	+	+	+	+	+	+	+
I	m	+	+	+	+	+	+	+	+	+	O
J	m	+	+	+	+	+	+	+	+	+	+
K	m	+	+	+	+	+	+	+	+	+	+
L	f	+	+	+	+	+	O	+	+	+	+
M	m	+	+	+	O	O	O	+	+	+	O
1	m	+	+	+	+	+	O	O	+	+	+
2	f	O	−	O	O	O	O	+	O	+	O
3	m	O	+	−	O	O	O	O	O	+	O
4	m	O	+	−	O	O	O	+	O	+	O
5	f	O	O	+	O	O	O	O	O	O	O
6	m	O	O	−	O	O	O	+	O	O	+
7	f	+	−	O	+	+	+	O	+	+	+
8	m	+	O	+	O	O	O	O	O	+	+
9	f	+	+	O	O	O	O	O	+	+	+
10	m	O	−	−	O	O	O	O	O	O	O

Note: + means "yes"; O means "no"; — means "decrease"

the movement was rendered precarious by making the girls one-legged and one-armed. In the third record the dancers are placed on both feet and dance back to back again, instead of spinning around in a circle. With each examination the movement became slightly more free and easy.

TABLE II.

GROUP AVERAGES OF SOME PERCEPTANALYTIC COMPONENTS AT OUTSET AND AT END OF TREATMENT—IN A GROUP OF 13 PATIENTS TREATED WITH PSYCHOANALYTICALLY ORIENTED PSYCHOTHERAPY AND IN A GROUP OF NON-PSYCHOANALYZED PATIENTS.

COMPONENT	POP GROUP		NON-POP GROUP	
	Rorschach *Outset*	Record *End*	Rorschach *Outset*	Record *End*
Sum resp.	41.6	76.8	24.2	27.3
Sum M	3.8	9.8	2.9	2.9
Sum CR	5.5	9.4	3.0	2.7
ΣC (wghtd)	4.8	7.5	2.9	3.1
Sum FC	2.0	5.1	1.1	.2
Σc (wghtd)	7.2	8.9	3.6	3.2
Sum W (all)	10.6	10.2	7.2	4.7
Sum good W	6.7	8.2	4.3	3.2
Time/resp.	34.4″	23.1″	54.3″	44.9″

To illustrate modifications of the compliant M, we can quote from the records of another POP patient who at the beginning of treatment responded to plate III as follows: "A couple of servants, sort of bowing. The whole reaction is an annoying one." At the termination of treatment this movement was changed to: "Two performing birds, fantastically dressed like in a formal full dress, prancing like in a puppet show." The patient then added a new M (reversed plate III): "A grotesque, fat, Dickens-like character." The compliant and flexor bowing was changed into an assertive prancing. The fact that this strutting was ascribed to birds and not to humans disclosed that the patient still felt somewhat uneasy in his new assertive role. The limitation of assertiveness was also shown in the surprise of the Dickens-like character. It is understandable that an adult who had been freed from habitual compliance in regard to others and who acquired a new habit of a rather ostentatious self-assertion would feel somewhat strange in his new role, at least at first.

Increasing the number of M is not necessarily desirable, and decreasing it is not necessarily undesirable. It is good to lose compliant or aggressive M and, in our POP group, the M that disappeared had been undesirable. One of these patients produced: " a pair of hands reaching out for aid" (plate I); "a lady sticking her tongue out at someone" (plate VI); and "penis going through the lips of the vagina" (plate IX). The first two M were absent from this female patient's last Rorschach. The last M was supplanted by "witches dancing around the cauldron." The first M signified humbleness; the second petty aggressiveness. Their disappearance was a gain. The third M revealed lack of sexual orgasm because of the great disproportion between the small penis and the much larger vagina. Although not the most desirable M (because hinting at homosexual tendencies), the "witches dancing around the cauldron" was an improvement. This new M was performed not by parts of bodies but by entire human figures, was more powerful, involved the entire plate, and its image fitted better the blot areas to which it referred.

COMPARISON OF OUR FINDINGS WITH RORSCHACH'S FINDINGS

In his *Psychodiagnostics,* Rorschach stated unequivocally that his perceptanalytic test did not have the power to probe into the unconscious (5). Later he revised this view in a study (appended to the *Psychodiagnostics*) in which he compared his "blind" conclusions from a patient's Rorschach record with those of Oberholzer who had had this patient under psychoanalysis. Here Rorschach stated that the human movement, the color, and the original responses revealed more about characteristic strivings and were more closely related to the unconscious than the form and popular responses. On this point our experience fully supports Rorschach. Our observations also confirm Rorschach's supposition that the extensor human movements probably are more favorable prognostically (not only in general, but specifically for success in psychotherapy) than the flexor human movements.

Our data show that improvement brought about by POP (and presumably also by psychoanalysis) is concurrent with changes in the M, making the M approach the M ideal, characterized by spontaneity, freedom, assertiveness and extensor movements of the whole human figure. This implies that patients with freer and more assertive M in their pre-treatment Rorschach tests need to change less to be freed of debilitating anxieties. The unhampered and non-aggressive assertive M seem to run parallel with the goal of a successful psychotherapy. It is important to keep in mind that this goal can hardly be reached without a prolonged and penetrating POP or psychoanalysis because character change is necessary to produce that degree of improvement which appears to us to warrant the descriptive terms "real" and "great."

Rorschach observed that small changes in his perceptanalytic test can correspond to basic personality changes in the patient. Therefore a minute, one might say microscopic, analysis of the essential aspects of the test records is advisable, in fact necessary. We have found that minute changes, particularly in the M, reflect great and fundamental changes in the patient's subjective feelings, in his overt behavior, and in his constructive accomplishments.

Another change after successful treatment reported by Rorschach is the equalization of human movement and color responses. We can corroborate this in our POP group. It is true of each one of these patients except the unimproved schizophrenic patient M. To make the number of their human movement and color responses more equal, the patients had to raise the number of their movement responses more than that of their color responses. As was his habit, Rorschach ended with a word of moderation: "Except as noted above, the importance of the test in psychoanalysis is probably more theoretical than practical." Here we definitely diverge from him. Our experience has been that the practical worth of perceptanalysis may even exceed its theoretical value.

SECONDARY RORSCHACH CHANGES

While during a successful psychoanalytic therapeutic procedure there are some personality changes which are gradual, consistent, and apparently lasting, there are others which are transient and sporadic. These modifications are prone to appear in the middle period of the psychoanalytic treatment and not in the initial and terminal phases.

Color Responses.

These answers did not change at all in the non-POP group. However, they changed noticeably in patients under POP. They reached their numerical peak in about the middle of treatment and dropped at the end of treatment although to a level which was significantly higher than the pretreatment level. Most of the transitory increase of color responses was due to a temporary appearance or temporary strengthening of negative, hostile, and aggressive feelings. Such emotions were associated with overt desires to sever or at least to decrease contacts with certain specific individuals in their personal environment. It should be noted that these hostile and aggressive feelings appeared after self-knowledge and conception of role-in-life had deepened, which could be read from the increase in number and from the modifications in the quality of the M. It seemed that the patients needed some time and practice in their freer and more mature roles before they could assume them with ease and without fear either of themselves or of others.

Bright Shading Responses.

The "fear of others" is manifested in the interpersonal relationships of the patient with his environment and in the transference relationship to the therapist. It represents the struggle of the instincts, gradually made more free and thus more strong, with the need for adequate self-control and for appropriate respect of the just rights of others. Since the bright shading responses were connected with this aspect of personality growth of our POP patients, they increased in the middle of the analysis and decreased at the end of it. The increase of the Σc was larger than that of the ΣC which signified not only intensified anxiety but also greater control over motor impulses. The fact that the Σc did not drop below ΣC throughout the treatment demonstrated that the release from inhibitions was not more rapid than the rise of our patients' capacity for an adequate control over the stronger and freer impulses. At various periods during the analysis this control seemed too severe for comfort and caused anxiety; however, it saved the patients from rash, imprudent, or regrettable actions, and its severity was transient.

The Animal Movement Responses.

These responses, symbolized by the letters FM, reveal past conceptions of role in life, that is, conceptions which have shaped the individual's adjustment to others in the past, presumably in very early childhood (3). However, the FM which find their way into a Rorschach record are not representative of all the FM of which the subject is capable; they are selected. The FM (like any other perceptanalytic component) must represent some present and actual psychological process and cannot be only a static record of past happenings. The FM produced are then parts of the past which are still alive although their influence upon covert and overt behavior is weaker than the influence of the M. It appears that the effect of the FM upon overt behavior increases as the consciousness and self-control of the individual diminishes (as a result of intoxication, extreme fatigue, sudden and acute anxiety, etc.) (3). The modifications of the FM during psychoanalytic treatment should differ from those of the M, and indeed they did so in our POP group. As a rule, most FM are assertive, the percentage of the compliant type of movement being much smaller among the FM than among the M. One of our POP patients had a compliant and passive FM at the onset of treatment and was freed from it at the termination of treatment. Nine of the 13 POP patients raised the number of their assertive FM. This corresponded to a decided rise in the patients' vitality and liveliness (3). Seven of these nine patients produced at least one compliant FM at the end of treatment, but their assertive FM greatly outnumbered the compliant FM. Some of the assertive FM changed into frankly aggressive FM. However three POP patients lowered the number of their assertive FM and augmented that of their compliant FM. The emergence of the compliant and aggressive FM may be interpreted as a sign of newly acquired knowledge of early experiences and attitudes, the previous denial of which had been possible at the cost of reduced energy which emerged from its repressed condition.

Much more significant and more conspicuous than the difference between the initial and the terminal FM is the difference between the changes in the FM which appear in the middle period of POP. In this middle period, the increase of compliant, passive, or sado-masochistic FM was greater than before and after POP. This coincided with the patients' strong feelings concerning their past attitudes and experiences which, previously repressed, became conscious. At first the patients responded with anxiety to the recall of their past struggles and defeats, reflected in the disturbing FM. No significant changes in this respect were observed in the non-POP group.

Inanimate Movement Responses.

These answers (in brief, m) also increased at first and either dropped out completely or decreased at the termination of therapy. The m are associated with the habit of psychological self-observation if they are limited to movements of inanimate objects or physical forces. It is not surprising that the m intensify during the analysis. The m disclose a conception of role in life which the individual feels to be very desirable but which he considers unattainable because of external difficulties or because of personal incapacity (3). Such conceptions either become realizable as a result of augmented character strength following a successful psychoanalysis or they disappear as being immature and exaggerated wishes.

CONCLUSIONS

The conclusions of each Rorschach examination agreed very closely with the psychotherapist's estimate of the patients' condition at the time. There were no major disagreements between the psychiatric and the perceptanalytic opinions. The agreement adds strength to the following conclusions:

Real character changes occur during POP and are reflected in the perceptanalytic Rorschach test. They are manifested chiefly in the number and in the type of human movement responses. The qualitative change is more important and signifies a greater personality improvement than the quantitative one.

Viewed through the repeated perceptanalytic records of our patients, the successful psychoanalytic treatment develops and strengthens creative imagination, broadens the understanding of human interrelationships, and makes the patient's dynamic conception of his role in life freer of inner inhibitions and of the fear of external retaliation.

The improvement takes place primarily through much deepened self-knowledge, and secondarily through improved ability for a more adequate and more purposeful curbing of impulsive acting-out.

Persons who have had successful and intensive psychoanalytic treatment tend to diminish whatever unrealistic strivings they had had. On the other hand, they learn how to plan more effectively for actions of which they are fully capable.

The non-analyzed neurotics frequently give up goals for which they have not sufficient power. These patients do not become more capable of pursuing goals requiring creative and constructive self-expression.

Emotional tension rises in the middle period of a psychoanalysis. The tension can be attributed in part to the patients' unfamiliarity with their expanded capacity for deeper and more varied psychosocial experiences.

The Rorschach records in our study show that the analyzed patients' range of psychological experiences, intellectual and emotional, inner and social, accompanied by a simultaneously heightened personality integration, widens greatly in the analytic psychotherapeutic group. Desire and capacity for constructive, cooperative, intelligent, and anxiety-free living with others, grows conspicuously. In some cases, traces of symptomatic difficulties seen at the outset of analysis remain. Nevertheless, the psychoanalysis of psychoneurotics is a liberating influence and procedure. This can be objectively demonstrated by perceptanalysis.

TABLE III

CLINICAL DIAGNOSTIC FORMULATIONS OF POP CASES
A to M

CASE A MALE AGE 48	1—CHRONIC INHIBITED and DEPRESSED STATE occurring in a— 2—CHRONIC COMPULSIVE OBSESSIVE NEUROTIC CHARACTER with— 3—Intense CASTRATION ANXIETY, PRECIPITATE ORGASM, and strong ASCETIC and MONASTIC TRENDS. 4—BUERGER'S DISEASE SYNDROME developing intercurrently with therapy.
CASE B MALE AGE 22	1—COMPULSIVE OBSESSIVE NEUROTIC CHARACTER with— 2—Intense INHIBITIONS in social, sexual, and intellectual spheres and with— 3—Strong ASCETIC TRENDS and OBSESSIVE INTELLECTUALIZATION and EROTICIZATION OF THOUGHT.
CASE C MALE AGE 31	1—CHRONIC NEUROTIC DEPRESSED and INHIBITED CHARACTER with— 2—Intense VAGINOPHOBIA, trends toward FROTTEURISTIC FIXATION, intense unresolved CASTRATION ANXIETY and OEDIPAL GUILT. 3—Intense "MARITAL DIFFICULTIES."
CASE D MALE AGE 27	*Borderline* 1—MIXED COMPULSIVE OBSESSIVE NEUROTIC INHIBITED and ASCETIC CHARACTER with IMPULSE NEUROTIC FEATURES. 2—Intense CYCLIC TRENDS toward HYPOMANIC ACTING OUT, ELATION, and MEGALOMANIACAL EXPANSIVENESS.

3—Strong trends toward ACUTE AND CHRONIC ALCO-
HOLISM with PATHOLOGICAL DRUNKENNESS associated with FUGUE-LIKE ACTING OUT and AMNESIA.

4—Occasional PARANOIDAL UNREALITY EPISODES with
intense IDEAS OF REFERENCE.

CASE E
MALE
AGE 40

1—CHRONIC RECURRENT ANXIETY and TENSION STATES
with HYPOCHONDRIACAL TRENDS occurring in a—

2—CHRONIC COMPULSIVE OBSESSIVE NEUROTIC CHARAC-
TER with strong ASCETIC TRENDS, VAGINOPHOBIA,
PSYCHOGENIC IMPOTENCE, and CHRONIC PRECIPI-
TATE ORGASM.

3—Strong unconscious repressed and denied PASSIVE
FEMININE and DEPENDENT HOMOSEXUAL STRIVINGS.

CASE F
MALE
AGE 40

1—Severe ACUTE MIXED REACTIVE and "CYCLOTHYMIC"
DEPRESSION with MULTIPLE PHOBIAS occurring in
a—

2—Long standing CHRONIC COMPULSIVE OBSESSIVE NEU-
ROTIC CHARACTER with—

3—Intense VAGINOPHOBIA, FROTTEURISM, FEMALE AM-
PUTEE FETISHISM, as well as FETISHISTIC and
"BISEXUAL" MASTURBATION ADDICTION.

4—Cigarette SMOKING ADDICTION.

CASE G
FEMALE
AGE 26

1—SUBACUTE and CHRONIC MIXED DEPRESSIVE and ANX-
IETY STATE with ALCOHOLISM occurring in a—

2—CHRONIC MIXED COMPULSIVE OBSESSIVE and IMPULSE
NEUROTIC CHARACTER with—

3—ALCOHOL and SMOKING ADDICTION, intense MASCU-
LINITY STRIVINGS, OVERT HOMOSEXUAL (F) TRENDS,
intramarital FRIGIDITY and AVERSION, and—

4—UNRESOLVED OEDIPAL GUILT toward mother.

5—Intense HYPERHYDROSIS with redness and swelling
of hands.

CASE H
FEMALE
AGE 43

1—OBSESSIONAL NEUROSIS with PHOBIAS and some CON-
VERSION HYSTERICAL FEATURES.

CASE I
MALE
AGE 23

Borderline

1—COMPULSIVE OBSESSIONAL NEUROSIS with—

2—Rare mild FUGUE STATES, moderately strong SCHIZOID

PERSONALITY TRENDS with occasional FEELINGS OF
UNREALITY.

CASE J
MALE
AGE 34

1—Intense ANXIETY HYSTERIA with PHOBIAS occurring
in a—

2—MIXED HYSTERICAL and COMPULSIVE OBSESSIVE NEU-
ROTIC CHARACTER with—

3—Intense repressed and denied PASSIVE, DEPENDENT,
and HOMOSEXUAL STRIVINGS.

CASE K
MALE
AGE 21

1—MIXED "ORGANIC" and PSYCHOGENIC EPILEPTIC
"GRAND MAL" CONVULSIVE SEIZURES occurring in
an—

2—Intense COMPULSIVE OBSESSIVE NEUROTIC CHARACTER
with intense trends toward RELIGIOSITY and strong
PARANOIDAL FEATURES.

CASE L
FEMALE
AGE 26

1—ATYPICAL AMBULATORY SCHIZOPHRENIA with MILD
PARANOIDAL FEATURES occurring in a—

2—Long standing COMPULSIVE OBSESSIVE NEUROTIC
CHARACTER with tendency toward—

3—PSYCHOPATHIC HYPOMANIC ACTING OUT, POLYMOR-
PHOUS PERVERSE SEX PRACTICES, SHOE FETISHISTIC
MASTURBATION, and DRUG ADDICTION.

CASE M
MALE
AGE 26

1—EARLY AMBULATORY SCHIZOPHRENIA of a MIXED
PARANOID and HEBEPHRENIC NATURE with—

2—Long standing CHRONIC SCHIZOID PERSONALITY
TRAITS with some COMPULSIVE OBSESSIVE FEA-
TURES.

BIBLIOGRAPHY

1. BECK, S. J., *Rorschach's Test*. Vol. I. "Basic Processes." New York, Grune & Stratton, 1944.
2. KLOPFER, B. AND KELLEY, D. M., *The Rorschach Technique*. Yonkers, (N. Y.), World Book Co., 1942.
3. PIOTROWSKI, Z. A., "A Rorschach compendium, revised and enlarged." *Psychiat. Quart.*, XXIV, 543–596, 1950.
4. ———, & LEWIS, N. D. C., "An experimental Rorschach diagnostic aid for some forms of schizophrenia." *Am. J. Psychiat.*, CVII, 360–366, 1950.
5. RORSCHACH, H. *Psychodiagnostics: A Diagnostic Test Based on Perception*. Bern, H. Huber, 1942.

► INDEX

Abraham, K., 160, 166, 216
Abreaction, in hypnoanalysis, 32–34
  indirect, in emergency therapy of
    depression, 330–331
  in narcotherapy, 11–12
Ackerman, N. W., 91
Acting-out, of borderline patient,
    313
Alcoholics Anonymous, 242, 243,
    251–252
Alcoholics Treatment Center, New
    York City, 244
Alcoholism, 239–258
  narcotherapy in treatment of, 16
  primary addict, 239–240
  secondary addict, 240–241
  symptomatic drinker, 239
  therapy, 241–258
    in acute phase, 244–245
    Alcoholics Anonymous, 251–252
    "Antabuse," 252–257
    aversion treatment, 252
    in free interval, 246–249
    with hangover, 245–246
    initial interview, 247–248
    physical and social rehabilita-
      tion, 248–249
    psychological study of patient,
      249–251
Alexander, F., 279
Ambivalence, of borderline patient,
    312–313
Amnesia, post-hypnotic, in hypno-
    analysis, 34–35
Analysis, basic steps in, 325–326
  of children, 280
    with atypical development, 119–
      132
  free painting as auxiliary tech-
    nique in. See Free painting
  goal of, 324
  of groups, 90–92
  of husband, wife and child, 103–
    118
  hypnosis in. See Hypnoanalysis
  indications, 325
  method of, 324
  as narcotherapeutic technique, 12
  of psychosomatic patient, 292–297

Analysis (*continued*)
  and psychotherapy, comparison of,
    324–326
  of schizophrenic, 159–179
    changing technique in, 162–172
    personal problems of psycho-
      therapist, 175–179
    problems of, 159–162
    setup and technique, 172–175
    telepathic hypothesis in, 45–57
    time of, 324
    transference situation, 325
Analyst. *See* Therapist
Animal movement responses, 356–
    357
"Antabuse" therapy for alcoholics,
    242, 243, 252–257
  precautions required, 255–256
  table of findings, 257
Anxiety, role of, in schizophrenia,
    171–172
  of therapist in treatment of schizo-
    phrenic, 177–178
Anxiety states, narcotherapy for, 10–
    13, 16
Appraisal in emergency psychother-
    apy of depression, 327–328
Arrested development, children of,
    119–132
Asthma, psychosomatic, 294–296
Aversion treatment for alcoholism,
    252

Bacon, S. D., 250
Barbiturates, use of, in diagnosis.
    See Narcodiagnosis and narco-
    therapy
Beck, S. J., 347
Bergler, E., 315
Blau, Abram, *The Master Hand*,
    cited, 208*n.*
Bleckwenn, W. J., 1
Blue Hills Clinic, Hartford, Conn.,
    254
Boggs, M. H., 248
Borderline states, 303–319
  case work with patients and rela-
    tives, 317–318